NUMERICAL COMPUTATION USING C

This is a volume in
COMPUTER SCIENCE AND SCIENTIFIC COMPUTING

Werner Rheinboldt, editor

NUMERICAL COMPUTATION USING C

ROBERT GLASSEY

Department of Mathematics
Indiana University
Bloomington, Indiana

ACADEMIC PRESS, INC.
Harcourt Brace Jovanovich, Publishers
Boston   San Diego   New York
London   Sydney   Tokyo   Toronto

This book is printed on acid-free paper. ∞

Copyright © 1993 by Academic Press, Inc.

ACADEMIC PRESS, INC.
1250 Sixth Avenue, San Diego, CA 92101

United Kingdom edition published by
ACADEMIC PRESS LIMITED
24-28 Oval Road, London NW1 7DX

Library of Congress Catalog Card Number: 92-33037

ISBN 0-12-286155-8

Printed in the United States of America
92 93 94 96 BC 9 8 7 6 5 4 3 2 1

TABLE OF CONTENTS

ACKNOWLEDGEMENTS

I wish to thank my wife Betsy for enduring many hours alone while I constructed this book. My son Tom deserves sincere thanks for not crashing my hard disk while (patiently?) waiting for his bedtime story . . . .

I wish to specially thank Bishara Shamee from whom I learned much about C and UNIX.

To my many friends and colleagues who offered advice and suggestions, I am most grateful. They include Kelly Alvey, Michele LeBlanc, John Willems, Scott Zasadil and Bill Ziemer.

Thanks also to Ms. Jenifer Swetland and the staff of Academic Press with whom it was a pleasure to work.

CHAPTER 0

INTRODUCTION

There are several reasons for my writing this book. Firstly, in numerical analysis classes at the senior–first year graduate level, I find that students who claim to know C do not in fact know it very well. In particular, pointers, arrays, dynamic memory allocation, etc., are troublesome.

Secondly, from my own experience of learning C, I found that the examples in existing texts were mostly system–oriented; few if any involved scientific computation. In 1990 I was shocked to read in *PC Magazine* a statement by a veteran programmer to the effect that, despite many years in the profession, he had never written a single computational program. Although there are many nice references on C, I do not know of any at the introductory level which are written from the viewpoint of a mathematician.

Furthermore, as I learned C, I wished for a mathematically oriented reference in which I could look things up quickly. It is certainly true that the recent excellent publication *Numerical Recipes in C* almost fits the bill; there it is assumed that the reader knows C already. In this book I will assume that the reader already knows some language and is familiar with the uses of loops, if–then–else statements, etc.

This book is not a text on the C language proper, nor is it a text on numerical analysis. It is intended to be a guide for learning C from the viewpoint of numerical analysis. As such it is a hybrid, perhaps to be used as a supplement in a course in numerical analysis. I intend it to be more or less brief and inexpensive, so that students can readily afford it. Indeed, I quote from [KR]: "C is not a big language, and is not well–served by a big book."

How does one learn a new language? The answer is: by reading a book,

1

by studying the code of others, and by sitting down at your terminal and enduring the edit–compile–run cycle until you get it right. The intended audience is probably split into two groups: one which uses a PC under DOS (or a Macintosh) to develop programs and another which uses UNIX. It is well–known that large–scale computation under DOS is impossible. Nevertheless program development on a PC is very convenient, and there are several nice C–compilers available. On the PC–level, I use the Microsoft "Quick C" (v. 2.5) compiler. For UNIX, I have in mind *gcc*, the GNU C–compiler. Both understand ANSI and are a pleasure to use. I omit the Borland product and all others simply because I have never used them.

While graphics are built into "Quick C," one can use *gcc* to write the results of a computation to a file and then feed the file to, say, GNU-PLOT, another GNU product which swallows files and produces nice two–dimensional graphics. The most recent version of this program (v. 3.0) can display three–dimensional graphs as well. These GNU products are excellent, the price is right and they work as advertised. Since I have not yet contributed to the Free Software Foundation, I feel this "plug" is warranted! Nothing in this book is compiler–specific; all programs should run on nearly any C–compiler, modulo a few minor changes.

In recent years several magnificent programs have appeared in the mathematical area: Mathematica, Macsyma, Maple, Derive, Gauss, Matlab, etc. In view of all of this power, should you still consider learning a language? The answer is an unqualified YES. The nature of this business is so specialized that you will not always be able to get one of these programs to do what you want. Moreover, the computation of solutions to large–scale Partial Differential Equations is an ad–hoc process for which the ability to write your own code is indispensable. If you require only small computations, BASIC is easy to learn and use. In my opinion, Microsoft "Quick Basic" v. 4.5 is a tremendous program and is to be highly recommended. For larger computations, of course, Fortran has been the standard in scientific computation, and superb libraries are available. These libraries are now available in C.

C is a general–purpose language which has been traditionally used in systems programming. Indeed, UNIX is written in C. C can be adapted to a broad spectrum of applications and boasts wide choices of data types, e.g., pointers, structures, etc. It contains a large set of operators and control devices, yet it is a "small" language. The standard run–time libraries contain code for dynamic memory allocation, input/output, etc. Moreover, C is to be recommended for its portability, efficiency and elegance, and is certainly in favor in academics and in the real world as well. There are some drawbacks from the scientific–computation point of view. For example, there is no built–in exponentiation function, nor is there a built–in facility for complex arithmetic. Of course, these computations are still possible in C, but a speed penalty is incurred.

A word or two about the plan of the book: Chapter 1 is an overview of the *C* language, put in terms of *mathematical* examples. Chapter 2 deals with the uses of *pointers* , their applications to memory allocation for vectors and matrices, etc. In Chapter 3 we cover certain smaller topics which did not seem to fit elsewhere, and some of the fine points. The last chapter of the book covers special topics, such as linear algebra, differential equations, etc. My intent is for you to find some nontrivial example programs here, as well as some of the mathematical background.

An indication of the proofs of those results which are not too detailed will be given. In my opinion, the only way to really understand an algorithm is to first prove it converges, and then to code it. Of course for most real problems encountered in practice, the idea of giving a rigorous proof may not be achievable, but there is nothing wrong with professing this as a goal.

As for background, that of an advanced undergraduate in mathematics or the physical sciences should be sufficient. An extensive knowledge of real analysis is not required, but familiarity with standard topics (such as the convergence of a sequence, the Mean–Value Theorem, Taylor's Theorem, etc.) is assumed.

Here are some comments about the programs. Undoubtedly there will be some errors, typos, etc. Rather than strive for the slickest possible coding, I have tried to make the programs simple and readable. Thus I do not claim that these programs are the best available, nor that they are optimized. If you can understand the coding of the basic form of an algorithm, then later on in life when you use a "canned program" you may feel fairly confident that you understand what is going on. (There is perhaps an analogy here to the study of special functions.) Each *C* function used in a program is (at least at the beginning of the book) explicitly included at the top of the file. While this is repetitious, it renders most of the programs self–contained. I have kept the number of special files to be "included" to an absolute minimum for simplicity. I encourage you to experiment with the programs, and to alter them to suit your needs. I would be pleased to hear about errors, bugs, etc.

The "tolerance" 5×10^{-20} is (arbitrarily) used to test a denominator before a division is performed. The "stopping criterion" in iteration loops varies in the programs. This tolerance may have to be adjusted (i.e., relaxed) if the data of a particular problem are "large." When the elements of a symmetric matrix are to be read from files, we always construct the data files by entering the first row, then the second row (from the diagonal to the right), etc. For the sake of uniformity we use *double precision* in most of the book (with the exception of the first few programs). This is consistent with calls to the functions in `math.h`, but can be easily changed.

A major topic for which *C* is employed is *string handling*. This is not discussed in this book, since the emphasis is on scientific computation. The manipulation of strings can be tricky; please consult the canonical reference [KR] for details. A related reference is [HS] which contains topic-oriented material on the C language proper. Both of these books contain descriptions of the standard libraries and are to be highly recommended.

There are other omissions in this book, e.g., unions, linked lists, the use of the bitwise operators, etc. Moreover, not all of the properties of the built-in functions (e.g. `printf`, `scanf`) are fully exposed. Therefore you will not become a C master by reading this book alone. Some topics have been omitted for considerations of length, others because I have never used them. Thus I urge you to consult other references for a more complete picture of C as a language; here we will use and study C with a specific goal in mind.

The numerical integration of Partial Differential Equations is an extremely interesting subject and is at the forefront of modern research in applied mathematics. The sheer size of many problems is daunting. Furthermore, the development of algorithms to accurately handle *nonlinear* phenomena is in its infancy. For these reasons a practitioner or student in the area of applied mathematics simply must be able to code his or her own work. The C language is a perfect environment for this and, modulo mutations, it is sure to be around for many years. A final quotation from [KR], which I have found to be appropriate, is "C wears well as one's experience with it grows."

SOME COMPILATION/RUN–TIME TIPS

1. Using Microsoft QC 2.5 on a PC

After entering your source code with the editor, just press F5 to compile and run. In my `autoexec.bat` file, I include the line

```
set cl=qcl /AS /O1
```

This uses the small memory model and optimizes loops. From the command line in the QC 2.5 directory, use `qcl filename.c`. The executable is then named `filename.exe` and is run by typing `filename` at the DOS prompt.

2. Using gcc on a Unix Machine

When using EMACS, type `ESC-x compile` after entering your code in the editor. In the minibuffer, enter the command

```
gcc filename.c -lm
```

(With older versions of *gcc* you may have include a switch as in `gcc -traditional filename.c -lm`.) A small window will open which lists compilation errors, if any. If errors are detected, enter the command `ESC-x next-error`. This positions you in the source code at the offending point, and you can take appropriate action. Once the compilation succeeds, exit to the command line. The executable has been called `a.out` and you run it by simply typing `a.out`.

Should the program fail and dump core, you need to use `dbx` as follows. First, recompile your program with the `-g` option. Then enter `dbx -r a.out core`. Several (perhaps undecipherable) messages flash by, along with some hex addresses. When it pauses, enter `where`. The explicit line(s) will then be tagged, and you can hope to fix things.

In the above, `-lm` links to the math library, and `-traditional` (if needed) allows *gcc* to understand ANSI. The latest version of *gcc* (v. 2.0) compiles ANSI *C* by default. Some other useful options for `gcc` are

```
-o outfilename       renames the executable to ''outfilename''
-O                              optimize for speed
```

In EMACS you can of course edit the compile command in your `.emacs` file to read as above. I suggest that you also edit your `.cshrc` (**c–sh**ell **r**un commands) by including a line like this making 'gc' an alias:

```
alias 'gc gcc \!* -lm'
```

Lastly is a caveat on the use of the Sun Microsystems *C* compiler. As of this writing (1991–92), Sun has not yet updated its compiler with a switch rendering it capable of understanding ANSI *C*. Therefore the programs in this book will not run under the Sun *C* compiler.

HOW TO OBTAIN THE PROGRAMS

All of the programs in this book are freely available on Internet. Here is the procedure for obtaining them:

Enter the command

```
ftp iu-math.math.indiana.edu
```
or
```
ftp 129.79.147.6 .
```

At the login prompt `login:`, enter `anonymous`. Any string will work for the password.

Change directories by entering the command

```
cd pub/glassey .
```

If you are using UNIX, enter at the `ftp` prompt `binary`. Then get the relevant file by entering

```
get csrcrtg.tar.Z .
```

Once you have obtained this file, you can uncompress it with the UNIX command

```
uncompress csrcrtg.tar.Z .
```

Then enter the UNIX command

```
tar -xvf csrcrtg.tar .
```

For convenience we also place in the same directory an uncompressed ASCII listing of the programs whose file name is `csrcrtg.txt`. After changing directories as above, enter at the `ftp` prompt

```
get csrcrtg.txt .
```

CHAPTER 1

STD TUTORIAL

FIRST PRINCIPLES

Please recall my philosophy that the only way to learn a language is to read a book (this one, or [KR], or another), to read the code of others, and then to sit down and write programs yourself. I assume that you are already familiar with (or are now studying) Numerical Analysis. Program line numbers are *not* used in C. Nevertheless, for reference purposes we display source code using line numbers. The program listings themselves appear in typewriter font.

We begin with

```
/* Comments are enclosed like this */
```

The first example program will use *Simpson's Rule* to approximate the value of the integral $I = \int_0^1 \exp(-x^2)\,dx$. As you know, Simpson's Rule looks like this:

$$(1.1) \qquad \int_a^b f(x)\,dx = \frac{(b-a)}{6}\left[f(a) + 4f\left(\frac{a+b}{2}\right) + f(b)\right] + E,$$

where the *error* $E = \frac{-(b-a)^5 f^{(4)}(\xi)}{2880}$ for some point $\xi \in (a, b)$. Let's ignore the error term for now so that I is approximately equal to

$$(1.2) \qquad \frac{[\exp(0) + 4\exp(-0.25) + \exp(-1)]}{6} \approx 0.74718.$$

We'll write a C program to compute this:

7

```
1 /* Simpson1.c */
2
3 # include <stdio.h>
4 # include <math.h>
5
6 main( )
7 {
8 float s;      /* floating point variable */
9               /* to hold the sum */
10 s=(exp(0.0)+4.0*exp(-0.25)+exp(-1.0))/6.0;
11 printf("Integral=%f\n",s);
12 }
```

There is a lot here! Firstly, every C program has a "central" body called "main." Notice the empty parentheses after "main." The body of the program is always enclosed in braces, { on line 7 and } on line 12. Each executable statement in a C program is terminated by a semicolon, as you see on lines 8, 10 and 11. Above the main part of the program on lines 3 and 4 you see two "include" files, whose appearance is heralded by the # symbol. The file math.h contains type definitions of standard mathematical functions such as $\exp(x), \sin(x)$, etc. The file stdio.h is a similar "header" file where the compiler finds the required information on standard input and output.   The program itself is simple. You must first define your variables in C. Here we have only one called s, which is a floating point number, hence the declaration float s on line 8. On line 10 s is computed according to the formula (1.2). It remains only to communicate the results, which one does by calling the function printf. (This stands for "print with formatting".) The line

```
printf("Integral=%f\n",s);
```

says: "print to the screen the value of the floating point variable s, calling it 'Integral'". Any desired string output (such as the word "Integral" here) is enclosed in quotes. The symbol %f is a float format specifier; the "\n" gives us a new line in the output. Please note the use of real floating point values: 1.0 instead of 1, etc.

Let's change a few things, but only one at a time. Suppose the function you are integrating is more complicated: $f(x) = \exp(\sqrt{1 + x^2} - x)$. We do not want to type this in three (or more) times, so we add at the top a *function definition*, or *function macro*, like this:

```
# define f(x)   (exp(sqrt(1.0+(x)*(x))-(x)))
```

There is a space after $f(x)$ and before the "(", but there must be no space between the "f" and the "(". Notice that the line itself is *not* terminated with a semicolon, and that the entire expression is enclosed within parentheses. The other relevant point is that each time the argument x appears, it is enclosed in its own set of parentheses. This is important; such a function–type macro will not execute correctly without these. Use parentheses liberally!

The entire program to compute $I = \int_0^1 f(x)\,dx$ now appears as:

```
1 /* Simpson2.c */
2
3 # include <stdio.h>
4 # include <math.h>
5 # define f(x) (exp(sqrt(1.0+(x)*(x))-(x)))
6
7 main( )
8 {
9 float s;   /* floating point variable */
10            /* to hold the sum */
11 s=(f(0.0)+4.0*f(0.5)+f(1.0))/6.0;
12 printf("Integral=%f\n",s);
13 }
```

It's even easier, isn't it? What if the function $f(x)$ were much more complicated? Then we'd write a separate *C–function* to find its value, and rewrite the Simpson program so that it receives this *C*–function as an argument (this is called a *pointer to a function*). This will be discussed in Chapter 2.

Perhaps you now think that the algorithm is too crude, which is true. Such an approximation over a larger interval is not likely to be very ac-curate. Therefore we now consider the *Composite Simpson's Rule*. The integral to be approximated is again written as $I = \int_a^b f(x)\,dx$. One parti-tions $[a, b]$ into equal subintervals

$$(1.3) \qquad x_i = a + ih, \quad i = 0, 1, \ldots, N, \quad \text{where} \quad h = \frac{b - a}{N}.$$

We can write the composite rule as

$$(1.4) \qquad I = \frac{h}{6} \sum_{i=1}^{N} \left(f(x_{i-1}) + 4f(x_{i-\frac{1}{2}}) + f(x_i) \right) - E$$

$$= \frac{h}{6} \left[f(a) + f(b) + 2 \sum_{i=1}^{N-1} f(x_i) + 4 \sum_{i=1}^{N} f(x_{i-\frac{1}{2}}) \right] - E,$$

where, for some point $\xi \in (a, b)$, the *error* E is given by

$$(1.5) \qquad\qquad E = \frac{1}{2880}(b-a)f^{(4)}(\xi)h^4.$$

This form of the error does not result directly, but comes from the following "mean–value" theorem: Given a continuous function f on an interval $[a, b]$ and a sequence of values $\{g_i\}_{i=1}^n$ all of one sign, there exists a point $\xi \in [a, b]$ such that

$$\sum_{i=1}^n f(x_i)g_i = f(\xi)\sum_{i=1}^n g_i.$$

This is quite important and merits a few lines of proof. Without loss of generality we can assume that $g_i \geq 0$ for all i. Let the function $f(x)$ take values in the interval $[m, M]$ for $x \in [a, b]$. Then

$$m\sum_{i=1}^n g_i \leq \sum_{i=1}^n f(x_i)g_i \leq M\sum_{i=1}^n g_i, \quad \text{i.e.,}$$

$$m \leq \frac{\sum_{i=1}^n f(x_i)g_i}{\sum_{i=1}^n g_i} \leq M.$$

This says that the number

$$\frac{\sum_{i=1}^n f(x_i)g_i}{\sum_{i=1}^n g_i}$$

lies between the extreme values of f, and thus, by the intermediate value theorem, is equal to $f(\xi)$ for some point ξ.

To code this we evidently need additionally two integers (`int`), N and i. Then we simply add up (over $1 \leq i \leq N$) contributions such as those in the previous program using a *for loop*. Here it is for $N = 10$ and $I(f) = \int_0^1 \exp(\sqrt{1+x^2} - x)\,dx$:

```
1 /* Simpson3.c */
2
3 # include <stdio.h>
4 # include <math.h>
5 # define f(x) (exp(sqrt(1.0+(x)*(x))-(x)))
6
7 main( )
8 {
9 int i;
10 float h,s;   /* step size and sum variable */
11
```

```
12 s=f(0.0)+f(1.0);      /* initialize the sum */
13 h=1.0/10.0;           /* use 10 points this time */
14
15 for (i=1;i<=9;i++){
16          s = s + 4.0*f((i-0.5)*h)+2.0*f(i*h);
17          }                /* end the for loop */
18
19          s = s + 4.0*f(9.5*h);
20          s = s * h/6.0;
21
22 printf("Integral=%f\n",s);
23 }                         /* end main */
```

The notation $i + +$ means increment i by one; similarly $i - -$ means to decrement i by one. (There are more sophisticated properties of these operators, to be discussed later.) Notice the three parts in the *for* loop on line 15 are separated by semicolons, and that the entire loop is enclosed in braces. (While this is not necessary for a body consisting of only one line, it is not a bad practice to always enclose the loop body in braces.) The only other change is the integer i defined on line 9. The variable s is then initialized on line 12. *C* allows one to initialize variables at the time of their definition, so we could shorten the program by replacing the lines

```
float h,s;              /* step size and sum variable */
s=f(0.0)+f(1.0);               /* initialize the sum */
h=1.0/10.0;                /* use 10 points this time */
```

by

```
float h=1.0/10.0,s=f(0.0)+f(1.0);
/* step size and sum variable */ .
```

There is some "type–mixing" above, e.g., what is the meaning of the expression $i * h$? We postpone this briefly; please see the discussion below.

C allows a shorthand to abbreviate operations such as $s = s + a$, $s = s * b$, etc. Thus we can write $s = s + a$ as $s + = a$, and $s = s * a$ as $s * = a$, etc. This is very convenient and may be more efficient; you'll get used to it soon. Thus the sum computation in the *for* loop above (on line 16) could be succinctly written as

```
s += (4.0*f((i-0.5)*h)+2.0*f(i*h));
```

By the properties in Chapter 3, an expression of the form x * = u+1.0 means x = x*(u+1.0).

Of course we can write **for** loops which run "backward"

```
for (i=N;i>=1;i--)
```

or which run "forward" by increments of 2, say, as in

```
for (i=1;i<=N;i += 2) .
```

For the last modification, we'll change the number of mesh points (i.e., N). We change it to suit the user's preference by asking for the number of points desired. This is one use of the scanf function. The two lines of code needed are:

```
printf("Enter the number of mesh points desired:   ");
scanf("%d",&N);  .
```

The printf statement simply prompts on the screen, but the scanf statement is a new construct. Firstly, the format specifier for an integer (*int*) is %d. Secondly, when using the function scanf for input, one must pass it the *address* of the variable desired. Therefore we precede its appearance in scanf with the *address of* operator &.

Here is then the final version for the integral I as above:

```
 1 /* Simpson4.c */
 2
 3 # include <stdio.h>
 4 # include <math.h>
 5 # define f(x) (exp(sqrt(1.0+(x)*(x))-(x)))
 6
 7 main ( )
 8 {
 9 int i,N;
10 float h,s=f(0.0)+f(1.0); /* step size, sum variable */
11
12 printf("Enter the number of mesh points desired:   ");
13 scanf("%d",&N);
14 printf("\n");        /* generate a new line in output */
15
16 h=1.0/(float)N;
17
18 for (i=1;i<=N-1;i++){
19         s += (4.0*f((i-0.5)*h)+2.0*f(i*h));
20 }                               /* end the for loop */
21         s += (4.0*f((N-0.5)*h));
22
23 printf("Integral=%f\n",s*h/6.0);
24 }                                      /* end main */
```

The function scanf can be very picky about its input. Be careful not to add any additional spaces when calling it; i.e., try to avoid errors such as `scanf(" %d",&N)` and `scanf("%d ",&N)`, in each of which there are "extra" spaces.

In the sum loop above (line 19), we see expressions like $f(i * h)$. In general, one must be very careful with mixing types, as is done here: h is a float, but h is multiplied by an integer i, so what is the result? The answer lies in the *promotion rules* which specify that, in this case, the integer is converted to a float (the "higher order") before the multiplication is performed. Then $i * h$ represents the multiplication of two floats, which is now clear. Notice that the sum from (1.4) (computed in the variable s) is multiplied by $h/6$ within the `printf` function on line 23.

Sometimes you will want to make a conversion explicitly. This is done using a *cast*. For example to convert an integer i to a float value, write simply `(float)i` in the code. See line 16 above. (The cast in line 16 is actually unnecessary by the same promotion rules.) We will often use casts on pointers later.

By the way, now seems a good time to point out all of the basic data types in C:

char: character (a single byte)
int: integer
long: long integer
float: single–precision floating point
double: double–precision floating point

How large these are depends on the machine you're using. Additionally, we can form structures and arrays of these types, pointers to them, etc. This comes later.

In terms of these, the promotion rules may be summarized by the "inequalities"

`char` < `int` < `long` < `float` < `double`.

Moreover, "unsigned" quantities have a higher "rank" than their "signed" counterparts. Please see the section on `printf` format specifiers below.

Now for some general comments.

Please be advised that C is *case sensitive*. All keywords appear in lower case (see Appendix IV). C ignores "whitespace" when processing files. This means that tabs, blank spaces and line breaks are simply skipped over. Thus you may enter source code in any form convenient for understanding. Some historical conventions include using upper case to define symbolic constants, and aligning grouping symbols (e.g., { and }) in the source code. You will often see the underscore character used to improve readability. When naming variables, not only must all keywords be excluded, but the first character must be a letter or an underscore. The remaining characters are unrestricted; at least the first 31 characters are significant.

As for the include file `math.h`, the compiler looks for the *prototypes* of various built–in functions. These prototypes tell the compiler what kind of arguments the function takes, what its return value is, etc. Here are some of the important functions whose types are found in `math.h`:

fabs(x), sin(x), cos(x), sinh(x), cosh(x), exp(x), log(x), pow(x).

(Here fabs(x) denotes absolute value.) There are many other useful functions in `math.h` such as `floor(x)` (the greatest integer $\leq x$, returned as a double), `ceil(x)` (which rounds its argument up to an integer, instead of down as `floor` does), etc. In order to determine the prototypes of a desired function, you should peruse the file `math.h`. In general, the functions in `math.h` use double precision.

Interestingly enough, C contains no built–in exponentiation operator, as Fortran does. Thus to exponentiate, call the power function `pow( )` in this manner: to compute $2^{1.5}$, use `pow(2.0,1.5);` . Do not use the power function unless you *must*. It is much too slow. If, for example you need to compute x^2, write it as $x * x$, etc. When you do use the power function, please be sure to cast its arguments to type double. According to the ANSI standard, if a proper prototype is present, an improper argument should be automatically cast to the correct type. Thus, suppose n is an integer; then the expression sin(n) should be correctly computed. How will you know if a given compiler is fully ANSI–compliant? You may not; therefore such an expression should be computed via sin(`(double)`n).

We briefly mention at this juncture two other mathematical functions. The `rand( )` function returns a (pseudorandom) integer i in the range $0 \leq i \leq 32,767$ on machines with 16–bit integers. This function is reseeded with the function `srand( )`. The modulus operator % returns the remainder on integer division. Thus the statement

```
int r=10%3;
```

assigns to `r` the value 1.

Exercise 1.1: Given a smooth function $f(x)$ on an interval $[a, b]$, let $I = \int_a^b f(x)\,dx$. Write programs similar to `simpson4.c` which implement the *composite trapezoidal rule*

$$I = h \sum_{i=1}^{N-1} f(x_i) + \frac{h}{2}\left(f(a) + f(b)\right) - \frac{f''(\xi)h^2(b-a)}{12}$$

and the *corrected composite trapezoidal rule*

$$I = h \sum_{i=1}^{N-1} f(x_i) + \frac{h}{2}\left(f(a) + f(b)\right) + \frac{h^2}{12}\left(f'(a) - f'(b)\right) + \frac{f^{(4)}(\xi)h^4(b-a)}{720}.$$

These should accept any (simple) integrand and should allow the user to specify the number of subdivision points desired. The notation is $h = \frac{b-a}{N}$ for some integer N, $x_i = a + ih$, $(i = 0, 1, \ldots, N)$ so that $x_0 = a$, $x_N = b$.

Exercise 1.2: (*Birthday Problem*) Assume that a year contains 365 days. A random sample of k people is gathered in a room. The probability p that all k birthdays are distinct is given by

$$p = \frac{(365)_k}{(365)^k} = \prod_{j=1}^{k-1} \left(1 - \frac{j}{365} \right).$$

Compute this probability for $k = 2, 3, \ldots, 25$ and notice that $p < \frac{1}{2}$ when $k = 23$.

DO WHILE LOOPS

A good example to illustrate these is *fixed–point iteration*. Here one seeks a solution x of $f(x) = 0$, where both x and $f(x)$ are scalar. It is customary to write our equation $f(x) = 0$ in the form $x = g(x)$. (This can always be achieved by taking $g(x) = x - f(x)$.) Beginning with an initial guess x_0, we consider the sequence $\{x_n\}$, defined by $x_{n+1} = g(x_n)$ $(n = 0, 1, \ldots)$. We make the following hypotheses:

  i)There is a $\ell < 1$ such that $|g(x) - g(y)| \le \ell |x - y|$ for all x, y with $|x - x_0| \le r, |y - x_0| \le r$;

  ii)$|x_0 - g(x_0)| = |x_0 - x_1| \le r(1 - \ell)$.

Then the fixed–point iterates $\{x_n\}$ all lie in the set $\{x : |x - x_0| \le r\}$, and $|x_n - \alpha| \le r\ell^n$, where α is the unique (on this interval) root of $x = g(x)$. Thus, the sequence $\{x_n\}$ converges to a fixed point α of g, which by construction is a root of $f(x) = 0$. Recall that i) is called a *Lipschitz Condition*. By the Mean Value Theorem, it is implied by the hypothesis that $g \in C^1$, i.e., that both g and g' are continuous on the above interval. Condition ii) may be thought of as saying that "the initial guess x_0 is good enough."

  The *proof* is simple enough to be given here. Since x_0 belongs to the interval, x_1 does too because $|x_0 - x_1| = |x_0 - g(x_0)| \le r(1 - \ell) \le r$ by ii). Using induction, we assume that $x_1, \ldots, x_n$ all lie within the given interval. Then we write $|x_{n+1} - x_n| = |g(x_n) - g(x_{n-1})| \le \ell |x_n - x_{n-1}|$. Iterate this to get $|x_{n+1} - x_n| \le \ell^n |x_1 - x_0| \le \ell^n r(1 - \ell)$. Therefore,

$$|x_{n+1} - x_0| \le |(x_{n+1} - x_n) + (x_n - x_{n-1}) + \cdots + (x_1 - x_0)|$$
$$\le (\ell^n + \ell^{n-1} + \cdots + 1)(1 - \ell)r = r(1 - \ell^{n+1}) \le r.$$

Thus, all x_n satisfy $|x_n - x_0| \le r$.

Since we do not know the limit α *a priori*, we could show that the sequence $\{x_n\}$ converges by showing it is a Cauchy sequence. Here is a simpler observation, which amounts to the same thing: write the identity

$$x_n = x_0 + \sum_{k=1}^{n} (x_k - x_{k-1}).$$

The left–hand side (i.e., our sequence) converges if and only if the right–hand side does, and this will be true if

$$\sum_{k=1}^{\infty} |x_k - x_{k-1}| < \infty.$$

However, we showed above that

$$|x_k - x_{k-1}| \leq r(1 - \ell)\ell^{k-1},$$

and this, when summed, converges as a geometric series, since $\ell < 1$. Now that we know convergence, say $x_n \to \alpha$, just let $n \to \infty$ in the definition $x_{n+1} = g(x_n)$ and use the continuity of g to get $\alpha = g(\alpha)$, as desired. Uniqueness is also easy: if there were two fixed points α, β in the set $\{x : |x - x_0| \leq r\}$, then we would have $|\alpha - \beta| = |g(\alpha) - g(\beta)| \leq \ell|\alpha - \beta|$ and this is impossible since $\ell < 1$.

To write this algorithm in C we first need to decide on a stopping criterion. An obvious choice is: iterate until $|x_n - x_{n-1}| < \epsilon$, where ϵ is some preassigned tolerance (e.g., $0.5 * 10^{-8}$.) This means iterate until you see no change in the results. This is fine if you know in advance the magnitude of the root, but a preferable criterion is to use a *relative* test such as

(1.6) $|x_n - x_{n-1}| < \epsilon|x_n|$, and/or $|f(x_n)| <$ FTOL,

where FTOL is another user–specified number.

Here is a standard routine to find the positive root of the equation $x = \cos(x)$:

```
1 /* fpi1.c */
2
3 # include <stdio.h>
4 # include <stdlib.h>
5 # include <math.h>
6 # define g(x) (cos(x))
```

```
 7
 8 main( )
 9 {
10 double x,y,e;          /* define the variables */
11 double tol=5.0e-10;    /* stopping tolerance */
12 int iter=0;                  /* iterate number */
13
14 /* prompt for input */
15 printf("Enter the starting approximation:");
16 scanf("%lf",&x);          /* get double input */
17 printf("\n");             /* display a new line */
18
19 do{                          /* do loop while */
20          y=g(x);
21          e=fabs(x-y);
22          x=y;
23          iter++;
24          if (iter>100){
25          printf("Maximum number of iterates exceeded.");
26          exit (1);
27                  }                        /* end if body */
28
29 }                                     /* end while body */
30 while (e>fabs(y)*tol);          /* test of while loop */
31
32 printf("root= %lf\n",y);
33 printf("iterates required = %d\n",iter);
34 }                                          /* end main */
```

Let's dissect the program. At the top (lines 3–5) are three standard include files, as well as the function macro definition for $g(x)$. The variables are defined as double precision; e will measure the relative error as discussed above. The tolerance is set fairly stringently, since we're using double precision.

Notice the **scanf** statement in line 16: we are getting double input, hence the format specifier %lf is used (lf stands for *long float*). Of course, the *address of* operator & is again required. Then comes the *do loop* (lines 19–30), enclosed in braces. We first evaluate g at x, and then calculate the error in the variable e. Then the next iteration is set up by putting $x = y$, and the iterate counter **iter** is incremented. The *if* statement checks for runaway iterates; we'll discuss this momentarily. The body of the loop ends with } (line 29) and the test of the loop appears as *while (condition)*. Here the condition (line 30) is that the error in successive iterates, e, exceeds

$|y| * tol$, which is exactly the relative error criterion mentioned above. The
printf statements first use the double format specifier %lf to print the final
value, and the next one prints an integer, so it uses %d.

Exercise 1.3: Write the equation $x^4 - x = 10$ in an appropriate form
$x = g(x)$ to find a root near $x = 2$, and alter the code just given to find it.

This version of the do–loop is *bottom–tested*; thus it always executes at
least once. Is there a problem with this? No — not in this case because the
probability is zero that the first guess is correct! The other standard form
of the *while* loop is top–tested, and may not execute at all. A good example
occurs when reading data from a file. However, this involves pointers, and
so will be postponed. For now, the top–tested while loop appears as

$$\text{while (condition)}\{$$
$$\text{body of loop}$$
$$\}$$

Here is an explicit code fragment to illustrate a simple case:

```
main( )
{
double x=0.0;
while(x<=3.14){
  printf("sin(%lf)=%lf\n",x,sin(x));
x += 0.05;
  }
}
```

The last line printed will contain the values x, $\sin x$ for $x = 3.1$.
Notice that in this form of such a loop there is no semicolon following
the condition of the while statement. When reading other programs you
may see something like this:

```
# define TRUE 1
  ⋮
while (TRUE){
  ⋮
}
```

Since such a test is always true, one needs to use an explicit construction
(such as the break statement) to terminate the loop. See the end of this
chapter.
The *if* statement in the code begins on line 24. The general form is:

```
if (condition){
    statements ...
}
```

If the condition is satisfied (i.e., evaluates as true), the body of the statement is executed. Otherwise, control returns to the next line following the loop body, as expected. In the present case, if the number of iterates exceeds 100, the `printf` statement (line 25) announces this on the screen, and the next line 26 allows a speedy exit. The `exit` statement allows one to terminate a program quickly and directly; possible values as arguments are 0 and 1, with 1 denoting abnormal termination, in general. The file `stdlib.h` is included for its prototype.

Compile and run this program, starting with an *arbitrary* value, and note the number of iterates required. Can you prove that for this function g the algorithm converges for *every* value of x_0?

Unless you started with a tremendously accurate initial guess, you may have noticed that some 50 iterates were required! A standard acceleration scheme, the *delta squared method* (or Steffensen iteration), is often employed. See the end of this chapter for the code, which is presented as an example of the `break` statement.

The last example is *Newton's method* for finding a root of the (scalar) equation $f(x) = 0$. In the fixed point iteration above, the error decreases *linearly* in the sense that $|x_{n+1} - \alpha| \leq \ell|x_n - \alpha|$. Thus, it is called a *first–order* method. Newton's method is second order at a simple root α of $f(x) = 0$, which basically means that $|x_{n+1} - \alpha| \leq c|x_n - \alpha|^2$ for some constant c. (The root α is *simple* if $f(\alpha) = 0$ but $f'(\alpha) \neq 0$.) Thus, the number of correct decimal places essentially doubles at each step.

In general, consider fixed–point iteration applied to $x = g(x)$ as above, and assume that $g(\alpha) = \alpha$, $g'(\alpha) = 0$. Applying Taylor's Theorem on the interval $|x - \alpha| \leq r$, we get

$$g(x) = g(\alpha) + \frac{1}{2}(x - \alpha)^2 g''(\xi)$$

for some point ξ between α and x. If μ is an upper bound for $g''(x)$ over the interval $|x - \alpha| \leq r$, we obtain the estimate

$$|x_{n+1} - \alpha| = |g(x_n) - g(\alpha)| \leq \frac{\mu}{2}|x_n - \alpha|^2,$$

which is the desired second–order convergence. Iterating this, we conclude that

$$|x_n - \alpha| \leq \left[\frac{\mu}{2}|x_0 - \alpha|\right]^{2^n - 1} |x_0 - \alpha|,$$

and hence if $\mu|x_0 - \alpha| < 2$, $x_n \to \alpha$ as $n \to \infty$, i.e., the iteration converges if the initial guess is sufficiently accurate.

The Newton iteration is this: given an initial approximation x_0, compute

(1.7) $$x_{n+1} = x_n - \frac{f(x_n)}{f'(x_n)} \qquad (n = 0, 1, \ldots).$$

Thus, in our earlier notation, $g(x) = x - \frac{f(x)}{f'(x)}$ and it is easy to see that $g'(\alpha) = 0$ when α is a root of $x = g(x)$. In the sketch we begin with an initial approximation x_0 and draw the tangent line to the graph of $y = f(x)$ at the point $(x_0, f(x_0))$. The point at which this tangent line crosses the axis is taken to be the next approximation x_1, as shown. Then the process is repeated with x_1 replacing x_0, etc.

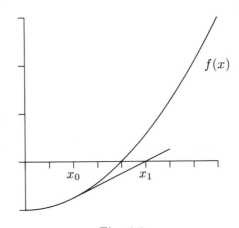

Fig. 1.1

The nontrivial theorem of Kantorovich (see Chapter 4 for the system version) says that, for a class of functions f, if the initial guess is sufficiently accurate, the sequence $\{x_n\}$ converges to a root of $f(x) = 0$. Here is a precise statement in the present one–dimensional case:

Let $f \in C^2$ satisfy the following:

i) $\left| \frac{1}{f'(x_0)} \right| \le a$;

ii) $|x_1 - x_0| = \left| \frac{f(x_0)}{f'(x_0)} \right| \le b$;

iii) $|f''(x)| \le c$ for $|x - x_0| \le 2b$.

Then if $2abc \le 1$, the Newton iterates converge quadratically to a root α of $f(x) = 0$.

The proof is too lengthy to be given here, but we show that the hypothesis $2abc \leq 1$ leads to the existence of a root of f on the interval $|x - x_0| \leq 2b$. Indeed, by Taylor's theorem we have

$$f(x_0 \pm 2b) = f(x_0) \pm 2bf'(x_0) + 2b^2 f''(\eta_\pm)$$

for some intermediate points $\eta_\pm$. Dividing by $f'(x_0)$ we get

$$\frac{f(x_0 - 2b)}{f'(x_0)} = \frac{f(x_0)}{f'(x_0)} - 2b + 2b^2 \frac{f''(\eta_-)}{f'(x_0)}$$
$$\leq \left| \frac{f(x_0)}{f'(x_0)} \right| - 2b + 2b^2 \cdot a \cdot c$$
$$\leq -b + 2b^2 ac = -b + b \cdot 2abc$$
$$\leq 0.$$

Similarly, using the plus sign we obtain

$$\frac{f(x_0 + 2b)}{f'(x_0)} \geq 0.$$

Thus, the intermediate value theorem now gives the result.

Here is the straightforward code, using again a relative error test, and checking for division by zero (the vanishing of $f'(x_n)$) as well as for run–away iterates.

```
1  /* Newton.c */
2
3  # include <stdio.h>
4  # include <stdlib.h>
5  # include <math.h>
6  # define TOL (5.0e-12)   /* tolerance for convergence */
7  # define f(x) (0.5*(x)-sin(x))          /* function f */
8  # define fp(x) (0.5-cos(x))         /* derivative of f */
9
10 main()
11 {
12         int i=0;                 /* iterate counter */
13         double x,y,z;
14
15         printf("Enter the initial approximation:  ");
16         scanf("%lf",&x);
17         printf("\n");
```

```
18
19          do{
20                  if (fabs(fp(x))<5.0e-20){
21                          printf("Division by zero.");
22                          exit(1);
23                          }
24
25                  y=x-f(x)/fp(x);   /* Newton iteration */
26                  z=fabs(x-y);
27                  i++;
28                  if (i>20){
29                          printf("Too many iterates.");
30                          exit(1);
31                          }
32                  x=y;
33              }while (z>fabs(y)*TOL);
34
35              printf("\n\n");
36              printf("root = %lf\n",y);
37              printf("iterates required:  %d\n", i);
38 }
```

This example is to find a positive root of $\sin x = \frac{x}{2}$. Sometimes you will need to find an extremely accurate initial guess, e.g., even when finding roots of the simple–looking equation $\tan x = x$.

Exercise 1.4: This exercise involves a polygonal approximation to π. Let a regular polygon of N sides be inscribed in the unit circle. If L_N denotes the length of one side, then an estimate for π is $\frac{NL_N}{2}$. Clearly a better estimate for π is obtained by using a polygon of $2N$ sides, each with length L_{2N}. We start with a polygon of four sides (i.e., a square). Thus, $L_4 = \sqrt{2}$.

i)Show that $L_{2N} = \left[2 \left(1 - \sqrt{1 - \frac{L_N^2}{4}} \right) \right]^{\frac{1}{2}}$.

ii)Compute an estimate for π by computing $\frac{NL_N}{2}$ and then doubling the number of sides. Repeat the procedure until "convergence" is obtained.

Be sure to include a termination statement, and pay attention to how you write L_{2N}. **HINT:** L_N will eventually be *extremely small*.

Exercise 1.5: In the classical *false position* method to find roots of $f(x) = 0$, one begins with two approximations x_0, x_1 and generates a sequence of (hopefully) better approximations via

$$x_{n+1} = x_n - f(x_n)\frac{x_n - x_0}{f(x_n) - f(x_0)} \quad \text{for} \quad n = 1, 2, \ldots.$$

Consider the following sketch in which we take the case that $f(x)$ is increasing and convex:

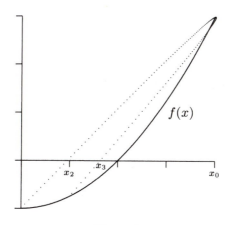

Fig. 1.2

We begin here with the two approximations $(x_0, f(x_0))$ and (for purposes of illustration) $(x_1, f(x_1)) = (0, f(0))$. The chord is drawn between these two points; the point at which this chord crosses the axis is taken to be the next approximation x_2. One then draws the chord between the two points $(x_0, f(x_0))$ and $(x_2, f(x_2))$. The next approximation is that point x_3 where this chord crosses the axis, as shown. Write a C program which achieves this approximation for a given function f. For such an f as above (increasing, convex) and for initial approximations x_0,x_1 as shown above with $f(x_0) \cdot f(x_1) < 0$, prove that this sequence must converge to the *unique* solution of $f(x) = 0$ over $[x_1, x_0]$.

Exercise 1.6: Consider the boundary–value problem

$$y'' + \lambda y = 0 \quad (0 < x < 1), \quad y(0) = 0, \, y(1) - y'(1) = 0.$$

Nontrivial solutions exist only for a discrete set of values of λ called *eigenvalues*. Attempt a solution to the equation of the form $y = \exp(rx)$ and show that the general solution is a linear combination of $\sin(\sqrt{\lambda}x)$ and $\cos(\sqrt{\lambda}x)$. Find a transcendental equation which the eigenvalues must satisfy and compute the first two positive eigenvalues.

IF–ELSE CONSTRUCTS

Such constructs are probably familiar from other languages; notice that "then" is *not* used in *C*. The standard form for a dichotomy (two choices) is

```
if (condition) {
    statements
}
else {
    other statements
}
```

As a simple example, consider this code fragment arising in solving a quadratic equation of the form $ax^2 + bx + c = 0$:

```
double discr=b*b - 4.0*a*c;
    if (discr<0.0){
        printf("complex roots\n");
}
    else {
        printf("real roots\n");
{
```

Another illustrative example is the *bisect method*. Here one has a continuous function $f(x)$ on an interval $[a, b]$ satisfying $f(a)f(b) < 0$, i.e., f takes opposite signs at the endpoints. From the intermediate value theorem, f must vanish somewhere on (a, b). So one considers the midpoint $c = \frac{a+b}{2}$ and computes $f(c)$ to determine its sign. If $f(a)f(c) > 0$, there must be a root in the interval (c, b). Otherwise there is a root in $(a, c]$. In either case, the "new" interval has length $\frac{b-a}{2}$. After n steps the root has been isolated to lie in an interval of length $\frac{b-a}{2^n}$. Thus, the bisect method always converges, but it does so *linearly* and hence slowly. However, at each step the root is *bracketed*, a desirable property. Here is a routine to achieve this:

```
1 /* Bisect.c */
2
3 # include <math.h>
4 # include <stdio.h>
5 # define f(x) ((x)*(x)*(x)-(x)+1.0)
6
7 main( )
8 {
9 double a,b,c,z;
```

```
10 printf("\n");
11 printf("Enter the left-hand endpoint:   ");
12 scanf("%lf",&a);
13 printf("\n");
14 printf("Enter the right-hand endpoint:   ");
15 scanf("%lf",&b);
16 printf("\n\n");
17
18 do{
19
20          c=(a+b)/2.0;
21
22          if (f(a)*f(c)>0.0)
23                   a=c;
24          else
25                   b=c;
26
27          z=fabs(b-a);
28
29 }while (z>5.0e-10);
30
31 printf("root = %lf\n",c);
32 printf("\n\n");
33 }
```

When you compile and run the program, the initial interval $a = -2$, $b = -1$ can be used.

Please notice line 22, on which the product $f(a) * f(c)$ is computed. To prevent overflow/underflow, one should compute only the algebraic signs of the two function values, since this suffices for the algorithm. We relegate this to an exercise later in this chapter.

What if there are several choices in a given situation? The format is this:

```
if (condition 1) {
statements
}
else if (condition 2) {
statements
}
else if (...) {
 .
 .
 .
}
```

```
else {
statements
}
```

Notice that else if is *two* words. Should some condition require no statement at all, use a semicolon:

```
else {
;
}
```

Here is an easy example: consider evaluating the function $t(x)$ given by

$$t(x) = \begin{cases} x & \text{if } -1 < x < 1 \\ -1 & \text{if } x \le -1 \\ 1 & \text{otherwise.} \end{cases}$$

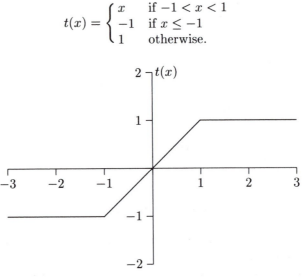

Fig. 1.3

Given a double value of x, this code fragment computes $t = t(x)$:

```
double t;
if (x ≤ −1.0)
      t = −1.0;
else if (x ≥ 1.0)
      t = 1.0;
else
      t = x;
```

We also mention here the *ternary* or *conditional* operator "(? :)." It is composed of three expressions on either side of the two symbols and is similar to an "if–then–else" statement. If the first condition evaluates as true, the expression is assigned the value of the second operand. Otherwise, the expression is assigned the value of the third operand.

Here are some examples which should help:

```
# define MAX(x,y)   ((x)> = (y)   ?    (x)  :  (y))
```

This macro returns the maximum of the two numbers x and y; the minimum is similarly written. The absolute value function $|x|$ could be written as

```
# define ABS(x)    ((x)> = 0.0   ?    (x)  :  -(x))
```

Note the essential use of parentheses around each variable in any such compiler directive. Naturally, these can be used in–line code, too:

```
double sgn=  ((x)> = 0.0)   ?    1.0   :    -1.0;
```

The first part of the conditional expression on the right–hand side here need not be enclosed in parentheses, due to an appropriate precedence rule. We do so anyway in the last example above to promote readability. The ternary operator is right–associative with respect to its first and third operands.

As our last example, we consider optimization of a function of one real variable. The algorithm may be called a "no–derivative line search via sectioning," or the "golden search." Only values of the function are used. Should derivative information also be available, more sophisticated methods are known; see [FL] or [NR]. It suffices to consider minimization.

A minimum of a function $f(x)$ is *bracketed* when a triple of points $\{a, b, c\}$ is known for which $f(b) < \min\{f(a), f(c)\}$. Consider three such points as given initial information. Thus, the value of the function at the middle point b is the best approximation at the current stage of the algorithm; this rule is maintained throughout the iteration.

Now we wish to refine the present approximation b to the point where the minimum is assumed, and do so by contracting the current bracketing interval $[a, c]$. Consider the following generic picture:

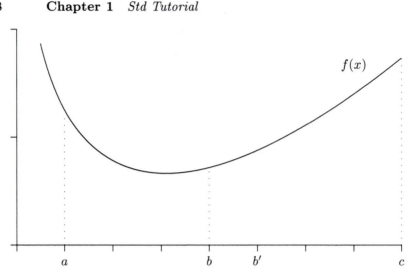

Fig. 1.4

The figure shows the original bracketing triple $\{a, b, c\}$ in the case $c - b > b - a$ which we focus on below. The next point b' to be inserted somewhere is also shown, and is taken to lie in the larger of the two intervals. In the bisect method for root finding, the "new" interval is one half the length of the original interval. In the current algorithm, it will be required instead that both potential new brackets have intervals in the same ratio. Thus, for any bracketing triple $\{a, b, c\}$ (with $c - b > b - a$) we require

$$(1.8) \qquad \frac{\text{long}}{\text{short}} = \frac{c - b}{b - a} \equiv R,$$

where $R > 1$ is fixed. What is the value of R? The new bracketing triples will be either $\{a, b, b'\}$ (if $f(b) < f(b')$ as shown) or $\{b, b', c\}$. (This case would arise if b were to fall to the left of the actual minimum in the sketch, and $f(b') < f(b)$.) Applying the rule of the algorithm to both of the possible new brackets we see that

$$\frac{\text{long}}{\text{short}} = \frac{b - a}{b' - b} = R = \frac{c - b'}{b' - b}.$$

Therefore $c - b' = b - a$ and hence

$$(1.9) \qquad 1 = \frac{c - b'}{b - a} = \frac{(c - b) - (b' - b)}{b - a} = R - \frac{1}{R}.$$

It follows that R satisfies the quadratic $R^2 - R - 1 = 0$ and thus

$$R = \frac{1 + \sqrt{5}}{2} \approx 1.618033989.$$

(Since $R > 1$ there is no ambiguity in the choice of sign for the radical.) Similar reasoning applies in the case $c - b < b - a$.

Now we can write an explicit formula for the new insertion point b'. If $[b, c]$ is the larger subinterval in the original bracketing triple, we can write

$$\frac{\text{long}}{\text{short}} = \frac{c - b'}{b' - b} = R$$

and solve this for b' to get

$$(1.10) \qquad b' = \frac{c + Rb}{R + 1} = b + \frac{c - b}{R + 1}.$$

If instead $[a, b]$ were the larger of the two subintervals, the point b' would be inserted to the left of b, and we would have

$$\frac{\text{long}}{\text{short}} = \frac{b' - a}{b - b'} = R,$$

and as above this can be solved for b' to get

$$(1.11) \qquad b' = \frac{a + Rb}{R + 1} = b - \frac{b - a}{R + 1}.$$

At each stage of the algorithm we thus have four points to monitor, the three points of the present bracket and the new point to be inserted. Below, our illustrations always depict the case in which $c - b > b - a$. We label them as $a = \xi_1 < b = \xi_2 < b' = \xi_3 < c = \xi_4$ with corresponding function values $f_i = f(\xi_i)$ $(i = 1, 2, 3, 4)$:

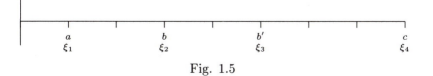

Fig. 1.5

Now consider the case in which $f(\xi_3) < f(\xi_2)$, i.e., the new bracket is $\{b, b', c\}$. We "blow–up" this new bracket and sketch it with the names of the new points $n\xi_1 = $ new ξ_1, etc.:

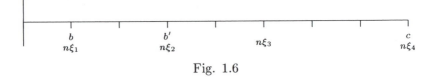

Fig. 1.6

Thus, in this case ξ_4 is unchanged. We need only compute the coordinate $n\xi_3$ in the next bracketing interval:

$$\frac{\text{long}}{\text{short}} = \frac{n\xi_4 - n\xi_3}{n\xi_3 - n\xi_2} = R,$$

which gives

$$n\xi_3 = \frac{n\xi_4}{R+1} + \frac{R}{R+1}n\xi_2.$$

The entire procedure for contracting the bracketing interval then takes the form (in the case $f(\xi_3) < f(\xi_2)$)

$\xi_1 = \xi_2;$
$\xi_2 = \xi_3;$
$\xi_3 = R * \xi_2/(R+1) + \xi_4/(R+1);$
$f_1 = f_2;$
$f_2 = f_3;$
$f_3 = f(\xi_3);$

In the case in which $f(\xi_2) < f(\xi_3)$, the new bracket is $\{a, b, b'\}$ and the next point $b' \equiv n\xi_2$ is inserted to the left of b. We leave it as an exercise to show that in this case the calculation of the new interval appears as follows:

$\xi_4 = \xi_3;$
$\xi_3 = \xi_2;$
$\xi_2 = R * \xi_3/(R+1) + \xi_1/(R+1);$
$f_4 = f_3;$
$f_3 = f_2;$
$f_2 = f(\xi_2);$

With this explanation the following procedure should be clear:

```
1 /* MIN_ONED.c */
2
3 /*
4 Minimization of a scalar function f(x) of one variable
5 via Golden Search Routine.
```

```
 6 Three distinct points a,b,c are to be input
 7 with f(b) < min{ f(a),f(c) }.
 8 */
 9
10 # include <stdio.h>
11 # include <math.h>
12
13 # define TOL 5.0e-8
14 # define ONE_OVER_RPLUS1   0.3819660112
15 # define R_OVER_RPLUS1     0.6180339888
16 # define f(x)  ((x)*(x)*(x)/3.0-(x)-1.0)
17
18 main()
19 {
20 double a,b,c,xi1,xi2,xi3,xi4,f1,f2,f3,f4,min_x,min_f;
21
22 printf("Enter the interval forming the bracket:\n");
23 printf("\n");
24 printf("Enter a:   ");
25 scanf("%lf",&a);
26 printf("\n");
27 printf("Enter b:   ");
28 scanf("%lf",&b);
29 printf("\n");
30 printf("Enter c:   ");
31 scanf("%lf",&c);
32 printf("\n");
33
34 xi1=a;
35 xi4=c;
36
37          /* initial configuration */
38          if (fabs(c-b)<fabs(b-a)){
39                  /* left interval bigger */
40                  xi3=b;
41                  xi2=b-(b-a)*ONE_OVER_RPLUS1;
42                  }
43          else{
44                  /* right interval bigger */
45                  xi2=b;
46                  xi3=b+(c-b)*ONE_OVER_RPLUS1;
47                  }
48
```

```
49 f2=f(xi2);
50 f3=f(xi3);
51
52 do{
53          if (f3 < f2) {
54                  xi1=xi2; f1=f2;
55                  xi2=xi3; f2=f3;
56                  xi3=xi2*R_OVER_RPLUS1+xi4*ONE_OVER_RPLUS1 ;
57                  f3=f(xi3);
58                  }
59
60          else {
61                  xi4=xi3; f4=f3;
62                  xi3=xi2; f3=f2;
63                  xi2=xi1*ONE_OVER_RPLUS1+xi3*R_OVER_RPLUS1;
64                  f2=f(xi2);
65                  }
66
67 }
68 while (fabs(xi4-xi1)>TOL*(fabs(xi2)+fabs(xi3)));
69
70 min_x=(f2 < f3) ?  xi2 :  xi3;
71 min_f=(f2 < f3) ?  f2 :   f3;
72
73 printf("Minimum Value = %lf\n",min_f);
74 printf("It occurs at x= %lf\n",min_x);
75 }
```

This is set up for a simple function $f(x)$ which has a minimum at $x = 1$. Here are two final comments. It is possible to give just the endpoints of an interval on which a minimum is sought; an extra routine then returns the "middle point" b automatically. See [NR] for such code. Secondly, for general use this code should be made into a C function which should accept the function f to be optimized as an argument. This will be an exercise in Chapter 2.

PRINTF FORMAT SPECIFIERS

So far we have used simply %d, %f, etc., in print statements. Here we discuss how to fine tune the output. On many machines an integer ranges from $-32,768$ to $32,767$ (this is essentially 2^{15} on each side). An *unsigned* integer N can vary from 0 to $65,535$ on the same machine. One declares an unsigned integer with the line

unsigned int N;

To display this value of N in `printf`, use the `%u` format specifier.

For larger integer values, use the *long* quantifier as in

```
long int N;
```

On the same machine as envisioned above, a long integer N satisfies $|N| <$ $2,147,483,647$ and is displayed in `printf` using the `%ld` format specifier.

How large is an integer on your machine? This one–line program (to be constructed within a `main` structure as usual) will tell you:

```
printf("integer=%d\n",sizeof(int));
```

On the same type of machine as above, a `float` contains four bytes while a `double` contains eight bytes.

Field width and precision specifiers are also supported. A statement such as

```
printf("%4d %10.6f\n",N,x);
```

produces (on each output line) an integer N in a field four digits wide, and a float x in a field at least ten digits wide with six digits after the decimal point. The "4" and the "10" are *minimum width specifiers*, while the "6" is called a *precision specifier*, and allows one to specify the number of decimal places displayed. The format %e is *exponential* and is useful when comparing significant digits. Thus, if $E=0.2718281828$,

```
printf("%12.7e\n",E);
```

produces 2.7182818e-001.

For null–terminated strings, use the `%s` specifier (see Chapter 3).

Other escape sequences often used with `printf` include

\a	(alert, or bell)
\b	(backspace)
\t	(tab)
\\	\ (backslash)

LOGICAL AND OTHER OPERATORS

The essentials are this:

&&	**AND**
||	**OR**
!	**(logical) NOT**
==	**EQUALITY**
! =	**INEQUALITY**

Be careful not to confuse EQUALITY: $a == b$ with ASSIGNMENT: $a = b$. The latter sets a equal to b, while the former tests to see if the two numbers a and b are in fact equal. Any nonzero integer is interpreted by the compiler to mean TRUE, while 0 means FALSE. Thus, the statement if (!x) is the same as if (x== 0) for an integer x. In expressions involving && or ||, evaluation is performed from left to right.

As a simple example, suppose that within a *do loop* you have a double variable e to measure the error in successive iterates. The loop will be exited when $e < TOL$, for some given number TOL. In addition, no more than 100 iterates are to be performed. Here is a code fragment which will do the job:

```
do {
  ⋮
}
while (e >TOL   &&   iter < 100);
```

Exercise 1.7: Write a short program which will compute the solution of the quadratic equation $ax^2 + bx + c = 0$ in every case.

C FUNCTIONS

Everything in C is a function, including main itself. The format of a C function is

return type   functionname   (parameter list)
{
    statements
    return (value)
}

Here "return type" indicates double, int, etc., and "parameter list" specifies the number and type of arguments the function expects. One calls a C function by simply writing its name (along with any arguments) in the main program. The word "call" itself is *not* used. Function arguments are passed *by value* in C, *not by reference*. This means that any arguments to a function are not changed by the function after the function call. In order to achieve a call by reference, one uses *pointers*. If a given function has no return value, its return type is "void"; similarly, a function which takes no arguments has "void" as the parameter list. We use the ANSI recommendation for C functions, as shown below. In particular, the code of the function itself appears outside of main, and a "function prototype" (essentially the first line in the format above) appears either before `main`, or in the first few lines of `main`.

The keyword `return` need not be present if the function simply ends without returning any value(s); we will see this later in Chapter 2. If it is explicitly used, `return` may appear anywhere in the function body.

As a simple example, suppose you want to write a C function which will return the value of the function $f(x) = \frac{1}{1+x^2}$. It might appear as

```
double f(double x)              /* function definition */
{
    double y=1.0/(1.0+x*x);
    return y;
}
```

The return type is double, and the function (also called f) expects a single argument x of type double. In the variable y the desired value is computed; this value is "returned" on the next line. A simple program to compute $f(2)$, say, follows. Please notice that *no semicolon appears* below at the end of the line (line 5) containing the function definition. However, notice that in `main` the line (line 13) containing the function prototype *does* indeed end with a semicolon. The actual function call appears on line 15.

```
1  /* Eval.c */
2
3  # include <stdio.h>
4
5  double f(double x)     /* defining code of function f */
6  {
7  double y=1.0/(1.0+x*x);
8  return y;
9  }
10
11 main( )
12 {
13 double f(double x);    /* function prototype */
14 double x=2.0;
15 double fnval=f(x);
16
17 printf("f(%lf)=%lf\n",x,fnval);
18 }
```

Before giving further examples, we make three points about "short-cuts." Firstly, in the definition of f, you may already see that the variable y is superfluous. Indeed, the code could be rewritten as

```
double f(double x)
{
   return (1.0/(1.0+x*x));
}
```

Secondly, there is no need for the variable fnval defined in main. In fact, the two lines

```
double fnval=f(x);
printf("f(%lf)=%lf\n",x,fnval);
```

could simply be replaced by the single line

```
printf("f(%lf)=%lf\n",x,f(x));
```

Lastly, the function prototype in line 13 could be written as

```
double f(double );
```

with the argument x omitted.

As an example of the phrase "call by value," consider this simple C function which computes the function $s(x) = x + 1$ for an integer x:

```
int s(int x)
{
   x += 1;
   return x;
}
```

If we call this function with the argument $x = 2$, say, the function will return the value 3, but x retains the value 2.

Here are a number of examples.

1. A function of two variables.

Suppose we want to compute the function $g(x, y) = \sin(xy)$. We could simply write

```
double g(double x, double y)
{
   return (sin(x*y));
}
```

Be sure to include the prototype double g(double x, double y); near the top of main.

2. Simpson's Rule, revisited.

Let's consider again the evaluation of the integral $I = \int_0^1 \exp(-x^2)\,dx$ by the simple (crude) version of Simpson's Rule:

$$\int_a^b f(x)\,dx \approx \frac{(b-a)}{6}\left[f(a) + 4f\left(\frac{a+b}{2}\right) + f(b)\right].$$

A C program using a function call to compute this approximation is

```
1 /* Simpson5.c */
2
3 # include <stdio.h>
4 # include <math.h>
5
6 double simpson(double a, double b)   /* function name */
7 {                              /* begin function definition */
8 double x=exp(-a*a);
9 double mid=(a+b)/2.0;
10
11 x += (4.0*exp(-mid*mid));
12 x += exp(-b*b);
13 x *= ((b-a)/6.0);
14
15 return x;
16 }                            /* end function definition */
17
18 main( )
19 {
20 double simpson(double a, double b);     /* prototype */
21 double a=0.0,b=1.0;                /* the endpoints */
22
23 printf("Integral=%lf\n",simpson(a,b));
24 }
```

3. Accurate computation of the expression $\sqrt{x^2 + y^2}$.

We can write

$$\sqrt{x^2 + y^2} = |x|\sqrt{1 + \left(\frac{y}{x}\right)^2} = |y|\sqrt{1 + \left(\frac{x}{y}\right)^2},$$

and the best form to use depends on the ratio of x to y. Here is a function which will do the job:

```
double sqr(double x, double y)
{
if (x == 0.0)
  return fabs(y);
else if (y == 0.0)
  return fabs(x);
else if (fabs(x) ≤ fabs(y))
  return fabs(y) * sqrt(1.0 + x * x/(y * y));
else
  return fabs(x) * sqrt(1.0 + y * y/(x * x));
}
```

The file **math.h** must be included whenever this is used. So that division by zero not be attempted, we test each argument to see if it vanishes. Of course *equality* of two floating point numbers is not to be expected in general, for reasons of binary representation. Therefore such tests are to be avoided whenever possible.

4. The Factorial Function.

The computation of $n! \equiv n(n-1)\cdots 1$ is nontrivial for large n. If $n > 13$ or so, one should use the fact that $n! = \Gamma(n+1)$ and evaluate the Gamma Function by special means. A nice way to do this appears in [NR]; see also [AS]. For cruder approximations, *Stirling's formula* is useful

$$n! \sim \sqrt{2\pi n}\, n^n e^{-n},$$

where the notation means the ratio of the two sides approaches one as $n \to \infty$. For now, we'll just use its definition; see the exercise involving the Gamma function later in this chapter. Here is a nonrecursive program for this:

```
1 /* Factor.c */
2
3 # include <stdio.h>
4
5 long factrl(int n)
6 {
7 int i;
8 long m=1;
9         for (i=2;i<=n;i++){
10                m *= ((long)i);   /* cast */
11 }
12 return m;
```

```
13 }
14
15 main( )
16 {
17 int n;
18 long factrl(int n);
19 printf("Enter an integer < 13:  ");
20 scanf("%d",&n);
21 printf("%d factorial=%ld\n",n,factrl(n));
22 }
```

Notice the `long` return type in line 5, and the cast in line 10 (this cast is again not necessary, but is included for emphasis). Moreover, the long `printf` format specifier `%ld` is essential in line 21.

5. Gauss–Chebyshev Integration.

Consider the numerical approximation of an integral of the form $I(f) = \int_{-1}^{1} \frac{f(x)}{\sqrt{1-x^2}} \, dx$. Typical composite rules cannot be applied directly since the error formulae demand computation of a certain high–order derivative of the integrand evaluated at some point in $(-1, 1)$. When we differentiate the integrand repeatedly, the result becomes more and more singular. Thus, a different method is required, and *Gaussian Integration* does the job. Gaussian rules can be derived by integrating the cubic Hermite interpolating polynomial for f—more on this later. For our present purposes, we simply quote the result: let $T_m(x) = \cos(m \arccos x)$ denote the *Chebyshev polynomial* of degree m, and define

$$(1.12) \qquad x_i = \cos\left[\frac{(2i-1)\pi}{2m}\right] = \text{ith zero of} \quad T_m(x) \quad (i = 1, 2, \ldots, m).$$

Then there is a point $\xi \in (-1, 1)$ for which

$$(1.13) \qquad I(f) = \int_{-1}^{1} \frac{f(x)}{\sqrt{1-x^2}} \, dx = \frac{\pi}{m} \sum_{k=1}^{m} f(x_k) + \frac{2\pi f^{(2m)}(\xi)}{2^{2m}(2m)!}.$$

The coefficients of the summands are all equal to $\frac{\pi}{m}$; we say that the *Gaussian weights* are all equal. Here is a simple program to implement this, which is set up for the case $f(x) = \cos(x)$:

```
1 /*  GAUSCHEB.C */
2
3 /* Gauss-Chebyshev Integration */
4 /* Integration of f(x)/sqrt(1-x*x) over (-1,1) */
```

```
 5
 6 # include <math.h>
 7 # include <stdio.h>
 8 # define PI (3.141592653589793)
 9
10 double f(double x)
11 {
12             return (cos(x));
13 }
14
15 main()
16 {
17 int i,m;                           /* define variables */
18 double s=0.0;
19 double f(double x);                 /* function prototype */
20
21 printf("\nEnter the desired number of nodes:      ");
22 scanf("%d",&m);
23
24 for (i=1;i<=m;i++)
25         s += (f(cos((2.0*i-1.0)*PI*(0.5)/(double)m)));
26
27 printf("\nIntegral= %10.10lf\n",s*PI/(double)m);
28 }   /* end main */
```

This should be easy to follow by now. The integrand is specified on lines 10–13 in a *C*–function, also called **f**. In lines 21–22 we get the number of nodal points desired, m, from the user. The `printf` statement begins with \n to get a new line in the output.

Here is another good example of Gauss–Chebyshev quadrature. The *Bessel function* $J_n(x)$ of order $n = 0, 1, \ldots$, is defined by

$$J_n(x) = \sum_{k=0}^{\infty} \frac{(-1)^k \left(\frac{x}{2}\right)^{n+2k}}{k!(n+k)!}.$$

Bessel functions arise often in problems involving cylindrical symmetry. In any special functions book you can find the integral representation

$$J_n(x) = \frac{\left(\frac{x}{2}\right)^n}{\Gamma(\frac{1}{2})\Gamma(n+\frac{1}{2})} \int_{-1}^{1} (1-t^2)^{n-\frac{1}{2}} \cos(tx)\, dt$$

and the asymptotic representation

$$(1.14) \qquad J_n(x) \sim \sqrt{\frac{2}{x\pi}} \cos\left(x - \frac{n\pi}{2} - \frac{\pi}{4}\right) \qquad (x \to \infty).$$

Here $\Gamma(x)$ is the Gamma function (cf. [LB]).

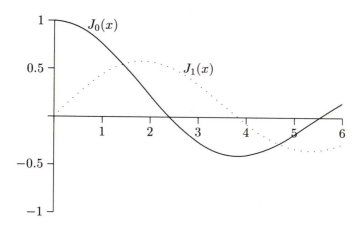

Fig. 1.7

Thus as special cases we have

(1.15)
$$J_0(x) = \frac{1}{\pi} \int_{-1}^{1} \frac{\cos(tx)}{\sqrt{1-t^2}}\, dt,$$

(1.16)
$$J_1(x) = \frac{1}{\pi} \int_{-1}^{1} \frac{t\sin(tx)}{\sqrt{1-t^2}}\, dt.$$

We have integrated by parts to get the latter representation.

   Now consider the problem of finding the first few zeroes of $J_0(x)$. We use Newton's method; thus, the derivative is required. It is well known that $J_0'(x) = -J_1(x)$. In the Gaussian formula above, what should the number of nodes m be? For the evaluation of $J_0(x)$, we have for the integrand the function $f(t) = \frac{1}{\pi}\cos(xt)$. Let's say that $x \le 6$ is known during the iteration. Then the error in computing $J_0(x)$ can be bounded by

$$\left| \frac{2\pi f^{(2m)}(\xi)}{2^{2m}(2m)!} \right| \le \frac{2|x|^{2m}}{2^{2m}(2m)!}.$$

It is not hard to see than when both $J_0(x)$ and $J_1(x)$ are so computed, the absolute value of the error cannot exceed

$$\frac{2(2m+1)3^{2m}}{(2m)!}.$$

When $m = 15$, this expression is less than 5×10^{-17}. Hence we can safely take $m = 15$ below. We begin with the approximation $x = 2.4$. Once the first root is refined, the next root is approximately $2.4 + \pi$, as follows from the asymptotic representation in (1.14). Here is the simple code for this computation:

```
1 /* BESSNUL.C */
2
3 /*
4 Computes the first two zeroes of the Bessel function
5 J_0(x) via the integral representation, Newton's method
6 and Gauss-Chebyshev Integration.
7 */
8
9 # include <math.h>
10 # include <stdio.h>
11 # define PI (3.141592653589793)
12
13 double f0(double t, double x)  /* integrand for J_0 */
14 {                              /* t=integration variable */
15         return (cos(t*x));
16 }
17
18 double f1(double t, double x)   /* integrand for J_1 */
19 {
20         return (t*sin(t*x));
21 }
22
23 main()
24 {
25 int i,j,m=15;                     /* define variables */
26                                   /* m=15 nodes used */
27 double e,y,x,s0,s1;
28 double f0(double t, double x); /* function prototypes */
29 double f1(double t, double x);
30
31 printf("\n");
32
33 for (j=1;j<=2;j++){        /* initial approximations */
34         x=2.4+(j-1)*PI;
35
36 do{
37
```

```
38  s0=0.0;s1=0.0;
39
40  for (i=1;i<=m;i++){
41          s0 += (f0(cos((2.0*i-1.0)*PI*(0.5)/(double)m),x));
42          s1 += (f1(cos((2.0*i-1.0)*PI*(0.5)/(double)m),x));
43          }
44
45  s0 /= ((double)m);
46  s1 /= ((double)m);
47
48  y=x+s0/s1;                      /* Newton iteration */
49  e=fabs(x-y);                    /* error test */
50  x=y;
51  }
52
53  while (e>fabs(x)*5.0e-10);
54
55  printf("Zero= %10.10lf\n",y);
56  }
57
58  } /* end main */
```

We conclude this section with several caveats. The first is that in *C*, *function definitions may not be nested.* That is, one may not define a function within the code of another function. The second is that, in *C* functions, the *order* in which function arguments are evaluated is not specified by the ANSI standard and may vary with compiler. For an explicit example, see [KR], p. 53. Lastly, you should not begin a function name with the underscore character, because such names may be reserved by particular compilers for special implementations.

Exercise 1.8: Write a *C* function to determine the sign of its variable argument, i.e., code the function sgn(x). Use it to rewrite the code given previously in this chapter for the bisect method. The point is to avoid overflow/underflow when computing the product $f(a) * f(c)$.

Exercise 1.9: Suppose that P dollars are borrowed from a financial institution at an annual rate of R percent. The loan is to be repaid over m years in equal monthly payments of y dollars. When we set $r = \frac{R}{100}$ the formula for y can be written as

$$y = \frac{rP(1 + \frac{r}{12})^{12m}}{12\left((1 + \frac{r}{12})^{12m} - 1\right)}.$$

Write a C function to compute this monthly payment and then use a simple C program to try it out on your mortgage or car loan, etc. Don't worry if you do not presently have a mortgage; you will.

C ARRAYS

An "array" is simply a collection of data elements of the same type. Perfect examples are vectors and matrices. By the way, you may have noticed that "strings" were not listed as a basic data type in C. This is because strings are arrays of characters (terminated by the null character "\0") in C.

Initialization of arrays is done like this: suppose we wanted to do a computation with a vector $x = (1.0, 1.5, 2.5)$. In `main` it is declared and initialized as follows:

```
double    x[3]={1.0,1.5,2.5};
```

In C arrays are *zero offset*, i.e., the indices start at 0. This means that, in the present case, the three elements of x are referred to as $x[0] = 1.0, x[1] = 1.5, x[2] = 2.5$. One must watch this in general; however, any indices can be achieved by using pointers, as we show later. Thus, the code fragment

```
# define ORDER 5
main( )
{
double y[ORDER]={2.0, 1.0, 0.0, −1.0, −2.0};
  ⋮
}
```

defines a five–vector y with elements $y[0], y[1], \ldots, y[4]$ and $y[0] = 2.0, y[1] = 1.0, \ldots, y[4] = -2.0$. In general, the size of an array must be defined by a *constant* as in either case above, but in functions which receive arrays as arguments, the argument may simply appear as $y[\ ]$.

For matrices a similar declaration is in effect. Suppose we wish to define and initialize the 2×2 matrix

$$A = \begin{pmatrix} 1 & \frac{1}{2} \\ \frac{1}{3} & \frac{1}{4} \end{pmatrix}.$$

One would use this line to do it:

```
double   a[2][2] = {{1.0, 0.5}, {0.3333333333, 0.25}};
```

The entries are assigned as follows:

$a[0][0] = 1.0, \quad a[0][1] = 0.5, \quad a[1][0] = .3333333333, \quad a[1][1] = 0.25.$

The matrix elements are stored in memory in increasing addresses in this manner. Notice also the double pairs of brackets [and] for each dimension and the "extra" leading { and following }.

Thus, we see that two–dimensional arrays are initialized row by row, starting from the top. Since the elements are stored by rows, we say that *row major order* is used (in contrast to Fortran). In order to see how the compiler accesses individual elements, consider an $p \times q$ array a_{ij} for which $0 \leq i \leq p - 1, 0 \leq j \leq q - 1$. As an explicit example let us take $p = 3$, $q = 4$:

$$a = \begin{pmatrix} a_{00} & a_{01} & a_{02} & a_{03} \\ a_{10} & a_{11} & a_{12} & a_{13} \\ a_{20} & a_{21} & a_{22} & a_{23} \end{pmatrix}.$$

Think of finding yourself in memory space at the address of the base element $a[0][0]$. How do we get to a particular element? To be specific, let us locate $a[1][2]$ (in the zero–offset notation above). We move to the right across the first row, and then partly across the second row, for a total of six spaces. For the element $a[1][2]$ considered, we write $r = 1$ and $c = 2$ (for row and column abbreviations). Then notice that the number of units moved through is

$$6 = 4 * 1 + 2 = q * r + c.$$

Similarly, if we were to locate element $a[2][1]$, again starting at the base element $a[0][0]$, we would have to move nine spaces, and

$$9 = 4 * 2 + 1 = q * r + c.$$

In general, for a $p \times q$ matrix a, the element $a[i][j]$ (with zero offset indices) is located by moving $q * i + j$ units from the base unit $a[0][0]$. We see that the number of rows is therefore irrelevant (since p does not enter into the calculation); only the number of columns is important. For this reason, when initializing or passing to a C function a two–dimensional array, it is sufficient to write, e.g., a[ ][10] where the second dimension is explicitly specified. This is a weakness of the language, but one which can be overcome by the use of pointers. Indeed, the procedure just described is *pointer arithmetic*; see Chapter 2.

C does *not* check array bounds; if you overrun them, your program may not run and/or return garbage, may dump core, etc. So be careful! The philosophy seems to be that the programmer is expected to know what he/she is doing. The ANSI standard allows arrays to be initialized within functions, as we will see later. (Some older compilers may require that the static keyword precede the array declaration).

When an array is passed to a C–function, the information actually transmitted is the *address* of the base element (that with lowest subscript) of the array. The rest of the array is accessed by the compiler via pointer arithmetic (see Chapter 2).

Examples

1. Evaluating a polynomial.

Consider a polynomial $p_N(x)$ of degree N given by

$$p_N(x) = \sum_{k=0}^{N} a_k x^{N-k} = a_0 x^N + a_1 x^{N-1} + \cdots + a_N,$$

where we assume that all of the coefficients a_k are real. Given a real number ξ, how do we evaluate $p_N(\xi)$? Well, you do *not* use the power form above. Instead, use *Horner's Rule* which tells us to compute a sequence $b_0, b_1, \ldots, b_N$ as follows:

(1.17) $b_0 = a_0, \ b_k = b_{k-1}\xi + a_k \qquad (1 \le k \le N).$

Then we know that $p_N(\xi) = b_N$. In fact, we can write

$$p_N(x) = (x - \xi)q_{N-1}(x) + R_0,$$

where q_{N-1} is a polynomial of degree $N - 1$ and, evidently, $R_0 = p_N(\xi)$. A bit of algebra shows that

$$q_{N-1}(x) = b_0 x^{N-1} + b_1 x^{N-2} + \cdots + b_{N-1}.$$

Notice that if ξ were a root of $p_N(x)$, then $R_0 = 0$ and we have *deflated* p_N, i.e., we have found in q_{N-1} a polynomial of degree one less which, except for the root ξ already known, has the same roots as p_N.

Let's write some C code for the evaluation of a special polynomial $P(x) \equiv p_3(x) = x^3 - x - 1$ at $x = 2$, say:

```
1 /* Evalpoly.c */
2
3 # include <stdio.h>
4 # define DEGREE 3
5
6 main( )
7 {
8 int i;
9 double x=2.0;
```

```
10 /* coefficients of polynomial */
11 double a[DEGREE+1]={1.0,0.0,-1.0,-1.0};
12 /* notation of Horner algorithm */
13 double b[DEGREE+1];
14
15          b[0]=a[0];
16          for (i=1;i<=DEGREE;i++){
17                  b[i]=a[i]+x*b[i-1];
18                  }
19
20 printf("P(%lf) = %lf\n",x,b[DEGREE]);
21 }
```

Notice that the degree is defined by the statement DEGREE 3 above main, and that the coefficients a_i are input on line 11. The rest is straightforward coding of the algorithm above.

2. Solution of an upper–triangular linear system.

Consider a linear system of the form $Ux = b$ where x, b are vectors of dimension n and U is an $n \times n$ matrix satisfying $u_{ij} = 0$ for $i > j$. Since all of the elements of U below the diagonal vanish, U is called *upper–triangular*. This is the final form achieved by Gaussian elimination for a general matrix; thus, we are now describing *back substitution*. Beginning with the last equation, we certainly have $x_n = \frac{b_n}{u_{nn}}$. Now component i of $Ux = b$ is by definition $\sum_{j=i}^{n} u_{ij} x_j = b_i$. Split off the $j = i$ term to write this as

$$(1.18) \qquad u_{ii} x_i + \sum_{j=i+1}^{n} u_{ij} x_j = b_i \qquad (i = n-1, n-2, \ldots, 1),$$

and hence

$$(1.19) \qquad x_i = \frac{b_i - \sum_{j=i+1}^{n} u_{ij} x_j}{u_{ii}} \qquad (i = n-1, n-2, \ldots, 1),$$

provided $u_{ii} \neq 0$ for all i.

We implement this by considering the special linear system $Ux = b$, where

$$U = \begin{pmatrix} 2 & 3 & -1 \\ 0 & -2 & -1 \\ 0 & 0 & -5 \end{pmatrix}, \qquad \text{and} \qquad b = (5, -7, -15).$$

Here is the code for it:

```
1 /* Uptri.c */
2
3 # include <stdio.h>
4 # include <stdlib.h>
5 # include <math.h>
6 # define N (int)3  /* order of system */
7
8 main()
9 {
10 int i,j;
11 double s=0.0;
12
13 /* coefficient matrix */
14 double u[N][N]={{2.,3.,-1.},{0.,-2.,-1.},{0.,0.,-5.}};
15
16 double b[N]={5.0,-7.0,-15.0};   /* right-hand side */
17
18 if (fabs(u[N-1][N-1])<5.0e-20){
19         printf("Singular Matrix.");
20         exit(1);
21         }
22
23 b[N-1] /= u[N-1][N-1];
24
25 for (i=N-1;i>=1;i--){
26         if (fabs(u[i-1][i-1])<5.0e-20){
27                 printf("Singular Matrix.");
28                 exit(1);
29                 }
30
31
32                 s=0.0;
33                 for (j=i+1;j<=N;j++){
34                         s += u[i-1][j-1]*b[j-1];
35                         }                 /* end j loop */
36                 b[i-1] = (b[i-1]-s)/u[i-1][i-1];
37
38         }                                 /* end i loop */
39
40 for (i=1;i<=N;i++)
41 printf("x[%d] = %12.8lf\n",i,b[i-1]);
42 }
```

U and b are defined and initialized on lines 14 and 16. Note the error test on lines 18–21 before solving for the last component (using shorthand!) on line 23. This error test appears in the i–loop as well. One particular item needs to be stressed. If you compare the indices in the code to those above, you will see that the indices in the code are uniformly retarded by 1. This is because the statement "double b[3]" defines the elements b[0],b[1],b[2]. The same holds for the matrix elements. This is often confusing and is a likely spot to commit an error. It will be "fixed" later using dynamic memory allocation and pointers. Moreover, to use this on other matrices, we should make a *function* out of it. Once again, this is facilitated by pointers, and so it will be postponed for now.

When you run this program, you should get the solution $x = (1, 2, 3)$.

Exercise 1.10: Write an analogous program which will compute the solution of a lower–triangular linear system.

Exercise 1.11: Given $N + 1$ distinct points $\{x_i\}_{i=0}^N$ and function values $\{f(x_i)\}_{i=0}^N$ the *linear discrete least squares* problem is to find a linear function $Q_1(x) = a_0 + a_1 x$ which minimizes

$$\sum_{k=0}^N (f(x_k) - Q_1(x_k))^2 \, .$$

Using elementary calculus, show that a necessary condition is the following 2×2 system for the unknown coefficients a_0, a_1 (all sums are taken over $0 \le i \le N$):

$$a_0 \left(\sum x_i^0 \right) + a_1 \left(\sum x_i \right) = \sum f(x_i)$$
$$a_0 \left(\sum x_i \right) + a_1 \left(\sum x_i^2 \right) = \sum x_i f(x_i).$$

Solve this system for the unknowns a_0, a_1 and write a C program to compute these coefficients, given specific data.

Exercise 1.12: Show how to implement Newton's Method for polynomials $p(x)$ by using the Horner scheme twice to compute first $p(x)$ and then $p'(x)$.

Exercise 1.13: Consider the evaluation of the *exponential integral* function $Ei(x) = \int_x^\infty \frac{\exp(-t)}{t} \, dt$ for *large positive* x. Power series methods are not effective, so one often uses an *asymptotic series*, described below, for the computation.

a) Show that $Ei(x) = \frac{\exp(-x)}{x} - \int_x^\infty \frac{\exp(-t)}{t^2} \, dt$. [Hint: integrate by parts.]

b)Continue the process begun in a) to show that

$$Ei(x) = \exp(-x)\left[\frac{1}{x} - \frac{1}{x^2} + \frac{2!}{x^3} - \frac{3!}{x^4} + \cdots + \frac{(-1)^{n-1}(n-1)!}{x^n}\right] + R_n,$$

where $R_n = (-1)^n n! \int_x^\infty \frac{\exp(-t)}{t^{n+1}} \, dt$.

c)Show that $|R_n| \le n! \exp(-x) x^{-(n+1)}$ and hence that $R_n \to 0$ as $x \to \infty$, for *fixed* n.

d)Show that the *asymptotic series* obtained in b),

$$Ei(x) \sim \exp(-x)\left[\frac{1}{x} - \frac{1}{x^2} + \frac{2!}{x^3} - \frac{3!}{x^4} + \cdots\right],$$

diverges for each fixed value of x!

e)Nevertheless, show that the *truncation error* R_n in using the result of b) to approximate $Ei(x)$ does not exceed the magnitude of the first omitted term. (This is the definition of an *asymptotic expansion*.)

f)Write a C program to compute $Ei(n)$ for $n = 5, 10, 15, 20, 25$ to six places using the above. Allow for a variable number of terms to be used from the series.

Exercise 1.14: (The *Gamma Function*) For $x > 0$ the Gamma function is defined by the integral

$$\Gamma(x) = \int_0^\infty e^{-t} t^{x-1} \, dt.$$

For large $x > 0$ we have the asymptotic representation

$$\Gamma(x) \sim \sqrt{2\pi} e^{-x} x^{x-\frac{1}{2}}\left[1 + \frac{1}{12x} + \frac{1}{288x^2} - \frac{139}{51840x^3} - \frac{571}{2488320x^4} + \cdots\right],$$

while for $0 < x \le 1$ we have

$$\Gamma(x+1) = 1 + \sum_{j=1}^{8} b_j x^j + \delta(x),$$

where $|\delta(x)| \le 3 \times 10^{-7}$ and the coefficients are given by

$b_1 = -0.577191652$ $b_5 = -0.756704078$
$b_2 = 0.988205891$ $b_6 = 0.482199394$
$b_3 = -0.897056937$ $b_7 = -0.193527818$
$b_4 = 0.918206857$ $b_8 = 0.035868343$.

See [AS]. Establish the property $\Gamma(x+1) = x\Gamma(x)$ in $x > 0$. Write a C program using arrays to approximate the value of the Gamma function for every x with $0.5 \le x \le 10$ in steps of 0.5. Then compute the function values for $x = 20$ to 50 in steps of 5. Recall that an asymptotic series has the property that the error committed by truncation to any number of terms is dominated in absolute value by the first neglected term.

Exercise 1.15: (*Elliptic Integrals*) For $0 \le m < 1$ the complete elliptic integral of the second kind is defined by

$$K(m) = \int_0^1 \frac{dt}{\sqrt{1-t^2}\sqrt{1-mt^2}} = \int_0^{\frac{\pi}{2}} \frac{d\theta}{\sqrt{1-m\sin^2\theta}}.$$

Set $m_1 = 1 - m$. For m as above we have the approximation

$$K(m) = \sum_{j=0}^{4} a_j m_1^j + \ln\left(\frac{1}{m_1}\right) \sum_{j=0}^{4} b_j m_1^j + \delta(x),$$

where $|\delta(x)| \le 2 \times 10^{-8}$ and the coefficients are given by

$a_0 = 1.38629436112$	$b_0 = 0.5$
$a_1 = 0.09666344259$	$b_1 = 0.12498593597$
$a_2 = 0.03590092383$	$b_2 = 0.06880248576$
$a_3 = 0.03742563713$	$b_3 = 0.03328355346$
$a_4 = 0.01451196212$	$b_4 = 0.00441787012.$

See [AS]. Write a C program using arrays to approximate the value of this elliptic integral for any m with $0.5 \le m \le 0.95$ in steps of 0.05.

3. An initial–value problem for a first–order ODE.

Consider the initial–value problem for a *scalar* ordinary differential equation

$$(1.20) \qquad\qquad y' = f(x,y), \qquad y(0) \quad \text{given}.$$

Of the many methods of solution, the *Runge–Kutta* method of order 4 (RK–4) is very popular. To numerically solve this problem on an interval $[0, T]$ we partition this interval by writing $x_i = ih$, $(i = 0, 1, \ldots, N)$, where $x_N = T$. Let's call the exact solution $y(x)$; our approximation to the value of $y(x_n)$ is written as y_n. As you may know, the (RK–4) method achieves the same accuracy as that of a *Taylor* method of order 4, but the often tedious computations of various partial derivatives of f, as required via Taylor, are avoided.

Here is the scheme. We begin with an approximation y_0 to $y(0)$, the given initial value. Then for $n = 0, 1, \ldots, N-1$ we are given y_n and proceed as follows. Compute

$$k_1 = hf(x_n, y_n)$$
$$k_2 = hf\left(x_n + \frac{h}{2}, y_n + \frac{k_1}{2}\right)$$
$$k_3 = hf\left(x_n + \frac{h}{2}, y_n + \frac{k_2}{2}\right)$$
$$k_4 = hf(x_n + h, y_n + k_3).$$

Then we advance in time using

(1.21)
$$y_{n+1} = y_n + \frac{1}{6}(k_1 + 2k_2 + 2k_3 + k_4).$$

This can be somewhat inefficient and/or inaccurate, since step size control should be taken into account. But for the purposes of an array example, it will suffice.

Here is code to implement this for the special case $y' = f(x, y) = x + y$ with $y(0) = 0$. The exact solution is $y(x) = e^x - x - 1$, as you can readily verify.

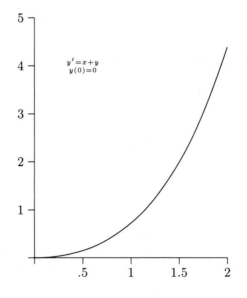

Fig. 1.8

```
 1 /* ODE1_RK4.c */
 2
 3 # include <stdio.h>
 4 # include <math.h>
 5 # define NUMGRIDPTS (int)50
 6 # define FINALTIME 2.0
 7
 8 double f(double x, double y)  /* enter f(x,y) here */
 9 {
10 return (x+y);
11 }
12
13 main()
14 {
15 int i;
16 double h=FINALTIME/NUMGRIDPTS;           /* step size */
17 double k1,k2,k3,k4;  /* to hold RK-4 intermediates */
18 double f(double x, double y);/* function prototype */
19
20 double x[NUMGRIDPTS+1],y[NUMGRIDPTS+1];
21
22 x[0]=0.0;y[0]=0.0;                   /* initial values */
23
24 printf("x=%12.6lf      y=%12.6lf\n",x[0],y[0]);
25
26 for (i=1;i<=NUMGRIDPTS;i++){
27         x[i]=x[0]+i*h;    /* array for grid points */
28         }
29
30 /* RK-4 */
31 for (i=1;i<=NUMGRIDPTS;i++){
32 k1 = h*f(x[i-1],y[i-1]);
33 k2 = h*f(x[i-1]+h/2.0,y[i-1]+k1/2.0);
34 k3 = h*f(x[i-1]+h/2.0,y[i-1]+k2/2.0);
35 k4 = h*f(x[i-1]+h,y[i-1]+k3);
36
37 y[i]=y[i-1]+(k1+2.0*k2+2.0*k3+k4)/6.0;
38
39 printf("x=%12.6lf      y=%12.6lf\n",x[i],y[i]);
40 }
41 }
```

In the two "defines," the number of grid points is taken to be 50, and the final time is 2. The function f is defined by a C–function (also called

f) on lines 8–11. The step size h appears on line 16. Please notice that on line 20 the arrays $x[\ ], y[\ ]$ are given dimension NUMGRIDPTS + 1, so that the values accessible are $x[0], \ldots, x[\text{NUMGRIDPTS}]$, etc. The initial values are input on line 22; lines 26–28 initialize the x–array. Finally, the RK–4 computation loop appears on lines 30–40 along with a `printf` statement after the advancement of each y_i.

To apply this to another equation, you need only change the function f and the initial value; of course the number of grid points and/or the final time are easy to alter as well. Try a *nonlinear* example, such as $y' = x^2 + y^2$, $y(0) = -1$.

C STRUCTURES

Structures in *C* allow us to construct new data types from old ones. A structure is a collection of related data items, perhaps of different types, grouped together under a single name. As such, they are a convenient tool for handling data. For example, as we will see later, memory for an entire structure can be allocated with a single one–line command.

The canonical example comes from database considerations. Suppose a professor keeps a log of students in a class. The relevant information may include the student's name, class year (1–4) and test score average. The first piece of data (the name) can be a char array, while the class year requires an integer and the average requires a float. Here is how one could define such a structure. By the way, this should take place above `main`:

```
struct student
{
    char name[12];
    int class;
    float average;
};
```

Note that each new data type declaration is terminated by a semicolon, and that the entire definition is, too. In the above, the keyword `struct` is followed by a structure tag (in this case "student") which allows other parts of the program to refer to that type. Now that a structure of type "student" has been defined, we can introduce variables of that type. For instance, in `main`, we can use

```
struct student gauss;
```

The *member of* operator "." identifies members of a structure by name. Thus, Mr. Gauss's data is referred to by using the expressions

```
gauss.name, gauss.class and gauss.average.
```

For instance, in the main program we could assign the structure data as follows:

```
strcpy(gauss.name, "Gauss, K" );
gauss.class=3;
gauss.average=0.999
```

The standard library function `strcpy` copies a string into an array, as shown. For its use, one must include the file `string.h`.

Alternatively we could have initialized the structure at the time of declaration by using

```
struct student gauss =
{
    "Gauss, K",
    3,
    0.999
};
```

Of course there will be many students, say 235, in the class. Thus, we need a statement of the form

```
struct student class[235];
```

This defines a 235–element array called "class." Each element of the "class" array is a structure of type "student." One refers to a particular element as follows: the expression

```
class[0].average;
```

gives the test average–member of the first structure in the array "class," etc.

Another simple example might arise if you were doing a computation in polar coordinates. In such a case, the following structure might be convenient:

```
struct polar
{
    double radius;
    double angle;
};
```

If you were writing a program using Gaussian Integration with, say, m nodes, weights `w[ ]` and abscissae `x[ ]`, this construction might be convenient:

```
struct gausquad
{
```

```
    int m;
    double x[m];
    double w[m];
};
```

One drawback of structures is that, although a particular construction may seem perfectly natural to the author of a program, others reading the code may find it anything but natural. Therefore if your code will be read and modified by others, it may be a good idea to hold the number of special data structures to a minimum.

Now we turn to the canonical example from mathematics: performing *complex arithmetic*.

COMPLEX ARITHMETIC

In some calculations complex arithmetic cannot be avoided. Classical examples are the two standard root finders *Laguerre's method* and *Muller's method*. Complex arithmetic is not built into the *C* compiler, so we must write our own arithmetic functions. These are conveniently defined in terms of a structure. In many *C* compilers, the file `math.h` contains the definition of `struct complex`. In any case we can define

```
struct complex
{
    double x;
    double y;
};
```

This construction is to appear above `main` (or in some include file, such as `math.h` or `cpxarith.c`; see Appendix I). Within `main`, we use, e.g., the declaration

```
        struct complex z,w;
```

which defines two complex variables z and w. Let $z = x_0 + iy_0$ be a complex number, where x_0 and y_0 are real. Similarly, write $w = u + iv$. Then the notation is

$$z.x = x_0, \quad z.y = y_0, \quad w.x = u, \quad w.y = v.$$

As you know, one has $z + w = (x_0 + u) + i(y_0 + v)$, $\quad z \cdot w = (x_0 u - y_0 v) + i(x_0 v + y_0 u)$, etc.

Let's begin with complex summation. The desired function will be called `cpxadd` and will receive two complex numbers as arguments. The return value is also a complex number; thus, the prototype will be

```
struct complex cpxadd(struct complex z, struct complex w);
```

Here is the appropriate code:

```
struct complex cpxadd(struct complex z, struct complex w);
{
  struct complex Z;
  Z.x=z.x+w.x;
  Z.y=z.y+w.y;
  return Z;
}
```

The two arguments are called z and w; the sum of the real parts is called $Z.x$; $Z.y$ denotes the sum of the imaginary parts. The function returns a structure of type complex, i.e., another complex number Z equal to $z + w$.

The composition of subtraction and multiplication functions is now probably clear. Here is division (n/d), which is slightly more difficult:

```
1  struct complex cpxdiv(struct complex n,struct complex d)
2  {
3  struct complex Z;
4  double temp1,temp2;
5
6  if (cabs(d)<(5.0e-20)*cabs(n)){
7          printf("division by zero in cpxdiv");
8          exit(1);
9          }
10
11 if (fabs(d.x)<=fabs(d.y)){
12          temp1=d.x/d.y;
13          temp2=d.y+temp1*d.x;
14          Z.x=(temp1*n.x+n.y)/temp2;
15          Z.y=(temp1*n.y-n.x)/temp2;
16          }
17
18 else{
19          temp1=d.y/d.x;
20          temp2=d.x+temp1*d.y;
21          Z.x=(n.x+temp1*n.y)/temp2;
22          Z.y=(n.y-temp1*n.x)/temp2;
23          }
24
25 return Z;
26 }
```

So that this piece of code can be easily understood, consider the following algebra given in the case $|d.x| \geq |d.y|$. We set temp$= \frac{d.y}{d.x}$ and write

$$
\begin{aligned}
\frac{n}{d} &= \frac{n.x + in.y}{d.x + id.y} \\
&= \frac{n.x\,d.x + n.y\,d.y + i(n.y\,d.x - n.x\,d.y)}{d.x^2 + d.y^2} \\
&= \frac{n.x\,d.x + n.y\,d.y + i(n.y\,d.x - n.x\,d.y)}{d.x^2(1 + \text{temp}^2)} \\
&= \frac{n.x + n.y \cdot \text{temp} + i(n.y - n.x \cdot \text{temp})}{d.x(1 + \text{temp}^2)}.
\end{aligned}
$$

Now just notice that the denominator here is equal to

$$
d.x + d.x \cdot \frac{d.y}{d.x} \cdot \text{temp} = d.x + d.y \cdot \text{temp}.
$$

Here is the complex exponential:

```
struct complex cpxexp(struct complex z)
{
    struct complex Z;
    Z.x=exp(z.x)*cos(z.y);
    Z.y=exp(z.x)*sin(z.y);
    return Z;
}
```

The complex square root is a bit tricky and should be given attention in detail. Let $z = x + iy$ be a complex number with both x, y real. We write $x = \Re z$ and $y = \Im z$. Setting $r = \sqrt{x^2 + y^2}$ and $\tan \theta = \frac{y}{x}$, we know that $z = re^{i\theta}$. There are several cases to be considered. Set $R = \sqrt{\frac{r + |x|}{2}}$. Then

(1.22)
$$
\begin{aligned}
z^{\frac{1}{2}} &= r^{\frac{1}{2}} e^{\frac{i\theta}{2}} \quad (-\pi < \theta < \pi) \\
&= r^{\frac{1}{2}} \cos \frac{\theta}{2} + ir^{\frac{1}{2}} \sin \frac{\theta}{2} \\
&= \pm r^{\frac{1}{2}} \sqrt{\frac{1 + \cos \theta}{2}} \pm ir^{\frac{1}{2}} \sqrt{\frac{1 - \cos \theta}{2}} \\
&= r^{\frac{1}{2}} \sqrt{\frac{1 + \frac{x}{r}}{2}} \pm ir^{\frac{1}{2}} \sqrt{\frac{1 - \frac{x}{r}}{2}} \\
&= \sqrt{\frac{x + r}{2}} \pm i\sqrt{\frac{r - x}{2}}.
\end{aligned}
$$

We have used here standard trigonometric identities; the choice of sign depends on the quadrant in which $\frac{\theta}{2}$ falls. Since $\cos \frac{\theta}{2} > 0$ in this range, the sign ambiguity occurs only in the imaginary part.

Consider the case in which $x = \Re z \geq 0$. Then

$$(1.23) \qquad \Im z^{\frac{1}{2}} = \pm\sqrt{\frac{r-x}{2}} = \pm\frac{\sqrt{r^2 - x^2}}{\sqrt{2(r+x)}} = \pm\frac{|y|}{2R} = \pm\frac{y}{2R}.$$

In the first and fourth quadrants (where $\Re z \geq 0$), y and $\sin \frac{\theta}{2}$ have the same sign. Thus, in this case,

$$(1.24) \qquad z^{\frac{1}{2}} = R + i\frac{y}{2R} \qquad (\Re z \geq 0).$$

Now consider the case in which $\Re z \leq 0$. Then we can write

$$\Re z^{\frac{1}{2}} = \sqrt{\frac{r+x}{2}} = \sqrt{\frac{r-|x|}{2}} = \frac{\sqrt{r^2 - x^2}}{\sqrt{2(r+|x|)}} = \frac{|y|}{2R}$$

and

$$\Im z^{\frac{1}{2}} = \pm\sqrt{\frac{r-x}{2}} = \pm\sqrt{\frac{r+|x|}{2}} = \pm R.$$

In the second quadrant, y and $\sin \frac{\theta}{2}$ are both positive. Thus, in this region,

$$(1.25) \qquad \Re z^{\frac{1}{2}} = \frac{y}{2R}, \qquad \Im z^{\frac{1}{2}} = R.$$

In the third quadrant, both y and $\sin \frac{\theta}{2}$ are negative so that

$$(1.26) \qquad \Re z^{\frac{1}{2}} = -\frac{y}{2R}, \qquad \Im z^{\frac{1}{2}} = -R.$$

It remains only to compute r (and hence R) accurately. If $|x| \geq |y|$ we write simply $r = |x|\sqrt{1 + \frac{y^2}{x^2}}$ so that

$$R^2 \equiv \frac{r+|x|}{2} = \frac{|x| + |x|\sqrt{1 + \frac{y^2}{x^2}}}{2}.$$

You will see this formula for R on line 13 in the code below. In the case $|x| < |y|$ we define temp $= \frac{|x|}{|y|}$ and write

$$(1.27) \qquad R^2 = \frac{r+|x|}{2} = \frac{|x| + \sqrt{x^2 + y^2}}{2}$$

$$= \frac{|y|}{2}\left(\text{temp} + \sqrt{1 + \text{temp}^2}\right),$$

which appears on line 9. At this point the following code will hopefully be clear:

```
1  struct complex cpxsqrt2(struct complex z)
2  {
3  struct complex Z;
4  double temp,R;
5  double absx=fabs(z.x),absy=fabs(z.y);
6
7  if (absx <= absy){
8          temp=absx/absy;
9          R=sqrt(absy)*sqrt((temp+sqrt(1.0+temp*temp))/2.0);
10         }
11 else {
12         temp=absy/absx;
13         R=sqrt(absx)*sqrt((1.0+sqrt(1.0+temp*temp))/2.0);
14 }
15
16 if (z.x >= 0.0) {
17         Z.x=R;
18         Z.y=z.y/(2.0*R);
19         }
20
21 else {
22         Z.x=absy/(2.0*R);
23         if (z.y >= 0.0)
24                 Z.y=R;
25         else
26                 Z.y=-R;
27
28 }
29 return Z;
30 }
```

The checking of quadrants as above is laborious and has been implemented in many compilers in the function

`double atan2(double y, double x).`

(Note the order of the arguments). If your compiler has this function in `math.h`, you can use the following simpler version of the complex square root function:

```
1  struct complex cpxsqrt(struct complex z)
2  {
```

```
3        struct complex Z;
4        double phi,r=sqrt(cabs(z));
5
6        double theta=atan2(z.y,z.x);
7        phi=theta/2.0;
8        Z.x=r*cos(phi);
9        Z.y=r*sin(phi);
10       return Z;
11 }
```

The standard inverse tangent function `atan` found in `math.h` uses angles in the range $-\frac{\pi}{2} \leq \theta \leq \frac{\pi}{2}$. Similarly one can write other familiar functions such as the logarithm, etc. You can find all of them in the file `cpxarith.c` in Appendix I. The function `cabs(z)` is defined after the following code; here is a program to try some of them out:

```
1 /* Cpxfunct.c */
2
3 # include <math.h>
4 # include <stdio.h>
5 # include <stdlib.h>
6 # include "cpxarith.c"
7
8 main()
9 {
10 /* define the variables */
11 struct complex z,w,sum,diff,prod,quot,sqr,expp,si,co;
12
13 /* function prototypes */
14 struct complex cpxadd(struct complex z,struct complex w);
15 struct complex cpxsub(struct complex z,struct complex w);
16 struct complex cpxmult(struct complex z,struct complex w);
17 struct complex cpxdiv(struct complex z,struct complex w);
18 struct complex cpxsqrt(struct complex z);
19 struct complex cpxexp(struct complex z);
20 struct complex cpxsin(struct complex z);
21 struct complex cpxcos(struct complex z);
22
23 z.x=3.0;z.y=4.0;        /* initializations */
24 w.x=1.0;w.y=6.0;
25
26 sum =cpxadd(z,w);
27 diff=cpxsub(z,w);
```

```
28 prod=cpxmult(z,w);
29 quot=cpxdiv(z,w);
30 sqr =cpxsqrt(z);
31 expp=cpxexp(z);
32 co  =cpxcos(z);
33 si  =cpxsin(z);
34
35 printf("sum          =%10.8lf+(%10.8lf)i\n",sum.x,sum.y);
36 printf("difference =%10.8lf+(%10.8lf)i\n",diff.x,diff.y);
37 printf("product    =%10.8lf+(%10.8lf)i\n",prod.x,prod.y);
38 printf("quotient =%10.8lf+(%10.8lf)i\n\n",quot.x,quot.y);
39
40 printf("sqrt(3+4i) =%10.8lf+(%10.8lf)i\n",sqr.x,sqr.y);
41 printf("exp(3+4i)  =%10.8lf+(%10.8lf)i\n",expp.x,expp.y);
42 printf("sin(3+4i)  =%10.8lf+(%10.8lf)i\n",si.x,si.y);
43 printf("cos(3+4i)  =%10.8lf+(%10.8lf)i\n",co.x,co.y);
44
45 }
```

We have explicitly listed all of the prototypes of the functions called at the top of the program (lines 13–21). Notice that the include file cpxarith.c is enclosed in double quotes. This is because it is of our own construction and is assumed to lie in the current source directory. See Chapter 3. The file cpxarith.c is listed in its entirety in Appendix I. The function cabs(z) gives the modulus (length) of the complex number z. It is ordinarily defined in math.h. If not, it is easy to write, using the definition $|z| = \sqrt{x^2 + y^2}$ for $z = x + iy$ (see the function called sqr earlier in this chapter).

Two complex numbers are introduced on lines 23–24, $z = 3 + 4i$ and $w = 1 + 6i$. These are then added, multiplied, etc. on the following lines. Before the print statements, several special complex–valued functions of z are called. Once these functions are defined, complex arithmetic is no worse than real arithmetic, the explicit function calls and related overhead notwithstanding. Notice that all functions in cpxarith.c pass arguments *by value*; when it is desired to pass by reference, a pointer to a structure of type complex is required. See Chapter 3.

THE SWITCH STATEMENT

The if and else if statements permit only one branch per keyword. In order to execute complex statements, a large number of such conditionals would have to be used. There is an alternative: the switch statement. It tests a single expression and provides different actions depending on varying input. A very common use would be in writing a menu program for a novice user. Another most important one is using command–line arguments. These are well–documented in nearly every C–book, so we will give another application, namely to *Gaussian Integration*.

Let $w(x)$ be a weight function on a (possibly infinite) interval $[a, b]$, i.e., assume $w(x)$ is nonnegative and integrable on this interval. Consider the problem of approximating the integral $I(g) = \int_a^b g(x)w(x)\,dx$. In the classical composite methods for a finite interval, we choose equally spaced nodes at which we evaluate the integrand and then compute a weighted sum of these values to get the approximate integral. In Gaussian quadrature, an approximation of the form $I(g) \approx w_1 g(x_1) + \cdots + w_m g(x_m)$ is sought which will be as accurate as possible; that is, among all such m–point formulae, the error in such an approximation will vanish when g is a polynomial of degree as high as possible.

The $\{x_k\}$ are called the *nodes* (or abscissae), and the $\{w_k\}$ are called the *weights*. It turns out that such an optimal distribution is attained when the $\{x_k\}$ are the m zeroes of the orthogonal (with respect to the function $w(x)$) polynomial $\phi_m(x)$ of degree m and thus are not equally spaced. Given the weight function w, this means that

$$(1.28) \qquad \int_a^b w(x)\phi_i(x)\phi_j(x)\,dx = 0 \quad \text{if} \quad i \neq j.$$

Familiar examples are the Legendre polynomials (with $w(x) = 1, a = -1, b = 1$), the Hermite polynomials (with $w(x) = \exp(-x^2), a = -\infty, b = \infty$), etc. We have seen yet another example previously, that of Gauss–Chebyshev quadrature.

The mathematical theorem states that for a function $g(x) \in C^{2m}[a, b]$, there exists a point $\xi \in (a, b)$ and a constant C_m such that

$$(1.29) \qquad I(g) = \int_a^b g(x)w(x)\,dx = \sum_{k=1}^m w_k g(x_k) + C_m g^{(2m)}(\xi).$$

For all special cases as above, the weights and abscissae are known and can be found in many places (cf., e.g., [HI] or [AS]). Notice that error term contains a derivative of order $2m$.

Typical formulae which arise in this manner are

$$\int_{-1}^1 g(x)\,dx = g\left(-\frac{1}{\sqrt{3}}\right) + g\left(\frac{1}{\sqrt{3}}\right) + \frac{g^{(4)}(\xi)}{135};$$

$$\int_{-\infty}^\infty e^{-x^2} g(x)\,dx = \frac{\sqrt{\pi}}{6}\left[g\left(\frac{-\sqrt{6}}{2}\right) + 4g(0) + g\left(\frac{\sqrt{6}}{2}\right)\right] + \frac{\sqrt{\pi} g^{(6)}(\xi)}{960}.$$

As you see, the use of larger values of m evidently generates greater accuracy, but the dependence of the constant C_m on m may nullify this.

We use this to illustrate the **switch** statement by estimating an integral of the form $I(g) = \int_a^b g(x)\,dx$ via *Gauss–Legendre integration* with the following code. First we make a preliminary change of variables so that the interval of integration becomes $[-1, 1]$: $x = \frac{b-a}{2}t + \frac{b+a}{2}$. Then

$$(1.30) \qquad I(g) = \int_a^b g(x)\,dx = \frac{b-a}{2} \int_{-1}^1 g\left(\frac{b-a}{2}t + \frac{b+a}{2}\right) dt.$$

We make the choice $g(x) = e^x \cos x$ below:

```
1 /*  gausleg.c */
2 /*  Gauss-Legendre Integration */
3
4 /*  Computes the integral of g(x) over a < x < b */
5 /*  Choice of m=2,3,4,5,6 or 8 nodes */
6 # include <math.h>
7 # include <stdio.h>
8
9 double g(double x)
10 {
11          return (exp(x)*cos(x));
12 }
13
14 main()
15 {
16 int i,m;
17 double a,b,s=0.0;
18
19 double g(double x);    /* function prototype */
20 double w[8],x[8];    /* weights and abscissae */
21
22 printf("\nEnter the left-hand endpoint:    ");
23 scanf("%lf",&a);
24
25 printf("\nEnter the right-hand endpoint:    ");
26 scanf("%lf",&b);
27
28 printf("\n");
29 printf("Number of nodes (2,3,4,5,6 or 8):    ");
30 scanf("%d",&m);
31
```

```
32 switch(m)
33 {
34 case 2:
35          x[0]=-.5773502692;x[1]=-x[0];
36          w[0]=w[1]=1.0;
37          break;
38 case 3:
39          x[0]=-.7745966692;x[1]=0.0;x[2]=-x[0];
40          w[0]=.5555555556;w[1]=.888888889;w[2]=w[0];
41          break;
42 case 4:
43          x[0]=-.8611363116;x[1]=-.3399810436;
44          x[2]=-x[1];x[3]=-x[0];
45          w[0]=w[3]=.3478548451;w[1]=w[2]=.6521451549;
46          break;
47 case 5:
48          x[0]=-.9061798459;x[4]=-x[0];
49          x[1]=-.5384693101;x[3]=-x[1];
50          x[2]=0.0;w[2]=.5688888889;
51          w[0]=w[4]=.2369268851;w[1]=w[3]=.4786286705;
52          break;
53 case 6:
54          x[0]=-.9324695142;x[5]=-x[0];
55          x[1]=-.6612093865;x[4]=-x[1];
56          x[2]=-.2386191861;x[3]=-x[2];
57          w[0]=w[5]=.1713244924;
58          w[1]=w[4]=.3607615730;
59          w[2]=w[3]=.4679139346;
60          break;
61 case 8:
62 default:        /* if some other value of m is chosen */
63          m=8;
64          x[0]=-.9602898565;x[7]=-x[0];
65          x[1]=-.7966664774;x[6]=-x[1];
66          x[2]=-.5255324099;x[5]=-x[2];
67          x[3]=-.1834346425;x[4]=-x[3];
68          w[0]=w[7]=.1012285363;
69          w[1]=w[6]=.2223810345;
70          w[2]=w[5]=.3137066459;
71          w[3]=w[4]=.3626837834;
72 }        /* end switch */
73
74          for (i=1;i<=m;i++)
```

```
75                        s += (g((0.5)*(a+b+(b-a)*x[i-1]))*w[i-1]);
76                        s *= ((b-a)*(0.5));
77
78 printf("\nUsing %d nodes:    Integral= %8.7lf\n",m,s);
79
80 }  /* end main */
```

The endpoints are prompted for in lines 22–26. The number of nodes m is requested from the user on lines 29–30, an integer m. The allowed values for m are 2, 3, 4, 5, 6 or 8. Arrays for the weights and abscissae are set up on line 20; we use x[8],w[8] because $m \leq 8$. Thus, the actual values we can refer to are x[0],x[1],...,x[7] with a similar statement for the array w, as we see used on line 75.

The switch statement in line 32 allows computation to be performed depending on the value of m, the "test expression." Its body is enclosed in braces. We use the keyword case followed by the value of m in this case, followed by a colon, as on lines 34, 38, 42, 47, 53 and 61. In each of the case bodies, the arrays x and w are explicitly specified. Every such body is terminated by the keyword break. The last case (line 62) is called default. It corresponds to a choice of m not in the above list. Once the data are known, the computation takes place on lines 74–76. Note that two assignments may be made in one statement, as, e.g., on lines 36, 45, etc.

Here are some generalities on the use of switch. The "case labels" always end with colons; each label must be a constant value (i.e., variables are not allowed.) The break statement ensures that the switch statement is exited correctly. Without the break, flow falls through to the next alternative. Note also the default label. If none of the case constants matches the value of the test expression, the code under the default label is executed. In general you need not include the default case. If it is absent, and if none of the case constants matches the test expression, execution continues after the closing right brace } of the switch statement. The order of case statements in switch is irrelevant, provided each is terminated by the break keyword.

BREAK, CONTINUE AND GOTO STATEMENTS

In addition to its use in a switch construct, the break statement allows immediate termination of a loop. Actually, break exits only from the innermost loop, so several may be required if your loops are nested. The continue statement, used within a loop, also interrupts flow control. In contrast to the break statement, continue ignores the remaining steps within a loop, and forces the next iteration of the loop to occur. We all know what goto accomplishes. However, the pundits proclaim that both continue and goto are to be avoided, in the hope of achieving more readable code. It is always possible to rewrite code segments (by changing the logic) so that continue need not be used. An "acceptable" use of the goto statement would be to exit from a deeply nested loop. If you must use the goto statement, its object is some other line with a label, followed by a colon. The goto statement is not used in this book.

Why do programmer–types eschew the goto statement? One is led to believe that the use of such a construct renders one's code "elementary" or "trivial." Here is a brief passage from [LE]: in a 1965 lecture, Professor E. Dijkstra

> "told how 'two programming department managers ... [had] communicated to me, independently ... that the quality of their programmers was inversely proportional to the density of goto statements in their programs. This [was] an incentive to do away with the goto statement.'"

Thus the "goto is harmful" mentality was born.

Here is some brief code from the bisect method to illustrate the use of break. It is set up for the function $f(x) = x^3 - x + 1$ beginning on the interval $[-2, -1]$ at the endpoints of which the function has opposite signs:

```
1  /* Bisect3.c */
2
3  # include <math.h>
4  # include <stdio.h>
5  # define f(x) ((x)*(x)*(x)-(x)+1.0)
6
7  main()
8  {
9          double a=-2.0;          /* left endpoint */
10         double b=-1.0;          /* right endpoint */
11         double c,z;             /* c is the midpoint */
12
13         do{
14         c=(a+b)/2.0;
15         if (fabs(f(c))<5.0e-20) break;
16         else if
17                 (f(a)*f(c)>0.0) a=c;
18         else
19                 b=c;
20         z=fabs(b-a);
21         }while (z>5.0e-11);
22
```

```
23          printf("root = %10.10lf\n",c);
24          printf("\n\n");
25 }
```

The do loop begins on line 13 in which the initial interval is continually cut in half until the desired tolerance is achieved. Now at some step it may happen that the midpoint c is (to working precision) a root of f, in which case we want to terminate the loop and print the result immediately. This is exactly what the **break** statement on line 15 allows us to do. Rather than test two floating–point values for equality, we use the **break** statement when $|f(c)|$ is suitably small.

For another example, consider coding the *delta squared* iteration. It is an acceleration device; we use it here to speed up fixed point iteration for $x = g(x)$. In pseudocode, it appears as

given x_0,   do{
compute $x_1 = g(x_0)$, compute $x_2 = g(x_1)$
compute $\delta x = x_1 - x_0$
compute $\delta^2 x = x_2 - 2x_1 + x_0$
compute $x' = x_0 - (\delta x)^2 / \delta^2 x$
compute $e = |x' - x_0|$
$x_0 = x'$ }
  while $(e > TOL * |x'|)$

The user–supplied TOL cannot be too strict, and a fairly accurate initial guess is required to ensure that the denominator above does not vanish. At a simple root α, this is known to be second–order convergent. Here is the full code:

```
1 /* Delta2.c */
2
3 # include <math.h>
4 # include <stdio.h>
5 # include <stdlib.h>
6 # define g(x) (cos(x))
7 # define TOL (5.0e-11)
8
9 main( )
10 {
11 double x,x1,x2,x3,xp,e;
12 int iter=0;
13
14 printf("Enter the starting approximation:   ");
15 scanf("%lf",&x);
16 printf("\n");
```

```
17
18 do{
19         x1=g(x);
20         x2=g(x1);
21         x3=x2-2.0*x1+x;
22
23         if (fabs(x3)<5.0e-20){
24                 x=x2;
25                 break;
26                 }
27
28         xp=x-(x1-x)*(x1-x)/x3;
29         e =fabs(xp-x);
30         x =xp;
31         iter++;
32         if (iter>20){
33                 printf("Too many iterates.");
34                 exit(1);
35         }
36
37 }
38 while (e>fabs(xp)*TOL);
39
40 printf("root = %lf\n",x);
41 printf("iterates required = %d\n",iter);
42 }
```

On line 23 we test the size of $x_3 = \delta^2 x$ so that division by a small number will not be attempted on line 28. If it is very small, the **break** statement on line 25 exits the loop immediately and line 40 is then executed.

As an example of the **continue** statement, suppose you are trying to roughly approximate the zeroes of the function $f(x) = x/2 - \sin(x^2)$ on the interval $[0, 2]$. This brief program evaluates the function in steps of 0.05 and prints out only the values of x and $f(x)$ when $|f(x)| \leq 5.0 \times 10^{-3}$. When $|f(x)| > 5.0 \times 10^{-3}$ the **continue** statement on line 10 simply forces the next value of x to be tested.

```
1 /* Cont_ex.c */
2
3 # include <stdio.h>
4 # include <math.h>
5 # define f(x) (0.5*(x)-sin((x)*(x)))
6
7 main ( )
```

```
 8 {
 9 double x;
10 for (x=0.0;x<=2.0;x += 0.05){
11          if (fabs(f(x))>5.0e-3)
12          continue;
13 printf("x=%lf fnvalue=%lf\n",x,f(x));
14 }
15 }
```

CHAPTER 2

POINTERS

DEFINITION AND EXAMPLES

Up to now, you may be thinking: "Every time this book gets to something interesting, the topic is postponed until later, because it involves pointers." True — and later is now. The importance of pointers cannot be overemphasized. They allow powerful constructions and permit modular structure.

A *pointer* is a variable that contains the *address* of some object in memory. This other object is normally another variable. Here are some of the common uses of pointers:

1. Allowing function calls by reference. (Recall that all function calls are performed by value in C.)

2. Allowing one function to receive another function as an argument.

3. Allowing a function to have multiple return values. (Sadly, in contrast to standard mathematical jargon, such constructs are still called "functions.")

4. Manipulating strings and, more generally, manipulating an array by moving pointers to its elements, instead of moving the elements themselves.

5. Accessing command–line arguments at run–time.

Among our purposes, pointers will be used to define (and allocate memory for) vectors and matrices. This question may already have occurred to you: "How can a vector be defined if its size is unknown?" Pointers and the dynamic memory allocation functions in the standard library (`malloc` and `calloc`) will solve this problem nicely.

Another useful application appears in statement 2 above. Suppose you have written a routine to implement the standard composite Simpson's Rule to evaluate $\int_a^b f(x)\,dx$ for a particular $f(x)$. How can we alter it so that it will work for *any* (sufficiently smooth) function? We achieve this by adding an additional argument to the Simpson routine: a *function pointer*. There is a standard (but perhaps arcane) syntax for doing this. Once you learn it, you will reuse it hundreds of times.

Let's begin by showing how to define a simple pointer variable. We use the *indirection operator* $*$. The expression

```
double *ptr;
```

defines a pointer variable `ptr` that can point to anything of type double. Suppose that we have a variable x in a program, which is of type double. Then we can initialize the pointer `ptr` with the line

```
ptr = &x;
```

Whenever using pointers, be sure to initialize them. "Dangling pointers" can cause serious problems, hang a PC, etc.

Now if you were to call `printf` with first x and then $*$ptr as arguments of type double, you would get the same (double) number. If you were to call `printf` with (correctly formatted) integer arguments &x and ptr, you would also get the same (possibly long) integer result. Try to think of this as follows: & means "address of,", while $*$ means "value of."

Now let's consider item 1 above—how to achieve a call by reference. This will be done in the context of defining a function which is to receive several arguments. To allow the function to change the arguments it is passed, follow this procedure:

Define the arguments in the parameter list as pointers, and when calling the function from `main`, use the ampersand operator & in the argument list.

This will be illustrated by two examples.

1. The *swap* function.

As you know, when performing pivoting in Gaussian elimination, it is necessary to interchange the contents of two vectors. Since this can be done within a loop one component at a time, it suffices to write a "swap function" which interchanges just two elements. Here is everyone's favorite such example:

```
void swap(double *x,double *y)
```

```
{
double temp;
temp=*x;
*x=*y;
*y=temp;
}
```

Notice that there is no "return value"; the only "action" taken is that the values of x and y are permuted. Furthermore, each argument is defined as a pointer to type double. Within the code, every time we wish to refer to the value of x, we use *x, etc. Now, in main suppose we have the declarations

$$\text{double } x=1.0, y=2.0;$$

Then we call the swap function with the line

$$\text{swap}(\&x, \&y);$$

Notice the use of the ampersand in the function call, after which we have $x = 2$, $y = 1$.

2. Newton's Method

Suppose you're writing code for Newton's method to find zeroes of a scalar function $f(x)$. At each step of the iteration, you require the values $f(x)$ and $f'(x)$. Given $f(x) = e^{-x} - x$, say, here is a function which does the job:

```
void func(double x, double *f, double *df)
{
*f=exp(-x)-x;                       /* value of the function */
*df=-exp(-x)-1.0;                   /* value of the derivative */
}
```

The return type is void because we are returning two values. If in main we have the declarations

$$\text{double } x=1.0, f, df;$$

then the line

$$\text{func}(x, \&f, \&df);$$

computes both values. Later reference to "f" gives the value of f(x)=f(1), while reference to "df" gives the value of the derivative of f at x=1. The syntax is the same as in the previous example.

FUNCTION POINTERS

Assume we have a routine (e.g., a numerical integration algorithm) which performs its work as soon as the function $f(x)$ to be integrated is specified. We want to make this routine work for *any* function. Then, for later use with different functions, we need only enter the definition of the integrand; the integration routine itself need never again be altered. There are two steps to be taken:

1. Define and initialize a function pointer in `main`.
2. Add a function pointer as an argument to the routine.

Let's say we're working with double values. Above `main`, we have the definition of the integrand, say

```
double f(double x)
{
return exp(-x*x);
}
```

Then, in `main`, we add this statement, which defines and initializes a function pointer (called `func_ptr`), which points to the above `f`:

```
double (*func_ptr) ( )=f;
```

Notice the double sets of parentheses, the latter being empty.

As for step 2 above, consider what such an integration routine requires: the endpoints `a` and `b`, an integer `m` specifying the number of subdivisions, and the integrand. Here is the desired routine for the *composite Simpson's Rule*:

```
 1 double num_integral(int m, double a, double b,\
 2                     double (*func_ptr) ())
 3 {
 4 int i;
 5 double h=(b-a)/m;
 6 double s=(*func_ptr)(a)+(*func_ptr)(b);
 7
 8 for (i=1;i<=m-1;i++){
 9 s += (4.0*(*func_ptr)(a+(i-.5)*h)+\
10               2.0*(*func_ptr)(a+i*h));
11 }
12 s += (4.0*(*func_ptr)(a+(m-.5)*h));
13 s *= (h/6.0);
14
15 return s;
16 }
```

Here the integer m+1 gives the total number of mesh points, and a<b are
the integration limits. The last argument is the function pointer; note again
the double sets of parentheses. Within the function itself, we simply add up
the individual contributions, as was done previously. In order to evaluate
the function pointer at any (double) point y, one uses the syntax

```
(*func_ptr)(y)
```

That's all there is to it. By the way, lines that are too long can be
continued by using the *line continuation character* \, as we have done on
line 9 above. Furthermore, no cast is necessary in line 5 (why?) Here is a
driver program for study:

```
 1 /*  Simptr2.c.    Composite Simpson Integration */
 2 /*  Computes the integral of f(x) over a < x < b */
 3
 4 # include <math.h>
 5 # include <stdio.h>
 6
 7 double f(double x)
 8 {
 9            return (exp(-x*x));
10 }
11
12 double num_integral(int m, double a, double b,\
13 double (*func_ptr) ())
14 {
15 int i;
16 double h=(b-a)/m;
17 double s=(*func_ptr)(a)+(*func_ptr)(b);
18
19 for (i=1;i<=m-1;i++){
20 s += (4.0*(*func_ptr)(a+(i-.5)*h)+\
21                   2.0*(*func_ptr)(a+i*h));
22 }
23 s += (4.0*(*func_ptr)(a+(m-.5)*h));
24 s *= (h/6.0);
25
26 return s;
27 }
28
29 main()
30 {
31 int m;
```

```
32 double integral,a,b;

33

34 /* function prototype */
35 double num_integral(int m, double a, double b,\
36 double (*func_ptr) ());

37

38 /* definition and initialization */
39 double (*func_ptr)()=f;

40

41 printf("\nEnter the left-hand endpoint:     ");
42 scanf("%lf",&a);

43

44 printf("\nEnter the right-hand endpoint:     ");
45 scanf("%lf",&b);

46

47 printf("\nEnter the desired number of nodes:    ");
48 scanf("%d",&m);

49

50 integral=num_integral(m, a, b, func_ptr);

51

52 printf("\nValue of Integral= %10.8lf\n",integral);

53

54 }
```

As you see, the main program is rather short. First, as always, we define our variables m, a, etc. The function prototype of num_integral follows. In the next line 39, we define the function pointer and then make it point to f. Note that there is no ampersand in the function call on line 50. The rest should be clear.

Now we give a similar program for the *secant method*. This seeks a root of a scalar equation $f(x) = 0$ as follows: we begin with two initial approximations x_0, x_1 and generate the sequence

$$(2.1) \qquad x_{n+1} = x_n - f(x_n)\frac{x_n - x_{n-1}}{f(x_n) - f(x_{n-1})} \quad \text{for} \quad n = 1, 2, \ldots.$$

Assume that α is a root of the smooth function $f(x)$. Recall the definition of the *divided differences*

$$(2.2) \qquad f[a, b] = \frac{f(b) - f(a)}{b - a}, \quad f[a, b, c] = \frac{f[a, b] - f[b, c]}{a - c}.$$

From the Mean–Value Theorem, $f[a, b] = f'(\xi)$ for some point ξ between a and b. Similarly, it can be shown that $f[a, b, c] = \frac{1}{2}f''(\nu)$ for an intermediate point ν.

In order to derive an error estimate, let $f(\alpha) = 0$ and rewrite the scheme as

$$(2.3) \qquad \alpha - x_{n+1} = \alpha - x_n + f(x_n) \frac{x_n - x_{n-1}}{f(x_n) - f(x_{n-1})}$$

$$= \alpha - x_n + \frac{f(x_n)}{f[x_n, x_{n-1}]}.$$

Now write $f(x_n) = f(x_n) - f(\alpha) = (x_n - \alpha)f[\alpha, x_n]$ and substitute in (2.3) to get

$$(2.4) \qquad \alpha - x_{n+1} = (\alpha - x_n)\left(1 - \frac{f[\alpha, x_n]}{f[x_n, x_{n-1}]}\right)$$

$$= (\alpha - x_n)\left(\frac{f[x_n, x_{n-1}] - f[\alpha, x_n]}{f[x_n, x_{n-1}]}\right)$$

$$= -(\alpha - x_n) \cdot (\alpha - x_{n-1}) \cdot \frac{f[x_{n-1}, x_n, \alpha]}{f[x_n, x_{n-1}]}.$$

It follows that

$$(2.5) \qquad \alpha - x_{n+1} = -(\alpha - x_n) \cdot (\alpha - x_{n-1}) \cdot \frac{f''(\nu_n)}{2f'(\xi_n)}.$$

Now assume that all iterates lie in some interval around α where $|f''|$ is bounded above and $|f'|$ is bounded below, explicitly

$$(2.6) \qquad \frac{|f''(\nu_n)|}{|f'(\xi_n)|} \le 2\mu.$$

We consider the *scaled error* $e_n \equiv \mu|\alpha - x_n|$ and assume that the initial guesses are sufficiently good in the sense that $\max(e_0, e_1) < \epsilon < 1$. Then from (2.5) we have the inequality

$$(2.7) \qquad e_{n+1} \le e_n \cdot e_{n-1},$$

and we get successively

$$e_2 \le \epsilon^2$$
$$e_3 \le e_2 e_1 \le \epsilon^3$$
$$e_4 \le e_3 e_2 \le \epsilon^{3+2} = \epsilon^5$$
$$e_5 \le e_4 e_3 \le \epsilon^{5+3} = \epsilon^8,$$

so that in general we have

$$(2.8) \qquad e_n \le \epsilon^{m_n},$$

where

(2.9) $m_0 = m_1 = 1$ and $m_{n+1} = m_n + m_{n-1}$ for $n \geq 1$.

This is the famous *Fibonacci* sequence. m_n is thus a solution of a second–order linear constant coefficient homogeneous difference equation. One seeks a solution in the form $m_n = \rho^n$ for some scalar ρ; the quadratic $\rho^2 - \rho - 1 = 0$ results whose roots are $\rho_{\pm} = \frac{1 \pm \sqrt{5}}{2}$. Using the initial conditions, we get for large n

(2.10) $$m_n = \frac{1}{\sqrt{5}}(\rho_+^{n+1} - \rho_-^{n+1}) \approx \frac{\rho_+^{n+1}}{\sqrt{5}} \approx 0.447214(1.618034)^{n+1}.$$

Thus, we see that the secant method converges at fractional order, much better than linear, but less than quadratic (like Newton). The great advantage is that the computation of $f'(x)$ can be avoided in cases where it is difficult (or impossible). If in the Newton algorithm you were to employ the finite difference approximation

$$f'(x_n) \approx \frac{f(x_n) - f(x_{n-1})}{x_n - x_{n-1}},$$

then the secant algorithm results.

   Here is a function pointer version of the secant method:

```
1 /* SECANT.C */
2
3 # include <math.h>
4 # include <stdio.h>
5 # include <stdlib.h>
6
7 double f(double x)        /* input the function f here */
8 {
9            return (cos(x)-x);
10 }
11
12 double secant(double (*func_ptr)(), double x1,\
13               double x2, double tol)
14 {
15           int iter=0;                 /* iterate counter */
16           double y1,y2,xnew,e;
17           do{
18                   y1=(*func_ptr)(x1);
```

```
19                  y2=(*func_ptr)(x2);
20                  if (fabs(y1-y2)<5.0e-20){
21                     xnew=x2;
22                     break;
23                     }
24
25                  xnew=x2-y2*(x2-x1)/(y2-y1);
26                  e=fabs(xnew-x2);
27                  iter++;
28                  if (iter>50){
29                     printf("Too many iterations.");
30                     exit(1);
31                        }
32                  x1=x2;
33                  x2=xnew;
34
35            }
36        while (e>fabs(xnew)*tol);
37
38        return xnew;
39 }
40
41 main()
42 {
43 double x,x1,x2;  /* x1,x2 are initial approximations */
44 double f(double x);            /* function prototype */
45 double secant(double (*func_ptr) (),\
46               double x1, double x2, double tol);
47
48 /* definition and initialization */
49 double (*func_ptr) ()=f;
50
51 printf("Enter the starting approximations:\n\n ");
52 printf("Enter x1:  ");
53 scanf("%lf",&x1);
54 printf("\n");
55
56 printf("Enter x2:  ");
57 scanf("%lf",&x2);
58 printf("\n");
59 printf("\nThe root equals %10.8lf\n",\
60               secant(func_ptr,x1,x2,5.0e-8));
61 }
```

As you see, this particular code is set up to solve $f(x) = 0$, where $f(x) = x - \cos x$. The two function prototypes are listed on lines 44–46 beneath the declaration of the variables. We then prompt for the initial approximations in lines 51–57 and call the secant routine within `printf`. The first argument of the secant function is a function pointer, declared as before. As we have done previously, we include the standard relative–error stopping test, and check for runaway iterates.

Eventually you may not need to be reminded of the presence of a function pointer via a "long" declaration such as

```
double (*func_ptr) ( )=f;
```

and you will perhaps use the shorter version

```
double (*f) ( )=f;
```

Finally we point out that the parentheses in a typical function pointer declaration (*f) ( ) are required because the prefix operator * has lower precedence than ( ). Therefore the parentheses in the declaration ensure the correct association (cf. Chapter 3).

Exercise 2.1: In Chapter 1 code was given in `min_oned.c` to minimize a function of one variable. Convert that code to a C function whose arguments would include the bracketing triple $\{a, b, c\}$ and a function pointer.

Exercise 2.2: In Chapter 1 code was given for Newton's method for finding zeroes of a scalar function $f(x)$. Convert that code to a C function utilizing a function pointer.

Exercise 2.3: Write a C function utilizing a function pointer which will implement the *composite midpoint rule*

$$\int_a^b f(x)\,dx = h\sum_{i=1}^N f(x_{i-\frac{1}{2}}) + \frac{h^2(b-a)f''(\xi)}{24},$$

where $h = \frac{b-a}{N}$, $x_i = a + ih$ $(i = 0, 1, \ldots, N)$.

Exercise 2.4: Let $f(x, y)$ be a smooth function defined on the unit square. Consider the problem of approximating

$$I(f) = \int_0^1 \int_0^1 f(x, y)\,dx\,dy$$

via iterated integration. That is, write $I(f)$ as

$$I(f) = \int_0^1 \left(\int_0^1 f(x, y) \, dx \right) dy$$

and approximate the inner integral by a composite Simpson rule: given an integer N, set $h = 1/N$ and $x_i = y_i = ih$ for $i = 0, 1, \ldots, N$. Then

$$I(f) \approx \frac{h}{6} \int_0^1 \left(f(0, y) + f(1, y) + 2 \sum_{i=1}^{N-1} f(x_i, y) + 4 \sum_{i=1}^{N} f(x_{i-\frac{1}{2}}, y) \right) dy.$$

Now approximate each of these y–integrals using the same formula. Write a C function which will compute this approximation. Its arguments should include N and a function pointer representing the integrand.

POINTER ARITHMETIC AND ARRAYS

Suppose we have in `main` the declaration

```
double x[  ]={2.0,1.0,0.0,-1.0,-2.0};
```

and the lines

```
int i;
double *vecptr;
vecptr=&x[0];
for (i=1;i<=5;i++){
    printf("x[%d]=%lf\n",i-1,*vecptr);
    vecptr++;
}
```

The result of running such a program would be

```
x[0]=2.0000000
```

$\vdots$

```
x[4]=-2.0000000
```

Thus, we see that once a pointer points to an array, we can get successive elements in the array by *pointer arithmetic*. (Recall the discussion of arrays in Chapter 1.) Above we have that `vecptr` points to the first element of the `x` array, `x[0]`. When the pointer is incremented, `vecptr` points to the *next* element of the array `x`, `x[1]`. The essential issue is that pointer arithmetic is automatically scaled by the compiler to point to the next array element;

the allotment of the appropriate number of bytes (e.g., for integers, doubles, etc.) is a detail taken care of for us.

Here is another code fragment to illustrate pointer arithmetic. Assume we have again defined the vector x as shown above. Consider the code

```
int i;
double *vecptr;
vecptr=&x[0];
for (i=1;i<=5;i++){
    printf("x[%d]=%lf\n",i-1,*(vecptr+i-1);
}
```

When executed, the result will be the same as that displayed above. Initially the pointer vecptr points to x[0]. At the end of the printf argument, you see the indirection operator * applied to the quantity (vecptr+i-1). Once again, pointer arithmetic is used to get the ith element in the array x. Of course, we want to print the *value* of the appropriate array element, and therefore the operator * is used. Within any such program we could of course refer to the value of x[2] by *(x+2), but this is not standard mathematical notation.

In general, *the name of an array is a pointer*; the address pointed to is that of the base element (i.e., lowest subscript).

VECTORS, MATRICES AND DYNAMIC MEMORY ALLOCATION

We have already noted the problem of how to properly dimension a vector when its size is not known *a priori*. In this section we deal with vectors and matrices by showing, in the context of pointers, how to allocate contiguous memory at run–time.

The standard library contains two useful functions malloc and calloc for this purpose. Each allocates contiguous blocks of storage via a pointer which must be cast to the appropriate type. calloc has the additional attractive feature of initializing all elements to zero. At the top of any such program, include the appropriate file. We use here malloc.h which is present in many popular compilers, including Microsoft Quick C (v. 2.5). Some compilers may store these functions in stdlib.h, which is the ANSI specification. If you get an error when trying to include malloc.h, simply include stdlib.h instead.

Suppose we wish to allocate n units of storage for double values. We employ a command like this:

```
double *t;
t=(double *) calloc(n,sizeof(double));
```

The first line declares t as a pointer to type double. The second line casts the pointer returned by calloc to type double, and gives us n units of storage, all initialized to zero. The calloc function returns a pointer to the first element of an array. The sizeof operator gets the appropriate machine size of the type requested. We're not quite done. Whenever you request memory allocation from a library routine, you must check that you do not get a NULL pointer. The NULL macro is to appear in stddef.h according to the ANSI standard, but may be found in stdio.h in many popular compilers. In Boolean expressions, NULL has the value "false." Consider this function v_alloc which allocates double values as above and checks for the validity of the pointer:

```
1 double *v_alloc(int n)
2 {
3 double *v;
4 v=(double *) calloc(n,sizeof(double));
5 if (v==NULL){
6 fprintf(stderr,"could not allocate memory.");
7 exit(1);
8 }
9 return v;
10 }
```

The first two lines are the same as above. Then if v points to NULL, an error message is printed to stderr, and the function is exited. (Notice that in this case the print function called is fprintf. This is the form used to print to files and will be covered later. Even if output is redirected, the message will appear on the terminal.) Some compilers may not recognize NULL. Should this occur, change if (v==NULL) to if (!v). The file stdlib.h must be included for stderr to be defined.

You may wish to use the function malloc in which case the relevant lines are slightly different:

```
double *t;
t=(double *) malloc(n*sizeof(double));
```

Thus, if you had statements like this in main

```
double *x;
x=v_alloc(n);
```

you would have n elements $x[0], \ldots, x[n-1]$ all initially equal to zero at your disposal. There are several notable features in this usage. Firstly, n may not be known until run–time (say as data input by the user). Secondly, in the program itself you can now simply refer to any component of the vector using standard mathematical notation. Thus, if you wanted to print the third element, you could use the line

```
printf("x[%d]=%lf\n",2,x[2]);
```

How would we deal with an $n \times n$ matrix A? Consider the above construction in the following formal sense: begin with a double x, and apply the indirection operator $*$: $x \rightarrow *x$. Then (after a call to calloc) a vector results. Thus one might expect that applying the indirection operator to (each element of) a vector will result in a matrix, i.e. that a matrix may be represented in the form $**a$. Indeed, consider this function

```
 1 double **m_alloc(int n)
 2 {
 3 int i;
 4 double **a;
 5
 6 a=(double **) calloc(n,sizeof(double *));
 7 if (a==NULL){
 8 fprintf(stderr,"could not allocate memory.");
 9 exit(1);
10 }
11 for (i=1;i<=n;i++){
12 a[i-1]=(double *) calloc (n, sizeof(double));
13         if (a[i-1]==NULL){
14            fprintf(stderr,"could not allocate memory.");
15            exit(1);
16            }
17         }
18         return a;
19 }
```

This function uses *multiple indirection*, which can be tricky. Line 4 declares a to be a *pointer to a pointer*. Line 6 defines a, using calloc, as n *pointers* to pointers of type double (whose size is not yet specified). You can think of this statement as defining pointers to the rows of $a = A$. In lines 7–10 the standard error test is seen. In lines 11–12, each a[i-1] is allocated as a vector of size n, as was done above. These statements fill out the rows, i.e., define the columns. If all goes well, a is returned on line 18. Since pointers to the rows have been allocated first, the prescription for getting to element a[i][j] via pointer arithmetic is the following: In memory space locate the address of the base element a, and add i. Then add j to this address, and return the value found there. Notice that the "size" n need not be known until run–time; only the address of the base element is required.

Suppose in the main program we wish to use a square matrix a of order n, and that n may not be known until run–time. We use the following lines to achieve this:

```
double **a;
a=m_alloc(n);
```

Again, in all later uses within the program we can refer to the elements of a in standard mathematical notation, e.g., a_{11} is a[0][0], a_{21} is a[1][0], etc. After giving an example, we will deal with the remaining problem of the choice of convenient indices. Why can we not simply use regular two–dimensional arrays? Please recall from Chapter 1 that the reason is that the compiler must be explicitly presented with the second dimension of such an array. Thus, a statement of the form, e.g., a[ ][10] must be entered. This is certainly unsuitable if the size of a is unknown *a priori* and is therefore useless in function argument lists.

1. Upper–triangular systems revisited.

Using pointers we can rewrite an upper–triangular system solver in a compact manner. Consider this program to do so:

```
 1  /* Uptriptr.c */
 2
 3  # include <math.h>
 4  # include <stdio.h>
 5  # include <stdlib.h>
 6  # include <malloc.h>
 7
 8  double *v_alloc(int n)
 9  {
10  double *v;
11  v=(double *) calloc(n,sizeof(double));
12  if (v==NULL){
13  fprintf(stderr,"could not allocate memory.");
14  exit(1);
15  }
16  return v;
17  }
18
19  double **m_alloc(int n)
20  {
21  int i;
22  double **a;
23
```

```
24 a=(double **) calloc(n,sizeof(double *));
25 if (a==NULL){
26 fprintf(stderr,"could not allocate memory.");
27 exit(1);
28 }
29 for (i=1;i<=n;i++){
30 a[i-1]=(double *) calloc (n, sizeof(double));
31          if (a[i-1]==NULL){
32              fprintf(stderr,"could not allocate memory.");
33              exit(1);
34              }
35          }
36          return a;
37 }
38
39 void uppertri (int n, double **u, double *b)
40 /* Solves Ux = b, U upper triangular*/
41 /* Solution returned in vector b.*/
42 /* Zero-offset indices used.    */
43
44 {
45 int j,k;
46 double s=0.0;
47
48 if (fabs(u[n-1][n-1])<5.0e-20){
49          printf("Singular Matrix.");
50          exit(1);
51          }
52
53 b[n-1] /= u[n-1][n-1];
54 for (k=n-1;k>=1;k--){
55
56          if (fabs(u[k-1][k-1])<5.0e-20){
57          printf("Singular Matrix.");
58          exit(1);
59          }
60
61          s=0.0;
62          for (j=k+1;j<=n;j++)
63          s += u[k-1][j-1] * b[j-1];
64
65          b[k-1] = (b[k-1]-s)/u[k-1][k-1];
66          }
```

```
67 }
68
69 main()
70 {
71 void uppertri(int n, double **u, double *b);
72 double *v_alloc(int n);    /* prototypes */
73 double **m_alloc(int n);
74
75 int i,j,N;
76
77 double **u;                /* matrix u */
78 double *b;                 /* vector b */
79
80 printf("Enter the order of the matrix:   ");
81 scanf("%d",&N);
82
83 u=m_alloc(N);
84 b=v_alloc(N);
85
86 printf("Enter the coefficient matrix:  \n");
87         for (i=1;i<=N;i++){
88                 for (j=i;j<=N;j++){
89                         printf("u[%d][%d]= ",i,j);
90                         scanf("%lf",&u[i-1][j-1]);
91                         }
92                 }
93
94 printf("Enter the right-hand side:  \n");
95         for (i=1;i<=N;i++){
96                 printf("b[%d]= ",i);
97                 scanf("%lf",&b[i-1]);
98                 }
99
100 uppertri(N,u,b);
101
102 for (i=1;i<=N;i++)
103 printf("x[%d] = %12.10lf\n",i,b[i-1]);
104 }
```

Notice the pointer declarations on lines 77–78 and the allocations on lines 83–84. Lines 86–98 just solicit the data in a manner we are familiar with. The only real work is in the function call on line 100; the results are then printed on lines 102–104. Notice the prototype of the function,

with **u for the matrix and *b for the vector. Within the function itself
the code is the same as that which we used before. In the argument list of
the function call to `uppertri`, notice that we pass just u and b (without
ampersands). This is because, by previous considerations, the name of an
array is identified with the address of the first element.

2. The scalar product.

Suppose you have two vectors x and y, each of length n, and you wish
to compute their inner (scalar) product. Assume that in `main` you have
already defined and allocated both vectors as above. Here is a simple
function which performs the calculation:

```
1 double dotprod(int n, double *x, double *y)
2 {
3 /* zero offset indices */
4 double s=0.0;
5 int i;
6 for (i=1;i<=n;i++){
7            s += x[i-1]*y[i-1];
8            }
9 return s;
10 }
```

If desired, array arguments to a C function may be written as arrays
instead of as pointers, e.g., in the form `x[]`. Be advised, however, that
arguments of array type are converted to pointers, and thus may be changed
after the function call.

MANIPULATION OF INDICES

We have seen that indices in C are *zero–offset* which means that if we
allocate N slots for a vector x, say, the actual elements are $x[0], \ldots, x[N-1]$.
Often we desire subscripts running from 1 to N. At other times you may
be displaying a function on an interval symmetric around the origin, say,
and desire $2N + 1$ subscripts, running from $-N$ to N. Let's see how this
can be achieved.

In allocating memory for vectors and matrices, we have used the functions `v_alloc(N)` and `m_alloc(N)`. One solution to this problem can be
obtained as follows. Suppose you have an array `x[ ]` which is to hold
$2N + 1$ values of a function on an interval centered at the origin. Given an
integer N, if you use the line

```
double *x;   x=v_alloc(2*N+1);
```

you will have $2N + 1$ elements $x[0], \ldots, x[2N]$. While it is possible to use these, problems of "translation" may arise, and errors may occur. A way around it is to define another pointer, say **nx** (the **n** stands for 'negative') like this:

```
double *x;   x=v_alloc(2*N+1);
double *nx=&x[N];
```

Throughout the rest of the program you refer only to the array **nx[ ]** whose elements now are $nx[-N], nx[-N+1], \ldots, nx[N]$. Figure 2.1 illustrates this with $N = 2$ so that there are five total units of storage. Think of each box as capable of storing one double value. The arrow on the left shows the original pointer returned by `calloc`. It points to the base element of **x**. The arrow in the middle shows the pointer **nx**. Notice that the present location is valid, as well as the two slots to the right and to the left. This is exactly as desired.

$x[0]$	$x[1]$	$x[2]$	$x[3]$	$x[4]$
$nx[-2]$	$nx[-1]$	$nx[0]$	$nx[1]$	$nx[2]$

Fig. 2.1

Exercise 2.5: Show how to define a nine–vector x with components $x[i]$ for $-2 \le i \le 6$.

Yet another way to alter the indices is to add additional arguments to the functions **v_alloc** and **m_alloc** which indicate the lowest and highest subscripts. Thus, statements of the form

```
double *x;
x=vecalloc(1,N);
```

would allocate N slots for the vector **x** which would now be given by

$$x[1], x[2], \ldots, x[N].$$

Similarly, statements such as

```
double **a;
```

```
a=matalloc(1,N,1,N);
```

would allocate N*N elements $\{a_{ij}\}$ for a square matrix a with indices i, j satisfying $1 \leq i, j \leq N$. The following code constitutes revised versions of routines in [NR]. (Adapted with permission from Cambridge University Press, Press, W.H., Flannery, B.P., Teukolsky, S.A. and Vetterling, W.T., *Numerical Recipes in C, The Art of Scientific Computation*, p. 706–707 (1989).)

We give two examples, first for vectors, and then for matrices:

```
 1 # include <malloc.h>
 2 # include <stdlib.h>
 3 # include <stdio.h>
 4
 5 double *vecalloc(int low,int high)
 6 {
 7 double *x;
 8
 9 x=(double *)calloc((unsigned)(high-low+1),sizeof(double));
10 if (x==NULL){
11 fprintf(stderr,"unable to allocate memory");
12 exit(1);
13 }
14 return (x-low);
15 }
16
17 double **matalloc(int rowlow, int rowhigh,\
18 int collow,int colhigh)
19 {
20 int k;
21 double **x;
22 x=(double **) calloc((unsigned) (rowhigh-rowlow+1),\
23 sizeof(double *));
24 if (x==NULL){
25 fprintf(stderr,"unable to allocate memory");
26 exit(1);
27 }
28 x -= rowlow;
29
30 for(k=rowlow;k<=rowhigh;k++) {
31 x[k]=(double *) calloc((unsigned) (colhigh-collow+1),\
32                        sizeof(double));
33 if (x[k]==NULL){
```

```
34 fprintf(stderr,"unable to allocate memory");
35 exit(1);
36 }
37 x[k] -= collow;
38 }
39          return x;
40 }
```

In the first function, `vecalloc`, the indices are to run from `low` to `high`. There are therefore `high-low+1` of them. This explains line 9. We use `unsigned` to achieve larger storage. Note also the cast to type `double`; an integer version, say, would be simple to write. On lines 10–13 we find the standard error test for `NULL` pointers. Finally, on line 14, pointer arithmetic is used and the pointer returned is `x-low`. Lines 21–28 of the `matalloc` function perform the same task for the rows of the matrix. Notice the multiple indirection (∗∗) which appears in lines 21 and 22. In lines 30–36, each row is allocated as in the `vecalloc` function above.

The one aspect which needs explanation here is the use of pointer arithmetic. It will be sufficient to consider the `vecalloc` function only. We do this in a special but representative case, that of allocation of a four–vector of double entries. Thus we will compare the two function calls

`a=v_alloc(4);`   and   `b=vecalloc(1,4);`

Each of these function calls defines and allocates four–vectors with components

$$a[0], a[1], a[2], a[3] \quad \text{and} \quad b[1], b[2], b[3], b[4]$$

respectively. Notice that the first lines of each of these functions are the same:

`double *x;  x=(double *)calloc(4,sizeof(double));`

We can neglect the error test, since it is the same in each. Now the `calloc` function returns a pointer to the first element of an array which has four elements. Thus, the line

`a=v_alloc(4);`

may be pictorially viewed as follows:

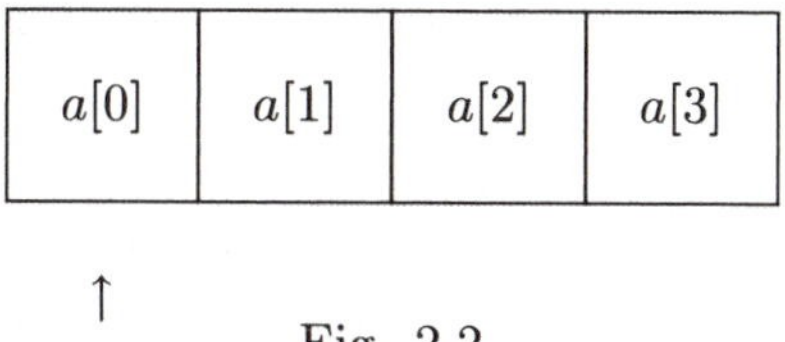

$a[0]$	$a[1]$	$a[2]$	$a[3]$

↑

Fig. 2.2

Here each box is thought of as containing enough storage for one double value.

Now consider the effect of moving the pointer one unit to the left, as shown below:

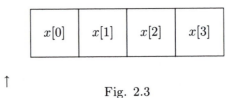

Fig. 2.3

This pointer no longer points to the allocated memory. In order to access the properly allocated first element, we now need to move one unit to the right to get the address of the base element. In the function call b=vecalloc(1,4) you will see on the last line that the return value in this case is x-1. This corresponds to moving the arrow one unit to the left as shown. Since we need to move one unit to the right to get the base element, this base element will be b[1], as desired.

Heuristically we are letting b=x-1 so that x=b+1, which translates index–wise into x[0]=b[1], x[1]=b[2], x[2]=b[3], x[3]=b[4], as desired.

Let's study several examples.

1. Tridiagonal linear systems.

Consider a tridiagonal system $Ax = b$ where the elements a_{ij} of A satisfy $a_{ij} = 0$ if $|i - j| > 1$. Thus, the only nonzero elements of A are on the diagonal and the first super– and subdiagonals:

$$A = \begin{pmatrix} \times & \times & 0 & 0 & \cdots & 0 \\ \times & \times & \times & 0 & \cdots & 0 \\ 0 & \times & \times & \times & \cdots & 0 \\ \vdots & \vdots & \vdots & \vdots & \cdots & \times \\ 0 & 0 & 0 & 0 & \cdots & \times \end{pmatrix}$$

Here by an "×" we mean a nonzero element. Gaussian elimination is simple for such a system. Let A be $N \times N$ and let b be an N–vector. We call the diagonal elements of A diag$_i$ for $1 \leq i \leq N$. The superdiagonal elements are sup$_i$ for $1 \leq i \leq N - 1$ and the subdiagonal elements are sub$_i$ for $2 \leq i \leq N$. Then in long form the system appears as

(2.11)

$$\mathrm{diag}_1 x_1 + \mathrm{sup}_1 x_2 = b_1$$
$$\mathrm{sub}_2 x_1 + \mathrm{diag}_2 x_2 + \mathrm{sup}_2 x_3 = b_2$$
$$\mathrm{sub}_3 x_2 + \mathrm{diag}_3 x_3 + \mathrm{sup}_3 x_4 = b_3$$

$$\vdots \qquad \vdots \qquad \vdots = \vdots$$

$$\text{sub}_{N-1}x_{N-2} + \text{diag}_{N-1}x_{N-1} + \text{sup}_{N-1}x_N = b_{N-1}$$

$$\text{sub}_N x_{N-1} + \text{diag}_N x_N = b_N$$

Provided $\text{diag}_1 \neq 0$, we can solve the first equation for x_1 in terms of x_2 and b_1. Using this, we can eliminate x_1 from the second equation, which will then involve only the unknowns x_2 and x_3, i.e., the second equation will then take the form $d_2' x_2 + \text{sup}_2 x_3 = b_2'$. Now, if $d_2' \neq 0$ we can use the same process to solve the second equation for x_2 and, with this result, we can eliminate x_2 from the third equation. We continue this process, eliminating the variable x_k from equation $(k+1)$ for $k = 1, 2, \ldots N - 1$. Then the last equation involves only x_N and can be solved directly. Since the next–to–last equation involves only x_N (now known) and x_{N-1}, we can now solve it for x_{N-1}, etc.

Here is pseudocode for the procedure just described. Let equation i be

$$(2.12) \qquad \text{sub}_i x_{i-1} + \text{diag}_i x_i + \text{sup}_i x_{i+1} = b_i \quad \text{for} \quad i = 1, 2, \ldots, N$$

with the understanding that $\text{sub}_1 = \text{sup}_N = 0$.

For $k = 2, \ldots, N$ {
provided $\text{diag}_{k-1} \neq 0$, compute $m = \text{sub}_k / \text{diag}_{k-1}$
compute $\text{diag}_k = \text{diag}_k - m \cdot \text{sup}_{k-1}$; compute $b_k = b_k - m \cdot b_{k-1}$
}
provided $\text{diag}_N \neq 0$, compute $x_N = b_N / \text{diag}_N$
for $k = N - 1, \ldots, 1$ {
provided $\text{diag}_k \neq 0$,
compute $x_k = (b_k - \text{sup}_k \cdot x_{k+1}) / \text{diag}_k$ }

As an explicit example, let's find the solution of the 20×20 system $Ax = b$ where $b_i = \delta_{i1}$ and A is the Dirichlet matrix, i.e., all diagonal elements equal 2, and all super– and subdiagonal elements equal -1. Here is the code:

```
1 /* TRDG.C */
2
3 # include <malloc.h>
4 # include <math.h>
5 # include <stdio.h>
6 # include <stdlib.h>
7
8 void tridiag(int n, double *sub, double *diag,\
9 double *sup, double *b)
10 {          /* solution returned in vector b */
```

```
11          int k;
12          double m,det;
13          for (k=2;k<=n;k++){
14                  if (fabs(diag[k-1])<5.0e-20){
15                  printf("Division by zero in tridiag");
16                  exit(1);
17                  }
18                  m=sub[k]/diag[k-1];
19                  diag[k] -= m*sup[k-1];
20                  b[k] -= m*b[k-1];
21                  }
22
23          det=diag[1];
24          for (k=2;k<=n;k++){
25                  det *= diag[k];
26                  }
27          if (fabs(det)<5.0e-20){
28                  printf("Singular matrix in tridiag");
29                  exit(1);
30                  }
31
32          b[n] =b[n]/diag[n];
33          for (k=n-1;k>=1;k--)
34                  b[k] =(b[k] - sup[k]*b[k+1])/diag[k];
35 }
36
37 double *vecalloc(int low,int high)
38 {
39 double *x;
40 x=(double *)calloc((unsigned)(high-low+1),sizeof(double));
41 if (x==NULL){
42 fprintf(stderr,"could not allocate memory.");
43 exit(1);
44 }
45 return (x-low);
46 }
47
48 main()
49 {
50 void tridiag(int n, double *sub, double *diag,\
51 double *sup, double *b);
52 double *vecalloc(int low,int high);
53 int j,n=20;
```

```
54 double *sub, *diag, *sup, *b;
55 diag=vecalloc(1,n);
56 sup=vecalloc(1,n);
57 sub=vecalloc(1,n);
58 b  =vecalloc(1,n);
59
60 for (j=2;j<=n-1;j++){
61         diag[j]=2.0;
62         sub[j]=sup[j]=-1.0;
63         b[j]=0.0;
64         }
65
66 diag[1]=diag[n]=2.0;
67 sub[1]=sup[n]=0.0;
68 sub[n]=sup[1]=-1.0;
69 b[1]=1.0;
70 b[n]=0.0;
71
72         tridiag(n,sub,diag,sup,b);
73         printf("\n\n");
74         for (j=1;j<=n;j++)
75                 printf("x[%d] = %10.10lf\n",j,b[j]);
76         printf("\n\n");
77
78         }
```

On lines 8, 9 the function header appears. Notice that many values will be returned (in the vector b) so the return type is void. The arguments are the order n and the three vector arrays, each in pointer form. The forward elimination code is on lines 13–21 and is a straightforward version of the above discussion. Please notice that indices are as expected; that is, they run over 1 to n. On lines 23–26 the determinant is computed. Back substitution is on lines 32–34. In main itself, we begin with the prototypes on lines 50–52. The four arrays are declared as pointers in line 54 and are allocated immediately afterward (lines 55–58) in a manner already discussed. The rest of the program through line 70 is just entering the data; the real work is done in the function call on line 72, after which we need only print the results. Note that on lines 66–68 we make two assignments on one line, as is allowed in C. One note of caution needs to be added: if you were to call **tridiag** many times in succession (as often happens in partial differential equations when advancing one step in time), the coefficients **diag** will be altered upon return.

Because of the importance of tridiagonal systems, we briefly give hypotheses under which such a matrix is invertible. Roughly, one requires that the matrix be diagonally dominant in the following sense. Let A have elements as above (the diagonal elements are diag_i for $1 \leq i \leq n$, etc.). Sufficient conditions for such a tridiagonal A to be invertible are:

$$|\text{diag}_1| > |\text{sup}_1| > 0$$
$$|\text{diag}_n| > |\text{sub}_n| > 0$$
$$|\text{diag}_i| \geq |\text{sup}_i| + |\text{sub}_i|, \quad (i = 2, \ldots, n-1)$$
$$\text{sub}_i \cdot \text{sup}_i \neq 0 \quad (i = 2, \ldots, n-1)$$

Here is the essence of the proof. Let us attempt the standard factorization $A = LU$, where L is lower–triangular and U is unit upper–triangular:

$$L = \begin{pmatrix} a_1 & 0 & 0 & \cdots & 0 \\ \text{sub}_2 & a_2 & 0 & \cdots & 0 \\ 0 & \text{sub}_3 & a_3 & \cdots & 0 \\ \vdots & \vdots & \vdots & \vdots & \vdots \\ 0 & 0 & 0 & \cdots & a_n \end{pmatrix}$$

$$U = \begin{pmatrix} 1 & c_1 & 0 & \cdots & 0 \\ 0 & 1 & c_2 & \cdots & 0 \\ 0 & 0 & 1 & \cdots & 0 \\ \vdots & \vdots & \vdots & \vdots & \vdots \\ 0 & 0 & 0 & \cdots & 1 \end{pmatrix}$$

Now multiply L by U and force equality with A; we get easily

$$(2.13) \qquad a_i = \text{diag}_i - \text{sub}_i c_{i-1}, \quad c_i = \frac{\text{sup}_i}{a_i} \quad (1 \leq i \leq n).$$

(Recall that $\text{sub}_1 = \text{sup}_n = 0$). Now we use $\det A = \det L \cdot \det U$ and note that $\det U = 1$. Thus, $\det A = \prod_{i=1}^{n} a_i$, and it is enough to show that $a_i \neq 0$ for every i.

By hypotheses, $|\text{diag}_1| > |\text{sup}_1| > 0$ and $a_1 = \text{diag}_1 - 0 = \text{diag}_1$. Therefore, $a_1 = \text{diag}_1 \neq 0$ by hypothesis. Similarly, $a_2 = \text{diag}_2 - \text{sub}_2 c_1$, so that by the hypothesis of diagonal dominance

$$(2.14) \qquad |a_2| \geq |\text{diag}_2| - |c_1||\text{sub}_2|$$
$$\geq |\text{sup}_2| + |\text{sub}_2| - |c_1||\text{sub}_2|$$
$$= |\text{sup}_2| + (1 - |c_1|)|\text{sub}_2|.$$

We will thus have $a_2 \neq 0$ then provided $|c_1| \leq 1$. However, by definition of c_1 we can derive strict inequality:

$$(2.15) \qquad |c_1| = \left| \frac{\text{sup}_1}{a_1} \right| = \left| \frac{\text{sup}_1}{\text{diag}_1} \right| < 1$$

by hypothesis. It then follows element by element that all a_i are nonzero, and hence A is invertible.

Exercise 2.6: Write a C function to solve a lower–triangular linear system with natural indices i running over $1 \le i \le n$.

2. Fixed–point iteration for systems.

This is a system version of the one–dimensional algorithm in Chapter 1. The independent variable is $(x_1, \ldots, x_n) \in R^n$, and the system can be compactly written as $x = g(x)$ where g is a vector–valued function; i.e., the system is

$$(2.16) \qquad \begin{aligned} x_1 &= g_1(x_1, \ldots, x_n) \\ x_2 &= g_2(x_1, \ldots, x_n) \\ &\vdots \qquad \vdots \\ x_n &= g_n(x_1, \ldots, x_n). \end{aligned}$$

We use the maximum norm for a vector x : $||x|| = \max_{1 \le i \le n} |x_i|$. One begins with an initial approximation x_i^0 for each i, $1 \le i \le n$ and iterates according to the algorithm

$$(2.17) \qquad x^{k+1} = g(x^k) \quad (k = 0, 1, \ldots).$$

The code we present below requires three vectors: x (the present approximation), y (the next iterate) and g (the value of g at x). We define each as a pointer and allocate via **vecalloc** as was done previously. Here is the rather straightforward version for the solution of the system $x = g(x)$ on R^2 with $g_1(x_1, x_2) = \sinh(x_2)$, $g_2(x_1, x_2) = (0.5)\cosh(x_1)$:

```
1 /* FPITN.C */
2
3 /*
4 Fixed point iteration for a system of the form
5 x=g(x), x = (x[1],x[2],...,x[N]),
6 g(x) = (g[1](x),...,g[N](x)) in R^N.
7 */
8
9 # include <math.h>
10 # include <stdio.h>
11 # include <stdlib.h>
12 # include <malloc.h>
```

```
13 # define MAX(a,b) ((a)>=(b) ?  (a):(b))
14 # define TOL 5.0e-11
15 # define N (int)2            /* number of equations */
16
17 void fung(double *x, double *g) /* enter g here */
18 {
19 /* assume form x=g(x), x = (x[1],x[2],...,x[N]) */
20
21         g[1] = sinh(x[2]);
22         g[2] = (0.5)*cosh(x[1]);
23         /* solution near (0.6,0.6) */
24 }
25
26 double *vecalloc(int low,int high)
27 {
28 double *x;
29 x=(double *)calloc((unsigned)(high-low+1),sizeof(double));
30 if (x==NULL){
31 fprintf(stderr,"could not allocate memory.");
32 exit(1);
33 }
34 return (x-low);
35 }
36
37 main()
38 {
39 double *x,*y,*g;   /* define vectors as pointers */
40 double e,norm_x;    /* e measures max-norm error */
41                     /* norm_x = max-norm of x */
42
43 int k,iter=0;                    /* iterate counter */
44 void fung(double *x, double *g);
45 double *vecalloc(int low,int high);
46
47 x=vecalloc(1,N);                 /* allocate memory */
48 y=vecalloc(1,N);
49 g=vecalloc(1,N);
50
51 printf("Enter the starting approximations:\n\n");
52 for (k=1;k<=N;k++){
53         printf("x[%d] = ",k);
54         scanf("%lf",&x[k]);
55         printf("\n");
```

```
56              }
57
58  do{
59              fung(x,g);              /* evaluate g at x */
60              for (k=1;k<=N;k++){
61              y[k]=g[k];
62              }
63
64              e=fabs(x[1]-y[1]);
65              for (k=2;k<=N;k++){
66              e = MAX(e,fabs(x[k]-y[k]));
67              }
68              for (k=1;k<=N;k++){
69              x[k]=y[k]; /* prepare for next iteration */
70              }
71              norm_x=fabs(x[1]);
72              for (k=2;k<=N;k++){
73                      norm_x=MAX(norm_x,fabs(x[k]));
74                      }
75
76              iter += 1;
77              if (iter>200){
78                      printf("Too many iterations.");
79                      exit(1);
80                      }
81  }
82  while (e>TOL*norm_x);
83
84  for (k=1;k<=N;k++){
85              printf("x[%d] = %12.10lf\n",k,y[k]);
86              }
87  printf("\n");
88  printf("iterates required:    %d\n",iter);
89  }
```

Notice that the indices run over the natural values $1 \leq i \leq N$. Line 15 contains N, the order of the system. The function g is entered on lines 17–24. The return type is void; the arguments are a pointer x (a vector, the independent variable) and a pointer g (a vector equal to the value of g at x). Within this function fung we write g_1 as g[1], etc., and the notation is that of standard mathematics. Line 39 defines the pointers to x, y and g as described above; the allocations then occur on lines 47–49. Lines 51–56 merely solicit the starting approximations. The function g is evaluated in line 59 via fung. The rest of the do while loop is hopefully clear.

If you begin this program with values near 0.6, 0.6, you will converge to a solution after 48 or 49 iterations. Just as in one dimension, g must be Lipschitz in a neighborhood of the starting approximation, which is itself assumed to be sufficiently accurate. While this may be the world's simplest algorithm, it should promote familiarity with pointers and their relationship to vectors and matrices.

3. Gauss–Seidel iteration for linear systems.

Consider an $n \times n$ linear system $Ax = b$ where n may be large but A itself is sparse, i.e., has many zeroes. Such systems arise often in partial differential equations, in which case the diagonal elements of A may be large in comparison to the off–diagonal elements. More precisely, A is called *diagonally dominant* if

$$(2.18) \qquad \mu \equiv \max_{1 \le i \le n} \sum_{\substack{j=1 \\ j \ne i}}^{n} \left| \frac{a_{ij}}{a_{ii}} \right| \quad < \quad 1.$$

To derive an iteration in this case, we write each of the equations

$$\sum_{j=1}^{n} a_{ij} x_j = b_i \qquad (i = 1, 2, \ldots, n)$$

in the form

$$a_{ii} x_i + \sum_{\substack{j=1 \\ j \ne i}}^{n} a_{ij} x_j = b_i \qquad (i = 1, 2, \ldots, n).$$

Thus, for $1 \le i \le n$ we can write

$$x_i = \frac{1}{a_{ii}} \left(b_i - \sum_{\substack{j=1 \\ j \ne i}}^{n} a_{ij} x_j \right)$$

which suggests the *Jacobi iteration*

$$x_i^{(m+1)} = \frac{1}{a_{ii}} \left(b_i - \sum_{\substack{j=1 \\ j \ne i}}^{n} a_{ij} x_j^{(m)} \right) \qquad (i = 1, 2, \ldots, n), \quad (m = 0, 1, \ldots).$$

This is easily shown to converge for *any* initial approximation x_i^0 if $\mu < 1$ but is much too slow in practice. A standard acceleration device is to use instead the *Gauss–Seidel* iteration. It is based on this simple idea: when computing $x_i^{(m+1)}$ above we have already updated the previous components of x, i.e., we have already computed $x_j^{(m+1)}$ for $j < i$. This suggests the iteration (for $m = 0, 1, \ldots$ and $i = 1, 2, \ldots, n$)

$$(2.19) \qquad x_i^{(m+1)} = \frac{1}{a_{ii}} \left(b_i - \sum_{j=1}^{i-1} a_{ij} x_j^{(m+1)} - \sum_{j=i+1}^{n} a_{ij} x_j^{(m)} \right),$$

which is that of Gauss–Seidel. We will show below that if μ as defined above in (2.18) is less than unity, this iteration converges and at a faster rate than that of Jacobi. In fact, an important theorem along these lines states that, given a symmetric A with positive diagonal entries, the Gauss–Seidel iteration converges for *any* initial vector $x^{(0)}$ if and only if A is positive definite. You can find a proof in [IK].

Here is a proof of convergence when $\mu < 1$. Set $e^{(m)} = x - x^{(m)}$ where x is the solution to $Ax = b$. Subtracting the Gauss–Seidel iterate $x^{(m)}$ from the solution x component–wise, we get for $m = 0, 1, \ldots$

$$(2.20) \qquad e_i^{(m+1)} = -\sum_{j=1}^{i-1} \frac{a_{ij}}{a_{ii}} e_j^{(m+1)} - \sum_{j=i+1}^{n} \frac{a_{ij}}{a_{ii}} e_j^{(m)} \qquad (i = 1, 2, \ldots, n).$$

Set

$$(2.21) \qquad \kappa_i^1 = \sum_{j=1}^{i-1} \left| \frac{a_{ij}}{a_{ii}} \right|, \qquad \kappa_i^2 = \sum_{j=i+1}^{n} \left| \frac{a_{ij}}{a_{ii}} \right|$$

with $\kappa_1^1 = \kappa_n^2 = 0$. Then

$$(2.22) \qquad \mu = \max_{1 \le i \le n} \sum_{\substack{j=1 \\ j \ne i}}^{n} \left| \frac{a_{ij}}{a_{ii}} \right| = \max_{1 \le i \le n} (\kappa_i^1 + \kappa_i^2)$$

and hence $\kappa_i^1 + \kappa_i^2 \le \mu$ for any i. Taking absolute values above in (2.20), we have

$$(2.23) \qquad |e_i^{(m+1)}| \le \kappa_i^1 \|e^{(m+1)}\|_\infty + \kappa_i^2 \|e^{(m)}\|_\infty.$$

Let k be that index for which $|e_k^{(m+1)}| = \|e^{(m+1)}\|_\infty$. Then

$$\|e^{(m+1)}\|_\infty \le \kappa_k^1 \|e^{(m+1)}\|_\infty + \kappa_k^2 \|e^{(m)}\|_\infty$$

from which we conclude

$$(2.24) \qquad \|e^{(m+1)}\|_\infty \le \nu_k \|e^{(m)}\|_\infty \quad \text{where} \quad \nu_k = \frac{\kappa_k^2}{1 - \kappa_k^1}.$$

Now we claim that $0 \leq \max_k \nu_k \leq \mu < 1$. If so, then by iteration we have the inequality

$$(2.25) \qquad \|e^{(m)}\|_\infty \leq (\max_k \nu_k)^m \|e^{(0)}\|_\infty \to 0 \quad \text{as} \quad m \to \infty.$$

For the claim we have the simple algebra

$$\kappa_i^1 + \kappa_i^2 - \nu_i = \kappa_i^1 + \kappa_i^2 - \frac{\kappa_i^2}{1 - \kappa_i^1} = \frac{\kappa_i^1 \left(1 - (\kappa_i^1 + \kappa_i^2)\right)}{1 - \kappa_i^1} \geq \frac{\kappa_i^1(1 - \mu)}{1 - \kappa_i^1} \geq 0.$$

Hence

$$\nu_i \leq \kappa_i^1 + \kappa_i^2 \leq \max_i(\kappa_i^1 + \kappa_i^2) \equiv \mu < 1.$$

Below we write standard code to implement the Gauss–Seidel algorithm:

```
1  /* gsiter.c */
2
3  # include <stdlib.h>
4  # include <math.h>
5  # include <malloc.h>
6  # include <stdio.h>
7  # define MAX(a,b) ((a)>=(b) ?   (a):(b))
8  # define TOL 5.0e-10
9
10 double *vecalloc(int low,int high)
11 {
12 double *x;
13
14 x=(double *)calloc((unsigned)(high-low+1),sizeof(double));
15 if (x==NULL){
16 fprintf(stderr,"unable to allocate memory");
17 exit(1);
18 }
19 return (x-low);
20 }
21
22 double **matalloc(int rowlow, int rowhigh,\
23 int collow,int colhigh)
24 {
25 int k;
26 double **x;
27 x=(double **) calloc((unsigned) (rowhigh-rowlow+1),\
28                              sizeof(double *));
```

```
29 if (x==NULL){
30 fprintf(stderr,"unable to allocate memory");
31 exit(1);
32 }
33 x -= rowlow;
34
35 for(k=rowlow;k<=rowhigh;k++) {
36 x[k]=(double *) calloc((unsigned) (colhigh-collow+1),\
37                     sizeof(double));
38 if (x[k]==NULL){
39 fprintf(stderr,"unable to allocate memory");
40 exit(1);
41 }
42 x[k] -= collow;
43 }
44         return x;
45 }
46
47 double maxnum(int m, double *x)
48 {
49 /* returns the maximum norm of vector x */
50 /* indices run over 1 to m */
51 int k;
52 double z;
53
54         z=MAX(fabs(x[1]),fabs(x[2]));
55         for (k=3;k<=m;k++)
56                 z=MAX(fabs(x[k]),z);
57         return z;
58 }
59
60 void gauseid(int N, int *iter, double **a, double *b)
61 {        /* solution returned in vector b */
62 int i,j;
63 double *e,*x,*y;
64 double s,t;
65 e=vecalloc(1,N);                    /* error vector */
66 x=vecalloc(1,N); /* current vector approximation */
67 y=vecalloc(1,N);    /* next vector approximation */
68
69 do{
70
71 for (i=1;i<=N;i++){
```

```
72          if (fabs(a[i][i])<5.0e-20){
73                  printf("Singular matrix.");
74                  exit(1);
75                  }
76          s=0.0;
77          for (j=1;j<=i-1;j++){
78          s += a[i][j]*y[j];
79          }
80          t=0.0;
81          for (j=i+1;j<=N;j++){
82          t += a[i][j]*x[j];
83          }
84
85          y[i]=(b[i]-s-t)/a[i][i];
86          }
87
88 for (i=1;i<=N;i++)
89          e[i]=fabs(x[i]-y[i]);
90
91 for (i=1;i<=N;i++){ /* set up next iteration */
92          x[i]=y[i];
93          }
94
95 (*iter)++;
96
97          if ((*iter)>500){
98                  printf("Too many iterates.");
99                  exit(1);
100                 }
101 }
102
103 while (maxnum(N,e) > TOL*maxnum(N,x));
104 /* relative error test in maximum norm */
105
106 for (i=1;i<=N;i++){
107          b[i]=y[i];
108          }
109
110 }
111
112 main()
113 {
114 double *vecalloc(int low,int high);
```

```
115 double **matalloc(int rowlow, int rowhigh,\
116                          int collow,int colhigh);
117 double maxnum(int m, double *x);
118 void gauseid(int N, int *iter, double **a, double *x);
119 double **a;
120 double *b,*x;
121 int iter=0,i,j,N;
122
123 printf("Enter the order of the matrix:   ");
124 scanf("%d",&N);
125 printf("\n\n");
126
127 a=matalloc(1,N,1,N);
128 b=vecalloc(1,N);
129 x=vecalloc(1,N);
130
131 printf("\n\n");
132 printf("Enter the coefficient matrix A row by row:\n\n");
133
134 for (i=1;i<=N;i++){
135         for (j=1;j<=N;j++){
136             printf("a[%d,%d] = ",i,j);
137             scanf("%lf",&a[i][j]);
138             printf("\n\n");
139         }
140 }
141
142 printf("Enter the given right-hand side b[ ]:\n\n");
143
144 for (i=1;i<=N;i++){
145             printf("b[%d] = ",i);
146             scanf("%lf",&b[i]);
147             printf("\n");
148         }
149
150 gauseid(N,&iter,a,b);
151
152 for (i=1;i<=N;i++){
153         printf("x[%d]=%10.10lf\n",i,b[i]);
154         }
155
156 printf("\n");
157 printf("%d iterates were required.\n\n",iter);
```

```
158
159 }
```

Scanning the code, you will find nothing new until line 47 where the function `maxnum` appears. Its arguments are an integer m, the size of the vector x, which is itself declared as a pointer. It simply computes the maximum norm of the vector x, a calculation which was used several times in the previous program.

On lines 60–110 we find a function `gauseid` which implements the algorithm described above. Its arguments are N, the size of the vector b (and the order of the matrix $A = a$), a pointer to an integer `iter` (to keep track of the total number of iterates), and the matrix a and vector b, each defined as pointers. The rest of the function code is straightforward; notice only line 95, where the *value* of the iterate counter is required. Thus, we see there the expression `(*iter)++`.

We employ the usual relative error test on line 103. In `main` the required prototypes appear on lines 114–118; the coefficient matrix a and right–hand side b are defined on lines 119–120. After the order N is obtained from the user in lines 123–124, the allocations are performed on lines 127–129. Lines 132–148 request data from the user. Thus, the only real work appears in the function call on line 150. Once we learn about `FILE` pointers, you may prefer to rewrite this code so that it reads the matrix data from a file. When N is large, such item by item data entry is tedious and is prone to errors.

We conclude this section with a brief discussion of the difference between a true two–dimensional array and an array of pointers. Consider the two statements

`double x[2][4];   double *y[2];`

The first defines a 2×4 matrix x with elements

$$x[i][j] \quad \text{for} \quad 0 \le i \le 1, \ 0 \le j \le 3.$$

The second statement (that defining y) allocates two pointers without initializing them. Thus, y is a type of array with two rows, but the length of these rows has not been specified. Indeed, these lengths could be any integral value. Therefore, the second construction is more general. However, in standard mathematical usage this form does not arise often; thus, matrix usage is well–handled by multiple indirection (e.g., `double **a;`) and a call to the `matalloc` function.

Exercise 2.7: Rewrite the standard fixed–point iteration for a system $x = g(x)$ (given in `fpitn.c`) utilizing the idea of the Gauss–Seidel iteration.

COMMAND–LINE ARGUMENTS

Accessing command–line arguments is a typical use of pointers. We have in mind here a program, already compiled, which for execution requires several pieces of data to be input by the user. Let's say the executable file is called `stabf` (an example to be introduced later, which will return all eigenvalues of the symmetric linear system $Ax = \lambda Bx$ via Sturm sequences.) The information required is the order of the matrices, say N (N = 33 in the example below), and two data files, say `a.dat` and `b.dat`, which contain the elements of the matrices A and B, respectively. Assuming the data files lie in the current working directory, one runs the program by issuing the command

```
stabf 33 a.dat b.dat
```

Note that spaces delimit the entries.

Here is how one prepares code for command–line arguments. Firstly, declare `main` differently as

```
main(int argc, char *argv[ ])
```

Here `argc` is an integer which indicates the *number* of command–line arguments. The second, `char *argv[ ]` is a pointer to an array of strings. By convention, `argv[0]` is actually the name of the program that is to be executed. Thus, the integer `argc` is in fact one greater than the number of command line arguments entered after the name of the executable file. This means that the first argument typed on the command line after the filename is in fact the second element of the array `argv[ ]`. In the example above, we have `argc=4`, `argv[0]=stabf`, `argv[1]=33`, `argv[2]=a.dat` and `argv[3]=b.dat`.

Since file reading and writing are typical applications of command–line arguments, we discuss that briefly before giving an example.

FILE I/O: READING AND WRITING FILES

One opens a file with the `fopen` command. This returns a *file pointer* by means of which you access the file in all future operations. Since a pointer is returned, you must check that it is valid before proceeding. Once all desired file activity has been concluded, one closes a file with the `fclose` command.

Firstly, you must always include the file `stdio.h` when using file operations. In `main` itself you must declare files to be used by, e.g., the statement `FILE *fp;`. Here are lines which open a file called `a.dat` for (ASCII) writing and check to see that all is well:

```
FILE *fp;
if ((fp=fopen("a.dat","w")) != NULL){
```

```
other statements
⋮
}
else {
printf("Error opening file a.dat");
}
```

Please notice carefully that the expression fp=fopen(...) is enclosed in its own set of parentheses *before* the comparison to the NULL pointer is made. This ensures that the file is indeed opened. These statements could be replaced by the lines

```
if (!(fp=fopen("a.dat","w"))){
printf("Error opening file %s\n",a.dat);
}
else {
other statements
⋮
}
```

(Recall that NULL has the value FALSE in logical expressions.)

To open an existing file for reading instead, replace "w" above by "r". To open an existing file for appending, use instead "a". Generally one can use the standard I/O functions (e.g., printf) for file operations by preceding their names with an f. Thus, to write the integer 10 (say) to the file as above, one uses the line

```
fprintf(fp,"%d\n",10);
```

Notice the use of the file pointer fp here as the first argument to fprintf. Suppose that you want to read pairs of (double) values from a file, which has already been declared by a FILE *fp; statement in main. You can use the following command to do this: assume that k is an integer and that you have already allocated two double vectors x,y of sufficiently large size:

```
k=0;
while (!feof(fp)){
fscanf(fp,"%lf %lf\n",&x[k],&y[k]);
k++;
(other statements) ...
}
```

Here the while condition (!feof(fp)) means we continue reading pairs of data from the file until all are exhausted (i.e., until the end of file is found.)

Consider now this code fragment which combines command–line arguments with the opening of files for the example above using stabf:

```
 1 # include <stdio.h>
 2 # include <stdlib.h>
 3
 4 main(int argc, char *argv[ ])
 5 {
 6 int N;
 7 FILE *fpa,*fpb;
 8
 9 if (argc!=4){
10          printf("Usage:    stabf order afile bfile");
11          }
12
13 else if (!(fpa=fopen(argv[2],"r"))){
14          printf("STABF: Error opening file %s\n",argv[2]);
15          }
16
17 else if (!(fpb=fopen(argv[3],"r"))){
18          printf("STABF: Error opening file %s\n",argv[3]);
19          }
20
21 else{
22          N=atoi(argv[1]);
23
24 (other statements ...)
25
26 }        /* end else */
27
28 (other statements )
29
30 }        /* end main */
```

Notice the form of main and the two file pointers declared on line 7. In the command line itself we are to use

stabf 33 a.dat b.dat

and thus argc must be 4. Lines 9–11 check that the correct number of command–line arguments are present. Lines 13–15 open the file argv[2] which, in this case, is the file a.dat; lines 17–19 do the same thing for argv[3], which is b.dat here. Instead of using NULL we have used a logical device to check that the file pointers are correctly returned. Lastly, notice line 22. The first command–line argument is the order N of the matrices, so `argv[1]=33`. The program obtains the ASCII representation of N from the user, which is then converted to an integer value via the function `atoi`. Please include the header file `stdlib.h` so that the prototype of `atoi` can be found (see Chapter 3).

Exercise 2.8: Rewrite the Gauss–Seidel code in `gsiter.c` (given previously in this chapter) so that the elements of the coefficient matrix A, and those of the right–hand side b, are read from files at the command line.

Exercise 2.9: Given $n + 1$ points $\{x_k\}_{k=0}^n$ and two set of values $\{f(x_k)\}_{k=0}^n$, $\{f'(x_k)\}_{k=0}^n$, the *Hermite Interpolating Polynomial* is a polynomial $P(x)$ of degree $2n+1$ or less which satisfies $P(x_k) = f(x_k)$, $P'(x_k) = f'(x_k)$ for $k = 0, 1, \ldots, n$. One knows (cf. [IK]) that

$$P(x) = \sum_{i=0}^n L_i^2(x) \left[f(x_i)(1 - 2L_i'(x_i)(x - x_i)) + f'(x_i)(x - x_i) \right],$$

where

$$L_i(x) = \prod_{\substack{j=0 \\ j \neq i}}^n \frac{x - x_j}{x_i - x_j}.$$

Given a collection of data points as above, write a C function whose arguments include these data arrays and which will evaluate $P(x)$ for $x_0 \leq x \leq x_n$ in appropriate steps. Write the results out to a file.

Exercise 2.10: (*Bernoulli's Method*) Let

$$P_n(x) = \sum_{k=0}^n a_k x^{n-k}$$

have real coefficients and real roots $r_1, \ldots, r_n$ with $|r_1| > |r_2| > \cdots > |r_n|$. Consider the difference equation

$$a_0 x_k + a_1 x_{k-1} + \cdots + a_{n-1} x_{k-n+1} + a_n x_{k-n} = 0$$

whose characteristic equation is $P_n(x) = 0$. Since the roots are distinct, we can write the general solution of this difference equation in the form

$$x_k = c_1 r_1^k + c_2 r_2^k + \cdots + c_n r_n^k$$

for arbitrary constants $c_1, \ldots, c_n$. Assume that initial values can be chosen so that $c_1 \neq 0$, and show that $\lim_{k \to \infty} x_{k+1}/x_k = r_1$. Implement this with a C program which will compute the dominant root of such a polynomial. Use as initial values $x_{-n+1} = x_{-n+2} = \cdots = x_{-1} = 0$, $x_0 = 1$. These can be shown to imply the condition $c_1 \neq 0$. There are many variations which handle dominant complex roots, multiplicities, etc. See the references.

Exercise 2.11: (*Graeffe's Method*) Let $P_n(x)$ be as in the above exercise with $a_0 = 1$. Thus, we can write, for $f_0(x) = P_n(x)$,

$$f_0(x) = \prod_{k=1}^{n} (x - r_k).$$

Now compute

$$(-1)^n f_0(x) f_0(-x) = (-1)^n \prod_{k=1}^{n} (x - r_k)(-x - r_k) = \prod_{k=1}^{n} (x^2 - r_k^2).$$

Thus,

$$f_2(x) \equiv (-1)^n f_0(\sqrt{x}) f_0(-\sqrt{x}) = \prod_{k=1}^{n} (x - r_k^2)$$

is a polynomial of degree n in x with roots $r_1^2, \ldots, r_n^2$. Similarly,

$$f_4(x) \equiv (-1)^n f_2(\sqrt{x}) f_2(-\sqrt{x}) = \prod_{k=1}^{n} (x - r_k^4)$$

has roots $r_1^4, \ldots, r_n^4$, etc. Thus, the roots of the successive f_m's are eventually widely separated.

Suppose that k "root–squarings" are performed, so that the roots of the final equation are $r_1^m, \ldots, r_n^m$, where $m = 2^k$. Let the final equation be of the form

$$f_m(x) = x^n - A_1 x^{n-1} + A_2 x^{n-2} + \cdots + (-1)^{n-1} A_{n-1} x + (-1)^n A_n = 0,$$

or

$$f_m(x) = (x - r_1^m)(x - r_2^m) \cdots (x - r_n^m).$$

Show that

$$r_1 = \lim_{k \to \infty} (A_1)^{\frac{1}{2^k}}, \qquad r_2 = \lim_{k \to \infty} \left(\frac{A_2}{A_1}\right)^{\frac{1}{2^k}}, \qquad \text{etc.}$$

Implement this procedure with a C function to find all roots of such a polynomial. First, establish the following recursion for the new coefficients in terms of the old ones: write

$$f_0(x) = \sum_{i=0}^{\infty} (-1)^i A_i x^{n-i}$$

with the conventions that $A_0 = 1$ and $A_i = 0$ for $i > n$. Show that

$$f_2(x) = \sum_{k=0}^{\infty}(-1)^k B_k x^{n-k},$$

where $B_k = 0$ for $k > n$ and otherwise

$$B_k = \sum_{i=0}^{2k}(-1)^{i+k} A_i A_{2k-i}.$$

Exercise 2.12: (*Muller's Method*) This scheme is a well–known root–finder, even for problems with complex roots. Let the problem be to find solutions to the scalar equation $f(x) = 0$ for x real. Assume that we are given three approximate solutions x_0, x_1, x_2. The idea of the scheme is to use this data to construct a parabola $p(x)$ passing through the points $(x_i, f(x_i))$ for $i = 0, 1, 2$. Using the Newton form of the interpolating polynomial, we can write

$$p(x) = f(x_2) + (x - x_2)f[x_2, x_1] + (x - x_2)(x - x_1)f[x_2, x_1, x_0].$$

(Recall the discussion of the secant method earlier in this chapter for a definition of the divided differences appearing here.) After some algebra, $p(x)$ can be rewritten in the form

$$p(x) = f(x_2) + (x - x_2)\xi + (x - x_2)^2 f[x_2, x_1, x_0],$$

where

$$\xi = f[x_2, x_1] + (x_2 - x_1)f[x_2, x_1, x_0].$$

Notice that ξ may be expressed in the simpler form

$$\xi = f[x_2, x_1] + f[x_2, x_0] - f[x_0, x_1].$$

Now use the quadratic formula to solve $p(x) = 0$ for a root in the form $x - x_2$ and then call $x = x_3$ to get the explicit formula

$$x_3 = x_2 - \frac{2f(x_2)}{\xi \pm \sqrt{\xi^2 - 4f(x_2)f[x_2, x_1, x_0]}}.$$

The sign is chosen to maximize the modulus of the denominator. Notice that complex quantities may arise, even if the actual solution is real. The algorithm then continues using x_1, x_2, x_3 as above. The scheme converges at fractional order ≈ 1.84; see [HO] for a proof of convergence.

Write a C function to carry out this procedure for a polynomial. You may wish to refer to the program implementing *Laguerre's Method* in Chapter 4.

Exercise 2.13: (*The Power Method*) Let A be an $n \times n$ symmetric matrix. Thus, A possesses an orthonormal basis of eigenvectors $\{e_i\}_{i=1}^n$ corresponding to eigenvalues $\{\lambda_i\}_{i=1}^n$. Given any vector $x^0 \in R^n$, there is an expansion $x^0 = \sum_{j=1}^n a_j e_j$ for suitable scalars a_j. Consider the iteration

$$x^{m+1} = Ax^m \quad (m = 0, 1, \ldots).$$

Thus,

$$x^m = A^m x^0 = \sum_{j=1}^n a_j A^m e_j = \sum_{j=1}^n a_j \lambda_j^m e_j.$$

Let (x, y) denote the usual inner product on R^n, and assume that there is a dominant eigenvalue:

$$|\lambda_1| > |\lambda_2| \geq |\lambda_3| \geq \cdots \geq |\lambda_n|.$$

Compute the quantities

$$(x^{m+1}, x^m) = \sum_{j=1}^n a_j^2 \lambda_j^{2m+1},$$

$$(x^m, x^m) = \sum_{j=1}^n a_j^2 \lambda_j^{2m}$$

and show that, provided $a_1 \neq 0$,

$$\frac{(x^{m+1}, x^m)}{(x^m, x^m)} \to \lambda_1 \quad \text{as} \quad m \to \infty.$$

For the corresponding eigenvectors, consider the normalized vector $y^m = \frac{x^m}{\|x^m\|}$ where $\|x\|^2 = (x, x)$. Show that, as $m \to \infty$, y^m converges to a normalized eigenvector corresponding to λ_1.

Implement this scheme via a C program to find the dominant eigenvalue of such a matrix. You may have to experiment with initial values to achieve convergence. (See [WI] for a reliable choice of initial values.)

Exercise 2.14: Consider the scalar symmetric integral equation

$$\phi(x) - \lambda \int_0^1 K(x, y) \phi(y) \, dy = 0,$$

where

$$K(x, y) = \begin{cases} (1 - x)y & \text{if } 0 \le y \le x \le 1 \\ (1 - y)x & \text{if } 0 \le x \le y \le 1. \end{cases}$$

Nontrivial solutions are called *eigenfunctions*; these exist only for special values of the parameter λ called *eigenvalues*. (There is some abuse of notation here; *proper values* would be a more appropriate term, because these proper values are the reciprocals of eigenvalues in the standard linear algebra context.) Set $h = 1/n$ for some positive integer n and approximate the integral by the midpoint rule. Use this to obtain a linear system for the approximation of the proper values. Use the power method above for $n = 2, 4, 8, 16, 32, 64$ to estimate the smallest proper value. (You can check your results by noting that $\phi'' + \lambda\phi = 0$ with $\phi(0) = \phi(1) = 0$.)

Exercise 2.15: Consider the initial–value problem for an autonomous system of two ODEs

$$y' = f(y, z) \qquad y(0) \text{ given } ; \qquad z' = g(y, z) \qquad z(0) \text{ given.}$$

A nonautonomous version of this is given in the program `odeivp_2.c` in Chapter 4. Modify that program for the present case, and compute the solutions for the Van der Pol equation

$$y' = z - y^3 + y, \qquad z' = -y$$

and for the pendulum equation

$$y' = z, \qquad z' = -\sin(y)$$

using several choices for initial values. Write the results to a file, and graph y vs. z. See [KH].

Exercise 2.16: (*The "Shooting" Method*) Consider a second–order boundary–value problem for the ordinary differential equation

$$y'' = f(x, y, y') \quad (0 < x < 1), \quad y(0) = y_0, \, y(1) = y_1,$$

where y_0, y_1 are given numbers. Please read the section in Chapter 4 about initial–value problems for a system of two ordinary differential equations. Thus, we may assume that an initial–value problem could be accurately solved, once the value of $y'(0)$ is known. Of course this value is unknown in the present case. Assume that we have two approximations to $y'(0)$, say β_0, β_1. We integrate the initial value problem for each of these approximations and call the "final" values $y(\beta_0, 1)$, $y(\beta_1, 1)$. To improve this approximation and refine the unknown slope, we employ inverse linear interpolation as follows. The linear interpolating polynomial $p(\beta)$ for the known points $(\beta_0, y(\beta_0, 1))$, $(\beta_1, y(\beta_1, 1))$ is given by

$$p(\beta) = \frac{(\beta - \beta_0)y(\beta_1, 1) + (\beta_1 - \beta)y(\beta_0, 1)}{\beta_1 - \beta_0}.$$

Now set $p(\beta) = y_1$, solve for β and call this solution β_2. In this manner one obtains

$$\beta_2 = \beta_0 + (\beta_1 - \beta_0)\left(\frac{y_1 - y(\beta_0, 1)}{y(\beta_1, 1) - y(\beta_0, 1)}\right).$$

Now integrate the equation again using the initial values $y(0) = y_0$, $y'(0) = \beta_2$ and call the resulting final value $y(\beta_2, 1)$. Interpolate again as above to find a new approximation β_3 to the slope $y'(0)$, etc.

Consider, for example, the special problem

$$y'' = y \quad (0 < x < 1), \quad y(0) = 0, \ y(1) = 1$$

whose exact solution is $y(x) = \frac{\sinh x}{\sinh 1}$. Write a C program to implement the shooting method in this case.

While there is no guarantee of convergence in general, much can be rigorously established (see [KL]).

Exercise 2.17: Consider the boundary–value problem

$$y'' = y + \epsilon \sin y \quad (0 < x < 1), \quad y(0) = 0, \ y(1) = 1.$$

In order to obtain a crude estimate of the solution, divide $[0, 1]$ into three subintervals, each of length $h = 1/3$, and define $x_0 = 0, x_1 = 1/3, x_2 = 2/3, x_3 = 1$. The value of the solution $y(x_i)$ is approximated by y_i, where the latter are computed by this centered finite–difference approximation to the ODE:

$$\frac{y_{n+1} - 2y_n + y_{n-1}}{h^2} = \frac{y_{n-1} + y_{n+1}}{2} + \frac{\epsilon}{2}(\sin y_{n+1} + \sin y_{n-1}) \quad (n = 1, 2).$$

Here we take $y_0 = 0$ and $y_3 = 1$. The result is the *nonlinear system* $F(y) = 0$, where $y = (y_1, y_2)$ and

$$F_1(y) = -2y_1 + (1 - \frac{h^2}{2})y_2 - \frac{h^2\epsilon}{2}\sin y_2$$

$$F_2(y) = (1 - \frac{h^2}{2})y_1 - 2y_2 + 1 - \frac{h^2}{2} - \frac{h^2\epsilon}{2}(\sin y_1 + \sin 1).$$

The parameter ϵ is to be sufficiently small, say $\epsilon = 0.0005$. Make an educated initial approximation, and write a C program to solve this system by fixed–point iteration.

Exercise 2.18: (*Steepest Descent Method*) Let A be an $n \times n$ symmetric positive definite matrix, and let b be an n vector. Write (x, y) for the usual inner product of two vectors in R^n. Consider the problem of minimizing the quadratic form

$$E(x) = \frac{1}{2}(x, Ax) - (x, b).$$

Clearly we have $\nabla E(x) = Ax - b$. We define the *residual* r by $r = -\nabla E$; recall that the gradient of a (scalar) function points in the direction of greatest increase of the function. Thus, the direction of "steepest descent" coincides with that of r.

The algorithm is this: given an initial approximation x^0, define

$$x^{k+1} = x^k + \alpha_k r^k,$$

where $\alpha_k \in R^1$ and $r^k = b - Ax^k$. We now compute $E(x^{k+1})$ as a function of the n real variables α_k:

$$
\begin{aligned}
E(x^{k+1}) &= E(x^k + \alpha_k r^k) \\
&= \frac{1}{2}(x^k + \alpha_k r^k, A(x^k + \alpha_k r^k)) - (x^k + \alpha_k r^k, b) \\
&= E(x^k) - \alpha_k(r^k, r^k) + \frac{1}{2}\alpha_k^2(r^k, Ar^k).
\end{aligned}
$$

Now compute $\frac{\partial E}{\partial \alpha_k}(x^{k+1})$ and set each result equal to zero; we get in this manner the formula

$$\alpha_k = \frac{|r^k|^2}{(r^k, Ar^k)}.$$

We see further that successive residuals are orthogonal: for by definition $r^k = b - Ax^k$ so that

$$r^{k+1} = b - A(x^k + \alpha_k r^k) = r^k - \alpha_k Ar^k.$$

From this we have $(r^k, r^{k+1}) = 0$.

With the explicit formula for α_k now known, we can write

$$
\begin{aligned}
E(x^{k+1}) &= E(x^k) - \frac{|r^k|^4}{(r^k, Ar^k)} + \frac{1}{2}\frac{|r^k|^4}{(r^k, Ar^k)^2}(r^k, Ar^k) \\
&= E(x^k) - \frac{1}{2}\frac{|r^k|^4}{(r^k, Ar^k)}.
\end{aligned}
$$

It follows that the sequence $\{E(x^k)\}$ is decreasing; since it is also bounded below (why?), it converges.

Code this algorithm as a C function. Try it on several symmetric positive definite matrices such as the Dirichlet matrix, etc.

Exercise 2.19: (*The Euler MacLaurin Expansion*) Let $f(n)$ for $n = 1, 2, \ldots$ be a smooth function decaying with sufficient rapidity at infinity, and consider the problem of numerically approximating the infinite sum

$$S = \sum_{n=1}^{\infty} f(n).$$

The Euler MacLaurin formula is an asymptotic expansion for computing S; see any text on Numerical Analysis (e.g., [IK]). The idea is to sum the first N terms directly and then to write an asymptotic expansion for the remainder. A special case is

$$S = \sum_{n=1}^{N} f(n) + \sum_{n=N+1}^{\infty} f(n)$$

$$= \sum_{n=1}^{N} f(n) + \sum_{n=0}^{\infty} f(n + N + 1)$$

$$\sim \sum_{n=1}^{N} f(n) + \int_{0}^{\infty} f(x + N + 1)\, dx$$

$$+ \frac{1}{2} f(N + 1) - \frac{1}{12} f'(N + 1) + \frac{1}{720} f'''(N + 1).$$

For the integral, write

$$\int_{0}^{\infty} f(x + N + 1)\, dx = \int_{0}^{1} f(x + N + 1)\, dx + \int_{1}^{\infty} f(x + N + 1)\, dx.$$

In the second (infinite) integral, introduce the change of variables $z = \frac{N+2}{x+N+1}$; then

$$\int_{1}^{\infty} f(x + N + 1)\, dx = (N + 2) \int_{0}^{1} f\left(\frac{N + 2}{z}\right) \frac{dz}{z^2}.$$

Each of the integrals is now taken over the set $[0, 1]$; they may be approximated by any numerical quadrature formula (e.g., the midpoint rule).

A typical choice is to take $N = 10$. Write a C program to achieve this approximation, and verify it on the two exact results

$$S = \sum_{n=1}^{\infty} n^{-4} = \frac{\pi^4}{90}, \qquad S = \sum_{n=1}^{\infty} n^{-2} = \frac{\pi^2}{6}.$$

Exercise 2.20: (*A Semilinear Wave Equation*)

Consider approximating the solution to the semilinear wave equation

$$u_{tt} - u_{xx} + F(u) = 0 \qquad (x \in R^1, t > 0),$$

with given initial values $u(x, 0) = \phi(x)$, $u_t(x, 0) = \psi(x)$. Assume that the data functions are smooth and of compact support. The scheme we use is due to Strauss and Vazquez; see [SR]. This scheme preserves a discrete energy, an analogue of the conservation of energy for the continuous problem:

$$E(t) = \int_{-\infty}^{\infty} \left(\frac{1}{2} u_t^2 + \frac{1}{2} u_x^2 + G(u) \right) dx = \text{const.},$$

where $G(u) = \int_0^u F(s)\, ds$. Given $\Delta t > 0, \Delta x > 0$, let $x_k = k\Delta x, t_n = n\Delta t$ and $u_k^n \approx u(x_k, t_n)$. The scheme is

$$\frac{u_k^{n+1} - 2u_k^n + u_k^{n-1}}{\Delta t^2} - \left(\frac{u_{k+1}^n - 2u_k^n + u_{k-1}^n}{\Delta x^2} \right) + \frac{G(u_k^{n+1}) - G(u_k^{n-1})}{u_k^{n+1} - u_k^{n-1}} = 0$$

with initial values

$$u_k^0 = \phi(x_k), \qquad u_k^1 = \phi(x_k) + \Delta t \psi(x_k).$$

When we multiply the scheme by $u_k^{n+1} - u_k^{n-1}$, sum over all k and sum the second term by parts, we find that the following expression is conserved:

$$E^n \equiv \sum_k \Delta x [(\frac{u_k^{n+1} - u_k^n}{\Delta t})^2 + \frac{(u_{k+1}^{n+1} - u_k^{n+1})(u_{k+1}^n - u_k^n)}{\Delta x^2}$$

$$+ G(u_k^{n+1}) + G(u_k^n)];$$

that is, $E^n = E^0$. One may show that the functional E^n is positive definite under the mesh restriction $\Delta t \leq \theta \Delta x$ for some $\theta < 1$.

Notice that to advance in time at any mesh point k, a scalar nonlinear equation in the unknown u_k^{n+1} must be solved. This may be done by Newton's method. Let's say we wish to solve on some time interval $[0, T]$.

Since finite speed of propagation is known, we have that $u = 0$ for $|x| > k+t$ where the initial functions vanish for $|x| > k$. A similar property can be shown to hold for the discrete solution. Write a C program to approximate the solution to this equation. Choose any initial values which are sufficiently smooth and have compact support, and take $F(u) = u + u^3$.

Exercise 2.21: (*Bairstow's Method*)

Consider a real–coefficient polynomial of degree n

$$P(x) = a_0 x^n + a_1 x^{n-1} + \cdots + a_{n-1} x + a_n,$$

and suppose we seek via iteration a quadratic factor $x^2 - ux - v$ beginning with approximations u_0 and v_0. This is useful in certain deflation routines. See [IK] for details which involve an application of Newton's method for a 2×2 system.

For $k = 0, 1, \ldots$ assume that the current approximations are u_k, v_k. The next iterates are obtained from the following procedure. Define two sequences $\{b_j^{(k)}\}$, $\{c_j^{(k)}\}$ by

$$b_j^{(k)} = a_j + u_k b_{j-1}^{(k)} + v_k b_{j-2}^{(k)} \quad (j = 0, 1, \ldots, n)$$
$$c_j^{(k)} = b_j^{(k)} + u_k c_{j-1}^{(k)} + v_k c_{j-2}^{(k)} \quad (j = 0, 1, \ldots, n-1)$$

with the conditions $b_{-2} = b_{-1} = c_{-2} = c_{-1} = 0$. Then we take

$$v_{k+1} = v_k + \frac{b_{n-1}^{(k)} c_{n-1}^{(k)} - b_n^{(k)} c_{n-2}^{(k)}}{(c_{n-2}^{(k)})^2 - c_{n-1}^{(k)} c_{n-3}^{(k)}}$$

$$u_{k+1} = u_k + \frac{b_n^{(k)} c_{n-3}^{(k)} - b_{n-1}^{(k)} c_{n-2}^{(k)}}{(c_{n-2}^{(k)})^2 - c_{n-1}^{(k)} c_{n-3}^{(k)}}.$$

Write a C function using pointers which will achieve the Bairstow factorization.

We conclude this chapter by reiterating several issues regarding pointers. Always be sure to initialize pointers. If you use the files `memalloc.c` and `memalloc.h` in Appendix II, remember that they provide `double` allocations for vectors and matrices. If you wish to construct a single precision version, simply change each occurrence of `double` to `float` (and rename the file!) Moreover, in these files the error checks are performed using comparison to the `NULL` pointer. If you encounter an error when these files are compiled, change `if (x==NULL)` to `if (!x)`. Another solution is to include the file stddef.h if it exists, in which case statements containing NULL may be kept.

Similarly, when performing error checking prior to FILE activities, we often compare the pointer returned by fopen( ) to the NULL pointer. Should this cause an error, use the device above. See the many examples in Chapter 4.

Lastly is a word on the various include files and their special implementations. In Microsoft Quick *C* (v. 2.5), the file malloc.h handles memory allocations, and is to be included when calls to malloc, calloc or realloc are required. However, some compilers do not provide the file malloc.h. In this case, the relevant information should be in stdlib.h; simply include this instead.

CHAPTER 3

FINE POINTS

In this chapter we elaborate on several constructs to show how the use of *C* can be fine–tuned.

THE INCREMENT OPERATORS

Given an integer i, we know that i++ means to increment i by one; similarly i-- means to decrement i by one. However, these operators may *precede* the variable on which they act, that is, one may see ++i or --i. These are *not* the same. The rule is this: for the form ++i, the value of i is incremented *first*; then the compiler uses the variable's contents. However, in the form i++, the value of i is used first, and then i is incremented. Consider this simple code fragment:

```
int i=1;
printf("initial value of i=%d\n",i);
printf("pre-increment value of i=%d\n",++i);
printf("post-decrement value of i=%d\n",i--);
printf("final value of i=%d\n",i);
```

When this code is run, the output is as follows:

```
initial value of i=1
pre--increment value of i=2
post--decrement value of i=2
final value of i=1
```

Thus, in the "pre–increment" line above, i is incremented before it is printed; similarly in the next line ("post–decrement") the present value

121

of i is printed before it is decremented.

Many times in the first two chapters, while in iteration loops, we have used for simplicity several lines to increment an iterate counter and to perform an error test, as in

```
iter++;
  if (iter>N){
    printf("Too many iterates");
    exit(1);}
```

Of course we now see that the first line is unnecessary and that the first two lines could be combined as

```
  if (++iter>N){
```

Do *not* use the increment operators in function–like macros. They can produce "side effects," which is a euphemism for hard–to–debug code. Actually "side effects" refer to the alteration of a variable as a result of evaluating some expression. These can occur, e.g., with the increment operators and certain function evaluations and can cause unexpected results which depend on the order in which the various components of an expression are calculated. For an explicit example, see [HS], pp. 40–41.

OPERATOR PRECEDENCE

Even if you know some other language, you will find a few surprises in C. Of course in the expression 5+6*3 the multiplication is performed first, as expected. As always, one can use parentheses to affect the order of any calculation.

String manipulation, a topic not covered in this book, can be tricky in C. Take a look at some of the "system code" in [KR]; you may find it difficult to read. Complications arise for instance when the increment and indirection operators are used in an expression. For example, suppose a C function contains a pointer to an integer *iter as an argument. Such a construction occurs often when one is monitoring the number of iterations, say, in a loop. We wish to increment this counter. Consider the following four expressions to do so:

1.   *iter $+ = 1$
2. $+ +$ *iter
3.   (*iter) $++$
4.   *iter $++$

The first three of these all have the same effect: each takes the value that iter points to and increments it. However, in line 4, the result is to increment the pointer iter itself (not what it points to). This is due to the associativity rules of the indirection * and increment $++$ operators: they associate from right to left, as seen below.

In general, the hierarchy can be represented as in the following table. The entries are given in decreasing order of precedence. It is not a complete list, but it does include all of the operators used in this book. For example, the bit–wise operators of *C* have been omitted:

\multicolumn{3}{c}{*C Precedence and Associativity Rules*}
Symbol	**Name**	**Associativity Direction**
( )	function call	left to right
[ ]	array element	left to right
− >	pointer member operator	left to right
.	structure member operator	left to right
!	logical NOT	**right to left**
++	increment	**right to left**
− −	decrement	**right to left**
*	indirection	**right to left**
&	address of	**right to left**
(type)	cast	**right to left**
sizeof	size in bytes	**right to left**
*	multiplication	left to right
/	division	left to right
%	integer remainder	left to right
+	addition	left to right
−	subtraction	left to right
<	less than	left to right
>	greater than	left to right
<=	less than or equal to	left to right
>=	greater than or equal to	left to right
==	equality	left to right
! =	inequality	left to right
&&	logical AND	left to right
||	logical OR	left to right
? :	conditional operator	**right to left**
=	assignment operator	**right to left**
+ =	shorthand addition	**right to left**
− =	shorthand subtraction	**right to left**
* =	shorthand multiplication	**right to left**
/ =	shorthand division	**right to left**
% =	shorthand remainder	**right to left**
,	comma operator	left to right

A final comment is in order on the topic of function–like macros or constants introduced with **define** compiler directives. On many compilers, the default value for such expressions is **double**. Thus, suppose that you define a function macro with the line

```
# define f(x) ((x)*(x))
```

and that subsequently in **main** you employ the line

```
float s=f(1.0);
```

An automatic type conversion occurs, because the values of f are double, yet s itself is only single precision. While this may often be harmless, it is something that one should be aware of.

THE for STATEMENT

If required, you can use several variables in a **for** loop. When doing so, one uses the *comma* operator to separate distinct entries. Here is a code fragment to illustrate such use:

```
int i,j;
for (i=0,j=100;i<=100;i += 2,j -= 2){
  printf("%d %d\n",i,j);}
```

The output will be as follows:

```
0    100
2    98
     ⋮
100   0
```

THE USE OF THE "SHORTHAND" OPERATORS

Let Ω denote any of the binary operators $+$, $-$, $*$, $/$. Let E_1 and E_2 be any arithmetic expressions. Then the shorthand operator expression

$$E_1 \, \Omega \; = \; E_2;$$

means

$$E_1 = (E_1) \, \Omega \, (E_2); \; ,$$

and the expression E_1 is computed just once. Notice the double parentheses here. As an example, the line

$$x_1 \, * = \; x_2 + x_3;$$

unambiguously means

$$x_1 \; = x_1 * (x_2 + x_3); .$$

The spacing around these operators also requires comment. Older compilers sometimes choke on expressions of the form `x-=x`, etc. One can fix this easily by providing spaces on either side of the operator, as in

`x -= x.`

We have tried to write these consistently in this manner throughout this book.

THE USE OF `stderr`

It is good practice to write your error messages to `stderr`. In this manner, error messages appear on the screen even if output is redirected. The file `stdio.h` must be included. Incidentally, this may be an appropriate place to mention a simple kind of redirection available in UNIX. Suppose you have written a program which writes its results to the standard output, i.e., to the screen. Then suddenly you realize that there is too much output going by too fast. If your executable file is called `a.out`, then to run the program and have its results written out to a file called, say, `out.dat`, enter at the prompt

`a.out > out.dat`

You can then peruse the output at your leisure with an editor or with the UNIX command

`more out.dat`

If the UNIX variable `noclobber` is set, you may have to redirect output with the command

`a.out >! out.dat`

THE USE OF THE `realloc` STATEMENT

Suppose you trying to differentiate a smooth function f numerically at some point $x = a$. The obvious approximation

(3.1)
$$f'(a) \approx \frac{f(a + h) - f(a)}{h}$$

is equal to $f'(a) + O(h)$. A better approximation is given by the centered difference quotient

$$f'(a) \approx \frac{f(a + h) - f(a - h)}{2h},$$

because this expression equals $f'(a) + O(h^2)$, as we know from the Taylor series expansion around a. One could continually decrease h, but eventually round–off error creeps in and ruins the procedure. Let's say we've made one calculation (with a given value of h) to get

$$D_h(f) = \frac{f(a+h) - f(a-h)}{2h}$$

as our approximation. When we cut h in half, we expect to get better results, i.e., the number

$$D_{\frac{h}{2}}(f) = \frac{f(a+\frac{h}{2}) - f(a-\frac{h}{2})}{h}$$

should be closer to $f'(a)$. An effective device is to use *extrapolation to the limit*. With both of these approximations in hand, it can be shown that the expression

$$D'_h(f) \equiv \frac{4D_{\frac{h}{2}}(f) - D_h(f)}{3}$$

equals $f'(a)$ with error $o(h^4)$ for a smooth function. (Notice the "little oh" notation; this means that $h^{-4}(D'_h(f) - f'(a)) \to 0$ as $h \to 0$.) This type of extrapolation can be continued. The method can be used on boundary–value problems, eigenvalue problems for differential equations, etc. We will encounter it later in *Romberg integration* and in the program sturmevl.c; the latter computes the lowest eigenvalue for a Sturm–Liouville operator under appropriate conditions.

Let's consider an application to, say, boundary–value problems for ordinary differential equations. Suppose we use finite differences to obtain the discrete solution vector, a double array called x. It corresponds to a particular value of h, say $h = 1/N$. Thus, in main you have defined and allocated a double vector x with the statements

```
double *x; x=vecalloc(0,N-1);
```

Here we employ the function vecalloc from the last chapter; it gives us the components x[0],x[1],...,x[N-1] for use. Now suppose that we wish to double N and increase the number of components of x accordingly. This is a natural use for the realloc function. Here is what to enter to achieve this:

```
N *= 2;
x=(double *)realloc(x,N*sizeof(double));
    if (x==NULL) {
        fprintf(stderr,"could not reallocate memory");
        exit(1);
}
```

An important point here is that whatever values have been previously assigned are unaltered. This would be relevant if, through use of realloc, you were to reduce the already allocated memory to a smaller block. Of course one must include the obligatory check for validity. Please recall also that the file `stdio.h` must be included for `stderr` to be defined.

CONDITIONAL COMPILER DIRECTIVES

Sometimes you may wish to write a macro or define a global constant with the `# define` statement. However, it is possible that when you do this, you might overwrite the corresponding value in some include file. It is easy to check; consider this example, where we want to define a logical variable TRUE:

```
# if !defined TRUE
  # define TRUE 1
# endif
```

Use the `# undef` directive to remove any definition previously made with the `# define` directive.

RECURSION

In C a function can call itself. A typical example is the Fibonacci sequence computation. We have encountered this in Chapter 2:

$$m_0 = m_1 = 1 \quad \text{and} \quad m_{n+1} = m_n + m_{n-1} \quad \text{for} \quad n \geq 1.$$

Here is a recursive function calculation:

```
 1 /* Fibon.c */
 2
 3 # include <stdio.h>
 4
 5 long f(int n)
 6 {
 7 long m;
 8 m=(n>1) ?  (f(n-1)+f(n-2)) :   1;
 9 return m;
10 }
11
12 main()
13 {
14 int i;
15 long f(int n);
16
17 printf("Enter a positive integer:     ");
18 scanf("%d",&i);
```

```
19 printf("Fibonacci(%d)=%ld\n",i,f(i));
20 }
```

After you have run this a few times for several large ($\approx$ 30) integers, you will realize that recursion is not fast. It is often more efficient to write a nonrecursive version of such a function. The cost is only a slight increase in code size. Here is a recursive rendition of the factorial function:

```
1 long factorl(int n)
2 {
3         if (n>1)
4                 return ((long)n*factorl(n-1));
5         else
6                 return 1;
7 }
```

LOCATION OF INCLUDE FILES

The paths to the standard `include` files were specified when your compiler was installed. Thus, a statement of the form

```
# include <math.h>
```

requires no further path specification. Suppose however that you wish to include some files of your own which reside in your current source directory. (We will use two of these many times in Chapter 4, specifically the files `memalloc.c` and `memalloc.h`.) To ensure that the compiler finds them, simply enclose them in double quotes, as follows:

```
# include "memalloc.c"
```

If you are using UNIX and do not know where a given file is, e.g., `math.h`, try this command:

```
find / -name math.h -print
```

While on this topic, a comment about the UNIX utility `grep` is in order. Suppose you have now located `math.h` and wish to find the prototype of the inverse tangent function `atan`. Assume that you have changed to the directory which contains `math.h`. Then after you enter the following command, all lines containing the string `atan` will be displayed:

```
grep atan math.h
```

puts vs printf

When a simple unformatted message is to be printed to the screen, one can use `puts` instead of `printf`. Much less overhead is involved. The function `puts` displays a character string. The function `gets` takes string input from the keyboard and places a null–character ('\0') at the end of the string, as is required in C. (The null character is used to find the end of a string, and is crucially important.) A string constant such as

```
# define GOODSTUFF "pde and numerical analysis"
```

is automatically given a null terminator by the compiler, but a character constant 'a' is not. If you were to define a character array with the line

```
char math[ ]="pde"
```

C adds the null character at the end, so that really the initialization of this array is more clearly shown in the line

```
char math[ ]={'p','d','e','\0'};
```

Notice that four slots are required here.

CREATING A PAUSE

On occasion you may wish to pause a program to allow user input or simply to let a user appreciate your beautiful graphics. Here is a (verbose) code fragment which will pause a program until the user strikes any key:

```
char ch;
 .
 .
 .
printf("Press return to continue\n");
do{
}
    while ((ch=getch()) == ' ');
```

We have defined ch as a variable of type char. In DOS one must include the file conio.h, which (for many compilers) is where the function getch() resides. In UNIX (at least for *gcc*), replace getch by getchar; this function resides in stdio.h. A shorter solution is simply to write

```
 .
 .
 .
printf("Press return to continue\n");
getchar( );
```

ASCII TRANSLATION

Sometimes you will use command–line arguments in your programs to request input from the user. When an integer is to be requested, use the function atoi to convert the ASCII representation of the integer to the form of an integer in C. Similarly, floating point values are converted using atof. Both of these functions are found in stdlib.h, which must be included in your program. atof is in math.h as well. If your input is a long integer, use atol which is also found in stdlib.h.

GLOBAL, AUTOMATIC AND STATIC VARIABLES

A *global* variable is one defined outside of all functions. Its value is then accessible to all functions in which it appears. The best advice is to not use global variables; they can be dangerous. It is all too easy to create a variable in another function with the same name, creating problems.

Local variables are those within a given function. They are also called *automatic* since they are automatically created by the compiler when the function is called and are automatically deleted by the compiler when the function is exited. Thus, their "life–span" is comprised of just one function call. *Static variables* are variables whose values are stored by the compiler from one invocation of the function to the next. They may be defined by simply preceding their name with the `static` keyword. By the way, character strings in functions should be initialized using the `static` attribute.

THE USE OF awk

Suppose you have run a program, all has gone well and you now have a file called `odeivp.dat`, say, containing the output. Assume that the format of this data file is such that on each line we have

xvalue   yvalue   zvalue

where *yvalue* denotes the value of the solution, and *zvalue* denotes the value of the derivative of the solution, at *xvalue*. You want to graph the function $y(x)$ but you don't care about the values of its derivative. Furthermore you have your hands on a good graphics program (e.g., GNUPLOT) which expects *pairs* of data to be present in the file (i.e., x and y values). How can we get rid of the unwanted data values of z?

Thus, we wish to write only columns 1 and 2 to another data file, say `ode2.dat`. We can do this with the UNIX command **awk** by entering this command:

```
(awk '{print $1,$2}' odeivp.dat)  >!    ode2.dat
```

This is a handy trick to know.

extern VARIABLES

Suppose a (double) x is declared in two source files, say `f1.c` and `f2.c`, but is initialized only in `f1.c`, say. In order to use this variable in `f2.c`, precede its declaration there with the **extern** keyword. That is, in the file `f2.c` one issues the command

```
extern double x;
```

NESTING RULES

We have seen in Chapter 1 that C functions may not be nested. Similarly comments may not be nested. Unfortunately it is a common (and convenient) practice to comment–out entire blocks of code. Should you attempt this on a block which already contains comments, an error will be generated. However, "include" files may be nested, typically to a depth of five or six levels.

COMMENTS REVISITED

DOS compilers often allow comments to be written as follows:

```
// this is a comment
```

Thus, all text following the double slash is ignored by the compiler. It is better not to use this form to comment code, since it is not supported by all compilers.

STRUCTURES REVISITED

Consider the following code fragment in which n is an integer, initialized to 50, say:

```
1  int n=50;
2  struct E_field{
3          struct complex new;
4          struct complex old;
5          };
6
7  struct E_field *E;
8
9  E=(struct E_field *)calloc(n,sizeof(struct E_field));
10         if (E==NULL){
11          fprintf(stderr,"could not allocate memory");
12          exit(1);
13          }
```

A structure E_field is defined, and a pointer to this structure is then defined on line 7. Notice how memory for the entire structure is allocated on lines 9–13. Thus, memory allocation for a pointer to a structure can be performed with a single command. This construction gives us two arrays of complex numbers

E[k].old, E[k].new   for $0 \le k \le n - 1$

We may refer to a member of this E_field structure by using the "structure member operator" . (a period). Given an integer k satisfying $0 \le k \le n-1$, we use, for example, the form

```
E[k].old.x=...
```

A related issue is illustrated in this brief code in which we assume that struct complex has been defined:

```
1 # include <math.h>
2 # include <stdio.h>
3 # include "cpxarith.c"
4
5 void cpxshow(struct complex *Z)
6 {
7 printf("Real=%lf\n",Z->x);
8 printf("Imag=%lf\n",Z->y);
9 }
10
11 main()
12 {
13          void cpxshow(struct complex *Z);
14          struct complex z;
15          z.x=1.0;
16          z.y=2.0;
17
18          cpxshow(&z);
19 }
```

The only thing this program does is to display a complex number. Notice however that it does so through a function called cpxshow which has as its only argument a *pointer* to struct complex. In main a complex variable z is defined and initialized on lines 14–16. Then the "display" function is called on line 18 (notice the ampersand there), and the program terminates. The only notable feature is that, in the body of the function cpxshow, we must use the *pointer member operator* $->$ to access a structure member with the pointer Z. This is constructed by using a "minus" sign, followed by the "greater than" symbol $>$. (Recall that the struct complex data type is defined by two double entries x (the real part) and y (the imaginary part)).

An advantage of passing a pointer to a structure (rather than the entire structure itself) to a function is that the values of members in the original structure can be altered. In the function cpxshow you may, if you wish, use the notation e.g., (*Z).x (instead of $Z->x$) in which the parentheses are necessary in view of the precedence rules. Recall that all functions in cpxarith.c pass their arguments by value.

CHAPTER 4

APPLICATIONS

In the example programs below please notice the various "include" files. In particular, you will see cpxarith.c, cpxarith.h and memalloc.c, memalloc.h. The last two files contain the code and headers, respectively, for appropriately allocating vectors and matrices of type double, with subscripts adjustable to the user's preferences.

THE CONJUGATE GRADIENT METHOD

Let $x \in R^n$ be a real n–vector, and A a real $n \times n$ *symmetric positive definite* matrix. Denote the inner product $\sum_{k=1}^{n} x_k y_k$ by (x, y). Consider the problem of minimizing the quadratic form

$$E(x) = \frac{1}{2}(x, Ax) - (b, x).$$

Applying straightforward calculus, we find a minimum occurs at the vector x where $Ax = b$. Although the method originated in minimization of scalar functions of several variables, we will use it to solve linear positive definite symmetric systems as above. These often arise in elliptic partial differential equations.

Here is the algorithm which, as stated below, must (theoretically) converge in no more than n steps. Given an initial vector approximation x^0:

compute $p^0 = r^0 = b - Ax^0$ ($r \equiv$ *the residual*)

k=0, do {

compute $\alpha_k = \frac{|r^k|^2}{(p^k, Ap^k)}$

compute $x^{k+1} = x^k + \alpha_k p^k$
compute $r^{k+1} = r^k - \alpha_k A p^k$
compute $\beta_k = \frac{-(r^{k+1}, Ap^k)}{(p^k, Ap^k)} = \frac{|r^{k+1}|^2}{|r^k|^2}$
compute $p^{k+1} = r^{k+1} + \beta_k p^k$
k=k+1   }

The name of the algorithm comes from the easily established fact that the "search directions" p^k are "A–conjugate," i.e., for $k \neq j$, we have $(p^k, Ap^j) = 0$. Moreover, distinct residuals are perpendicular: $(r^k, r^j) = 0$ for $k \neq j$. From this, one concludes that $r^n = 0$, i.e., that convergence must take place in n or fewer iterations.

We now show that the successive search directions are "A–conjugate": $(p^{k+1}, Ap^k) = 0$. Indeed, using the first definition of β_k in the scheme, we have

$$(p^{k+1}, Ap^k) = (r^{k+1} + \beta_k p^k, Ap^k)$$
$$= (r^{k+1}, Ap^k) + \beta_k (p^k, Ap^k) = 0$$

by the definition of β_k.

Furthermore, it is easy to see that successive residuals are perpendicular: $(r^{k+1}, r^k) = 0$. By what has just been established, we can write $(p^k, Ap^k) = (r^k, Ap^k)$. Therefore,

$$(r^{k+1}, r^k) = (r^k - \alpha_k Ap^k, r^k)$$
$$= |r^k|^2 - \alpha_k (Ap^k, r^k)$$
$$= |r^k|^2 - \alpha_k (p^k, Ap^k)$$
$$= |r^k|^2 - (r^k, r^k) = 0$$

by the definition of α_k.

Here is the major result:

Conjugate Gradient Convergence Theorem

Let $A = A^T$ be positive definite with eigenvalues lying in $[\lambda_{\min}, \lambda_{\max}]$ (thus, $\lambda_{\min} > 0$). Denote the error vector by $e^k = x - x^k$ where the x^k are computed via the above scheme, and $Ax = b$. Then

$$(e^k, Ae^k)^{1/2} \leq 2 \left(\frac{\sqrt{\lambda_{\max}} - \sqrt{\lambda_{\min}}}{\sqrt{\lambda_{\max}} + \sqrt{\lambda_{\min}}} \right)^k (e^0, Ae^0)^{1/2}.$$

As you see, the rate of convergence is determined by the "closeness" of $\lambda_{\min}$ and $\lambda_{\max}$. See [ST]. Special preconditioning devices may be employed to improve this, but we code just the standard method in the following.

In the `congrad` function, the arguments are the order `n` of the coefficient matrix `a`, the given right–hand side `b`, and a pointer to an integer `iter` to keep track of the number of iterates. The solution is returned in the vector b. The program uses command–line arguments to read the upper triangle of the coefficient matrix A row by row from a file, and then reads the given right–hand side b from another file:

```
1  /* CG.c */
2
3  # include <math.h>
4  # include <malloc.h>
5  # include <stdio.h>
6  # include <stdlib.h>
7  # include "memalloc.c"
8  # include "memalloc.h"
9  # define MAX(a,b) ((a)>=(b) ?  (a):(b))
10
11 /* Usage:    cg order afile bfile */
12
13 double dotprod(int n, double *x, double *y)
14 {
15 /* indices run over 1 to n */
16 double s=0.0;
17 int i;
18 for (i=1;i<=n;i++){
19          s += x[i]*y[i];
20          }
21 return s;
22 }
23
24 double maxnum(int m, double *x)
25 {
26 /* returns the maximum norm of vector x */
27 /* indices run over 1 to m */
28 int k;
29 double z;
30
31          z=MAX(fabs(x[1]),fabs(x[2]));
32          for (k=3;k<=m;k++)
33                  z=MAX(fabs(x[k]),z);
34          return z;
35 }
36
37 void conjgrad(int n, int *iter, double **a, double *b)
38 {
```

```
39 int i,j;
40 double alpha,beta,s,e;
41 double *x,*p,*rold,*rnew,*y;
42
43 x   =vecalloc(1,n);
44 p   =vecalloc(1,n);
45 rold=vecalloc(1,n);
46 rnew=vecalloc(1,n);
47 y   =vecalloc(1,n);
48
49 /* initializations */
50 /* initially x[i] =0 for every component i via calloc() */
51 for (i=1;i<=n;i++){
52         rold[i]=p[i]=b[i];
53         }
54
55 do {
56
57 /* compute Ap in vector y */
58 for (i=1;i<=n;i++){
59         s=0.0;
60         for (j=1;j<=n;j++){
61                 s += a[i][j]*p[j];
62                 }
63         y[i]=s;
64         }
65
66 e=dotprod(n,p,y);
67
68 if (fabs(e)<5.0e-20){
69         printf("division by zero\n");
70         exit(1);
71         }
72
73 alpha=dotprod(n,rold,rold)/e;
74
75 for (i=1;i<=n;i++){
76         x[i] += alpha*p[i];
77         }
78
79 for (i=1;i<=n;i++){
80         rnew[i] = rold[i]-alpha*y[i];
81         }
```

```
82
83  e=dotprod(n,rold,rold);
84
85  if (fabs(e)<5.0e-20){
86          printf("division by zero\n");
87          exit(1);
88          }
89
90  beta=dotprod(n,rnew,rnew)/e;
91
92  for (i=1;i<=n;i++){
93          p[i] = rnew[i]+beta*p[i];
94          }
95
96  for (i=1;i<=n;i++){
97          rold[i] = rnew[i];
98          }
99  (*iter)++;
100 }
101
102 while (maxnum(n,rnew) > 5.0e-9*maxnum(n,rold));
103
104 for (i=1;i<=n;i++){
105         b[i] = x[i];
106         }
107 }
108
109 main(int argc, char *argv[ ])
110 {
111 double dotprod(int n, double *x, double *y);
112 void conjgrad(int n, int *iter, double **a, double *b);
113 double maxnum(int m, double *x);
114 FILE *fpa,*fpb;
115
116 int iter=0,i,j,N;
117 double **a,*b;
118
119 printf("\n\n");
120 if (argc!=4){
121         printf("Usage:     cg order afile bfile");
122         }
123
124 else if (!(fpa=fopen(argv[2],"r"))){
```

```
125          printf("cg:    Error opening file %s\n",argv[2]);
126          }
127
128 else if (!(fpb=fopen(argv[3],"r"))){
129          printf("cg:    Error opening file %s\n",argv[3]);
130          }
131
132 else{
133          N=atoi(argv[1]);
134          a=matalloc(1,N,1,N);
135          b=vecalloc(1,N);
136
137          for (i=1;i<=N;i++){
138           for (j=i;j<=N;j++){
139           fscanf(fpa,"%lf",&a[i][j]);  /* read matrix */
140           printf("\n");
141             }
142          }
143          for (i=2;i<=N;i++){        /* symmetrize */
144          for (j=1;j<=i-1;j++)
145                 a[i][j]=a[j][i];
146          }
147
148          for (i=1;i<=N;i++){     /* read the RHS */
149                 fscanf(fpb,"%lf",&b[i]);
150                 printf("\n");
151                 }
152
153 conjgrad(N,&iter,a,b);
154
155 printf("\n\n");
156
157 for (i=1;i<=N;i++){
158          printf("x[%d] = %10.8lf\n",i, b[i]);
159          }
160
161 printf("\n\n");
162 printf("The computation required %d iterates.",iter);
163 printf("\n\n");
164 }
165 }
```

AN INITIAL–VALUE PROBLEM FOR A SYSTEM
OF TWO ORDINARY DIFFERENTIAL EQUATIONS

Consider the initial–value problem for a system of two ODEs

$$(4.1) \qquad y' = f(t, y, z) \qquad y(0) \text{ given}; \qquad z' = g(t, y, z) \qquad z(0) \text{ given}.$$

Let's say we want to solve this problem on an interval $[0, T]$. We partition this interval using $t_i = ih$, $i = 0, 1, \ldots, N$, where $t_N = T$, and write $y_n \approx y(t_n)$, $z_n \approx z(t_n)$.

There are many methods of solution. One of the most popular, the *Runge–Kutta* scheme of order 4, is as follows: We begin with approximations y_0, z_0 to the initial values $y(0), z(0)$ respectively. For $n \geq 0$, assume that we know y_n, z_n and advance in time by computing

$$(4.2) \qquad y_{n+1} = y_n + \frac{1}{6}(k_1 + 2k_2 + 2k_3 + k_4)$$

$$z_{n+1} = z_n + \frac{1}{6}(l_1 + 2l_2 + 2l_3 + l_4),$$

where

$$(4.3) \qquad \begin{aligned}
k_1 &= hf(t_n, y_n, z_n) \\
l_1 &= hg(t_n, y_n, z_n) \\
k_2 &= hf\left(t_n + \frac{h}{2}, y_n + \frac{k_1}{2}, z_n + \frac{l_1}{2}\right) \\
l_2 &= hg\left(t_n + \frac{h}{2}, y_n + \frac{k_1}{2}, z_n + \frac{l_1}{2}\right) \\
k_3 &= hf\left(t_n + \frac{h}{2}, y_n + \frac{k_2}{2}, z_n + \frac{l_2}{2}\right) \\
l_3 &= hg\left(t_n + \frac{h}{2}, y_n + \frac{k_2}{2}, z_n + \frac{l_2}{2}\right) \\
k_4 &= hf\left(t_n + h, y_n + k_3, z_n + l_3\right) \\
l_4 &= hg\left(t_n + h, y_n + k_3, z_n + l_3\right).
\end{aligned}$$

As you know, this generates the same accuracy as the Taylor scheme of the same order and is far preferable.

The general class of *Adams' methods* are $O(h^k)$–accurate and require only one function evaluation per step. They require a "starting procedure," for which a Runge–Kutta method is a natural choice. As a simple example, consider the scalar problem $y' = F(t, y)$ with an initial value given. We can write

$$(4.4) \qquad y(t_n) - y(t_{n-1}) = \int_{t_{n-1}}^{t_n} F(t, y(t)) \, dt,$$

but of course the right–hand side still depends on the unknown solution $y(t)$. Basically, *Adams–Bashforth* methods replace the integrand by an interpolating polynomial which interpolates, say, at $y_{n-1}, \ldots, y_{n-k}$. This interpolating polynomial can be written down explicitly, so its integral can be explicitly evaluated, which generates the scheme, which is explicit. Given a smooth enough function F, the truncation error is $O(h^{k+1})$ which leads to global error of $O(h^k)$.

Suppose now that we attempt this interpolation on the set of the k points $y_n, \ldots, y_{n-k+1}$. Then when we replace the left–hand side in (4.4) by $y_n - y_{n-1}$, the integral (4.4) becomes an *implicit* (perhaps nonlinear) equation for y_n. How should we solve it? As with any nonlinear root–finder, we need a decent initial guess. What is better than the Adams–Bashforth value? This leads to the *Adams–Moulton* scheme.

For the Adams–Moulton scheme of order 4, applied to our original system, we call

$$f_{n+1} = f\left(t_{n+1}, y_{n+1}, z_{n+1}\right), \text{ etc.}$$

We start with approximations y_0, z_0 to the initial values $y(0), z(0)$ and use the Runge–Kutta scheme of order 4 to compute y_1, y_2, y_3 and z_1, z_2, z_3. To solve the implicit schemes, use as *predictors*

$$(4.5) \qquad y_{n+1} = y_n + \frac{h}{24} \left(55f_n - 59f_{n-1} + 37f_{n-2} - 9f_{n-3}\right)$$

$$z_{n+1} = z_n + \frac{h}{24} \left(55g_n - 59g_{n-1} + 37g_{n-2} - 9g_{n-3}\right),$$

and the *correctors* are

$$(4.6) \qquad y_{n+1} = y_n + \frac{h}{24} \left(9f_{n+1} + 19f_n - 5f_{n-1} + f_{n-2}\right)$$

$$z_{n+1} = z_n + \frac{h}{24} \left(9g_{n+1} + 19g_n - 5g_{n-1} + g_{n-2}\right).$$

One iterates the last two equations in (4.6) (say by standard fixed–point iteration) until convergence is achieved, using the predictor to generate an initial approximation. Then we simply advance in time: $n \to n + 1$. Here is the full program:

```
1  /* ODEIVP_2.c  */
2
3  /*
4  Solves the Initial-Value Problem for the System
5  y'=f(x,y,z),z'=g(x,y,z)
6  with initial values y0=y(x0),z0=z(x0)
7  Uses RK-4 to start, then AM-4
8  The results are written to the file ODEIVP.DAT
9  */
10 # include <stdlib.h>
11 # include <stdio.h>
12 # include <math.h>
13 # include <malloc.h>
14 # include "memalloc.c"
15 # include "memalloc.h"
16
17 /* These choices for y''=2*y*y*y, y(1)=1,z(1)=-1 */
18 /* Here z=y' and the exact solution is y(x)=1/x */
19
20 double f(double x, double y, double z)
21 {
22 return z;
23 }
24
25 double g(double x, double y, double z)
26 {
27 return (2.0*y*y*y);
28 }
29
30 double P(double h, double x, double y, double z, double w)
31 /* predictor */
32 {
33 return (h*(55.0*x-59.0*y+37.0*z-9.0*w)/24.0);
34 }
35
36 double C(double h, double x, double y, double z, double w)
37 /* corrector */
38 {
39 return (h*(9.0*x+19.0*y-5.0*z+w)/24.0);
40 }
41
42 main()
43 {
```

```
44 FILE *fp;
45 if (!(fp=fopen("odeivp.dat","w"))){
46         puts("Error opening file odeivp.dat");
47         }
48
49 else{
50
51 int i,N,iter;
52 double x0,y0,z0;
53 double h,p1,p2,c1,c2,e,T;
54 double k1,k2,k3,k4,l1,l2,l3,l4;
55 double f(double x, double y, double z);
56 double g(double x, double y, double z);
57 double P(double h,double x,double y,double z,double w);
58 double C(double h,double x,double y,double z,double w);
59
60 double *x,*y,*z;
61
62 printf("Enter the initial time:  ");
63 scanf("%lf",&x0);
64 printf("\n");
65
66 printf("Enter the final time:  ");
67 scanf("%lf",&T);
68 printf("\n");
69
70 printf("Enter the step size h:  ");
71 scanf("%lf",&h);
72 printf("\n");
73
74 printf("Enter the initial value of y:  ");
75 scanf("%lf",&y0);
76 printf("\n");
77
78 printf("Enter the initial value of z:  ");
79 scanf("%lf",&z0);
80 printf("\n");
81
82 N=(int)floor(T/h)+1;
83
84 x=vecalloc(0,N-1);
85 y=vecalloc(0,N-1);
86 z=vecalloc(0,N-1);
```

```
87
88  x[0]=x0;y[0]=y0;z[0]=z0;
89  fprintf(fp,"x=%12.6lf y=%12.6lf z=%12.6lf\n",\
90                     x[0],y[0],z[0]);
91
92  for (i=1;i<=N-1;i++){
93          x[i]=x[0]+i*h;
94          }
95
96  /* RK-4 */
97  for (i=1;i<=3;i++){
98  k1 = h*f(x[i-1],y[i-1],z[i-1]);
99  l1 = h*g(x[i-1],y[i-1],z[i-1]);
100
101 k2 = h*f(x[i-1]+h/2.0,y[i-1]+k1/2.0,z[i-1]+l1/2.0);
102 l2 = h*g(x[i-1]+h/2.0,y[i-1]+k1/2.0,z[i-1]+l1/2.0);
103
104 k3 = h*f(x[i-1]+h/2.0,y[i-1]+k2/2.0,z[i-1]+l2/2.0);
105 l3 = h*g(x[i-1]+h/2.0,y[i-1]+k2/2.0,z[i-1]+l2/2.0);
106
107 k4 = h*f(x[i-1]+h,y[i-1]+k3,z[i-1]+l3);
108 l4 = h*g(x[i-1]+h,y[i-1]+k3,z[i-1]+l3);
109
110 y[i]=y[i-1]+(k1+2.0*k2+2.0*k3+k4)/6.0;
111 z[i]=z[i-1]+(l1+2.0*l2+2.0*l3+l4)/6.0;
112
113 fprintf(fp,"x=%12.6lf y=%12.6lf z=%12.6lf\n",\
114                 x[i],y[i],z[i]);
115 }
116
117 for (i=3;i<=N-2;i++){
118
119 p1=y[i]+P(h,f(x[i],y[i],z[i]),f(x[i-1],y[i-1],z[i-1]),\
120 f(x[i-2],y[i-2],z[i-2]),f(x[i-3],y[i-3],z[i-3]));
121 p2=z[i]+P(h,g(x[i],y[i],z[i]),g(x[i-1],y[i-1],z[i-1]),\
122 g(x[i-2],y[i-2],z[i-2]),g(x[i-3],y[i-3],z[i-3]));
123
124 iter=0;
125 do{
126
127 c1=y[i]+C(h,f(x[i+1],p1,p2),f(x[i],y[i],z[i]),\
128 f(x[i-1],y[i-1],z[i-1]),f(x[i-2],y[i-2],z[i-2]));
129 c2=z[i]+C(h,g(x[i+1],p1,p2),g(x[i],y[i],z[i]),\
```

```
130  g(x[i-1],y[i-1],z[i-1]),g(x[i-2],y[i-2],z[i-2]));
131
132  e=fabs(p1-c1)+fabs(p2-c2);
133
134  p2=c2;
135  p1=c1;
136
137  if (++iter>100){
138          fprintf(stderr,"Too many iterates.");
139          exit(1);
140  }
141
142  }
143  while(e>(fabs(c1)+fabs(c2))*5.0e-7);
144
145  y[i+1]=c1;
146  z[i+1]=c2;
147
148  fprintf(fp,"x=%12.6lf y=%12.6lf z=%12.6lf\n",\
149                          x[i+1],y[i+1],z[i+1]);
150
151  }
152  fclose(fp);
153  }
154
155  }
```

This code computes the solution of the scalar second–order equation $y'' = 2y^3$ with initial values $y(1) = 1, y'(1) = -1$. You can easily check that the solution is $y(x) = \frac{1}{x}$ in this case. Here we call $z = y'$; this constitutes the first equation, i.e., $f(x, y, z) = z$. Then from the second–order equation itself $z' = y'' = 2y^3$ so that $g(x, y, z) = 2y^3$. These functions are entered on lines 20–28. Lines 30–40 contain the explicit formulae for the predictors and correctors, as displayed above in (4.5) and (4.6).

A file pointer is declared on line 44; the results are to be written to the file **odeivp.dat**. The standard error test follows on lines 45–47. Three arrays are declared as pointers on line 60. They are initialized and allocated on lines 84–86 once the data has been solicited from the user (lines 62–79). Lines 96–111 incorporate the Runge–Kutta scheme of order four to compute the first three values of the discrete y, z. The results are written out to the file on lines 113–114. The **floor** function on line 82 returns (as a **double** value) the greatest integer less than or equal to its argument.

The predictors are computed on lines 119–122. Then, in a **do loop** from lines 125–143, the correctors are iterated until the desired stopping tolerance is achieved, and the "new" values of the discrete approximations are written to the file.

One finds in many textbooks the usage of only *one* iteration in the corrector loop. This is because it may be more efficient to adjust the step size than it is to perform several iterates. For reasons of simplicity, we prefer to allow several iterates rather than to monitor the step size. Naturally only non–stiff equations can be treated with this code.

A BOUNDARY–VALUE PROBLEM FOR A NONLINEAR ORDINARY DIFFERENTIAL EQUATION

Consider the scalar nonlinear boundary–value problem

$$(4.7) \qquad (p(x)y')' = f(x, y) \quad (0 < x < 1)$$

with boundary conditions $y(0) = \alpha \geq 0, \quad y(1) = \beta \geq 0 \quad (\alpha^2 + \beta^2 > 0)$. Notice that f is independent of y'. Here are the standing assumptions:

1. $p(x) > 0$ on $[0, 1]$, $p \in C^1$,
2. $f \in C^2$ for $y \geq 0$, $x \in [0, 1]$,
3. For $y \geq 0$, $\frac{\partial f}{\partial y} \geq 0$; $\frac{\partial^2 f}{\partial y^2} \geq 0$; $f(x, 0) \leq 0$.

It is not difficult to show that there exists a unique solution which is non–negative. See Wendroff's book [WE]. A scheme which uses monotonicity is also given there; we follow it below.

On $[0, 1]$ let $h = \frac{1}{N+1}$ for some integer N and set $x_i = ih$ for $i = 0, \ldots, N+1$. Let $u_i \approx y(x_i)$ where $y(x)$ is the exact solution. Abbreviate $p(x_i + \frac{h}{2})$ by $p_{i+\frac{1}{2}}$, etc. The scheme proposed is as follows:

$$(4.8) \quad p_{i+\frac{1}{2}} \left(u_{i+1} - u_i \right) - p_{i-\frac{1}{2}} \left(u_i - u_{i-1} \right) = h^2 f(x_i, u_i) \quad (i = 1, \ldots, N)$$

with the boundary conditions $u_0 = \alpha$, $u_{N+1} = \beta$. This is a system of N *nonlinear* equations for the unknowns u_i. It can be shown that this system possesses a unique solution for any $h > 0$. Indeed, the algorithm we present can be used to prove this fact. We employ an iterative scheme which converges monotonically to the solutions u_i.

For this purpose let the first approximation be $U_i^0 = \alpha + (\beta - \alpha)x_i$ for $i = 0, 1, \ldots, N+1$. Abbreviate $f(x_i, U_i^k)$ by f_i^k. Consider the sequence $\{U_i^k\}$ defined for $i = 1, \ldots, N$ by

$$(4.9) \qquad p_{i+\frac{1}{2}} \left(U_{i+1}^k - U_i^k \right) - p_{i-\frac{1}{2}} \left(U_i^k - U_{i-1}^k \right) =$$
$$h^2 \left[f_i^{k-1} + \frac{\partial f_i^{k-1}}{\partial u} (U_i^k - U_i^{k-1}) \right]$$

with $U_0^k = \alpha$, $U_{N+1}^k = \beta$. This iteration is to be performed for $k = 1, 2, \ldots$.
As for the additional notation, $\frac{\partial f_i^{k-1}}{\partial u} \equiv \frac{\partial f}{\partial u}(x_i, U_i^{k-1})$.

We see that this system for the $\{U_i^k\}$ is *linear tridiagonal*. It has been obtained by linearizing the nonlinear term. One can show by means of the *maximum principle* that $0 \le U_i^{k+1} \le U_i^k$ for all k, i. Therefore, the coefficient matrix is diagonally dominant and hence invertible (see Chapter 2 or [IK]) since by hypothesis $\frac{\partial f}{\partial u} \ge 0$ for such arguments. It follows that the limit $\lim_{k \to \infty} U_i^k$ exists for each $i = 0, 1, \ldots, N+1$. With the continuity assumptions given above, we can pass to the limit $k \to \infty$ in the scheme (4.9) for the $\{U_i^k\}$ to get the desired scheme for the $\{u_i\}$. The convergence $u_i \to y(x_i)$ can be shown via the maximum principle.

Before giving the code it may be useful to state the discrete maximum principle. The continuous version may be found in [IK] or [JO1]. Consider the discrete linear operator

$$(Ly)_i \equiv p_{i+\frac{1}{2}}(y_{i+1} - y_i) - p_{i-\frac{1}{2}}(y_i - y_{i-1}) - q_i y_i \quad (i = 1, \ldots, N).$$

Here $q_i \ge 0$ for each i. A statement of the maximum principle in this case is:

Assume $y_0 \ge 0$, $y_{N+1} \ge 0$, and $(Ly)_i \le 0$ for each i. Then $y_i \ge 0$ for each i.

Here is the listing **2bvpmax.c** which implements this scheme for the special problem

$$y'' = 2y^3 \quad (0 < x < 1); \quad y(0) = 1, \quad y(1) = \frac{1}{2}$$

whose exact solution is $y(x) = \frac{1}{1+x}$.

```
 1 /* 2BVPMAX.C */
 2
 3 /*
 4 Solution of a two-point BVP via a "monotone" method
 5 (maximum principle) for a second order nonlinear ODE.
 6 cf.  Wendroff's book [WE], p.  86 ff.
 7 Problem is (p(x)y')' = f(x,y), 0 < x < 1
 8 BC's:   y(0)=alpha>=0, y(1)=beta>=0, y(0)+y(1)>0
 9 Hypotheses are f(x,0) <= 0,
10 p(x) strictly positive on [0,1],
11 and in {y >= 0}:  Df/Dy >= 0; D^2f/Dy^2 >= 0.
12 Results are written to the file "2bvpmax.dat."
13 */
14
```

```
15 # define p(x) (1.0)
16 # define f(x,y) (2.0*(y)*(y)*(y))
17 # define fd(x,y) (6.0*(y)*(y))
18 /* fd(x,y) = Df(x,y)/Dy */
19 /* this particular example is for y'' = 2 y^3 on [0,1] */
20 /* with boundary conditions y(0)=1, y(1)=1/2 */
21 /* Exact solution is y(x) = 1/(1 + x) */
22
23 # include <stdio.h>
24 # include <stdlib.h>
25 # include <math.h>
26 # include <malloc.h>
27 # include "memalloc.c"
28 # include "memalloc.h"
29 # define MAX(a,b) ((a)>=(b) ?  (a):(b))
30
31 double maxnum(int m, double *x)
32 { /* zero offset indices */
33 int k;
34 double z;
35
36         z=MAX(x[0],x[1]);
37         for (k=2;k<=m-1;k++)
38                 z=MAX(x[k],z);
39         return z;
40 }
41
42 void tridiag(int n, double *sub, double *diag,\
43                 double *sup, double *b)
44 {
45         int k;
46         double m,det;
47         for (k=2;k<=n;k++){
48                 if (fabs(diag[k-1])<5.0e-20){
49                 printf("Division by zero in tridi
50                 exit(1);
51                 }
52                 m=sub[k]/diag[k-1];
53                 diag[k] -= m*sup[k-1];
54                 b[k] -= m*b[k-1];
55                 }
56
57         det=diag[1];
```

```
58              for (k=2;k<=n;k++){
59                      det *= diag[k];
60                      }
61              if (fabs(det)<5.0e-20){
62                      printf("Singular matrix in tridiag");
63                      exit(1);
64                      }
65
66              b[n] =b[n]/diag[n];
67              for (k=n-1;k>=1;k--)
68                      b[k] =(b[k] - sup[k]*b[k+1])/diag[k];
69 }
70
71 main ()
72 {
73 int i,k,N,iter=0;
74 double alpha,beta,s,h,H2;
75 double *x,*b,*u,*v,*sub,*diag,*sup,*e;
76 double maxnum(int m, double *x);
77 void tridiag(int n, double *sub, double *diag,\
78                      double *sup, double *b);
79 FILE *fp;
80 if (!(fp=fopen("2bvpmax.dat","w"))){
81         puts("Error opening file 2bvpmax.dat");
82         }
83
84 else{
85
86 printf("\n");
87 printf("Enter the number of interior mesh points:");
88 scanf("%d",&N);
89 printf("\n");
90
91 x    =vecalloc(0,N+1);
92 u    =vecalloc(0,N+1);
93 v    =vecalloc(0,N+1);
94 e    =vecalloc(0,N+1);
95 b    =vecalloc(1,N);
96 sub =vecalloc(1,N);
97 diag=vecalloc(1,N);
98 sup =vecalloc(1,N);
99
100 h=1.0/(N+1.0);
```

```
101 H2=h*h;
102
103 for (i=0;i<=N+1;i++)
104 x[i]=i*h;
105
106 printf("\n");
107 printf("Enter the left-hand boundary value:");
108 scanf("%lf",&alpha);
109 printf("\n");
110 printf("Enter the right-hand boundary value:");
111 scanf("%lf",&beta);
112 printf("\n\n");
113
114 for (i=0;i<=N+1;i++)
115 v[i]=alpha+(beta-alpha)*x[i];
116 /* this is the first approximation */
117
118 for (i=1;i<=N;i++)
119 b[i]=v[i];
120
121 sub[1]=sup[N]=0.0;
122
123 for (i=2;i<=N-1;i++){
124         sub[i]  = -p((i-.5)*h)/H2;
125         sup[i]  = -p((i+.5)*h)/H2;
126 }
127         sub[N]  = -p((N-.5)*h)/H2;
128         sup[1]  = -p((1.5)*h)/H2;
129
130 do{
131
132 for (i=1;i<=N;i++){
133         diag[i] = (p((i-.5)*h)+p((i+.5)*h))/H2\
134                   +fd(x[i],v[i]);
135         b[i]    = -f(x[i],v[i])+v[i]*fd(x[i],v[i]);
136         }
137
138 /* The following correct for the BC's in the */
139 /* tridiagonal system at the unknowns u[1],u[N] */
140
141 b[1] += (p(0.5*h)*alpha/H2);
142 b[N] += (p(1.0-0.5*h)*beta/H2);
143
```

```
144 tridiag(N,sub,diag,sup,b);
145
146 for (k=1;k<=N;k++){
147         u[k]=b[k];
148         e[k]=fabs(v[k]-u[k]);
149         }
150 for (k=1;k<=N;k++)
151         v[k]=u[k];
152
153         if (++iter>500){
154                 printf("Too many iterations.");
155                 exit(1);
156                 }
157
158 }  /* end do */
159
160 while (maxnum(N+2,e)>5.0e-8*maxnum(N+2,u));
161
162 fprintf(fp,"%12.8lf %12.8lf\n",0.0,alpha);
163 for (k=1;k<=N;k++)
164 fprintf(fp,"%12.8lf %12.8lf\n",x[k],u[k]);
165 fprintf(fp,"%12.8lf %12.8lf\n",1.0,beta);
166
167 }
168 fclose(fp);
169
170 }
```

A MORE GENERAL NONLINEAR BOUNDARY–VALUE PROBLEM

Consider the nonlinear boundary–value problem

$$(4.10) \qquad y'' = f(x, y, y'), \quad a < x < b, \quad y(a) = \alpha, \quad y(b) = \beta.$$

Assume that

$$(4.11) \qquad 0 < Q_1 \leq \frac{\partial f}{\partial y}(x, y, z) \leq Q_2, \quad \left| \frac{\partial f}{\partial z}(x, y, z) \right| \leq P$$

for all points (x, y, z). (If we had *a priori* bounds on the solution, these bounds would only be required to hold in some appropriately large set). Further assume there is a solution y in $C^4[a, b]$. Notice that the nonlinear term can now depend on y'.

We pick a uniform grid $x_j = a + jh$ for $j = 0, \ldots, N+1$ with $(N+1)h = b-a$. Consider the scheme (for $j = 1, \ldots, N$)

$$(4.12) \qquad \frac{u_{j+1} - 2u_j + u_{j-1}}{h^2} = f\left(x_j, \frac{u_{j-1} + u_{j+1}}{2}, \frac{u_{j+1} - u_{j-1}}{2h}\right)$$

with $u_0 = \alpha$, $u_{N+1} = \beta$. The standard centered difference is used to approximate y' in the last argument of f. Notice also the averaging in the y–argument of f; this is essential and allows convergence to be shown. This scheme appears in [IK].

Now notice that this scheme again generates a nonlinear system. Therefore, we need to supply an iteration to find its solution. Here is one that works: for $k = 0, 1, \ldots$ and $j = 1, 2, \ldots, N$, consider

$$(4.13) \quad u_j^{(k+1)} = \frac{1}{2}\left(u_{j-1}^{(k)} + u_{j+1}^{(k)}\right) - \frac{h^2}{2} f\left(x_j, \frac{u_{j+1}^{(k)} + u_{j-1}^{(k)}}{2}, \frac{u_{j+1}^{(k)} - u_{j-1}^{(k)}}{2h}\right)$$

with $u_0^{(k+1)} = \alpha$, $u_{N+1}^{(k+1)} = \beta$. We may begin with $u_j^{(0)} = \alpha + \frac{(\beta-\alpha)jh}{b-a}$. It is an exercise to show that the limit of the $\{u_j^{(k)}\}$ (as $k \to \infty$) exists and generates the desired solutions $\{u_j\}$, provided $h(P + hQ_2) \le 2$. Under the same condition we will now show that $|y(x_j) - u_j| = O(h^2)$ as $h \to 0$.

We abbreviate $y(x_j)$ by y_j. The *local truncation error* τ_j is the amount by which the exact solution $y(x)$ fails to satisfy the approximate scheme; thus, for $j = 1, \ldots, N$

$$(4.14) \qquad \frac{y_{j+1} - 2y_j + y_{j-1}}{h^2} = f\left(x_j, \frac{y_{j-1} + y_{j+1}}{2}, \frac{y_{j+1} - y_{j-1}}{2h}\right) + \tau_j.$$

The first goal is to show that $\tau_j = O(h^2)$. By Taylor's theorem, the left–hand side here is

$$y''(x_j) + \frac{h^2}{12} y^{(4)}(\xi_j)$$

for some intermediate point ξ_j. Thus, the definition of τ_j can be rewritten as

$$\tau_j = y''(x_j) + \frac{h^2}{12} y^{(4)}(\xi_j) - f\left(x_j, \frac{y_{j-1} + y_{j+1}}{2}, \frac{y_{j+1} - y_{j-1}}{2h}\right)$$

$$(4.15) \quad = f(x_j, y_j, y_j') - f\left(x_j, \frac{y_{j-1} + y_{j+1}}{2}, \frac{y_{j+1} - y_{j-1}}{2h}\right) + O(h^2)$$

$$= \frac{\widetilde{\partial f}}{\partial y}\left[y_j - \frac{1}{2}(y_{j+1} + y_{j-1})\right] + \frac{\widetilde{\partial f}}{\partial z}\left[y_j' - \frac{1}{2h}(y_{j+1} - y_{j-1})\right] + O(h^2),$$

where the tildes denote evaluation at some intermediate point on the line segment joining the indicated arguments. Using Taylor's Theorem in the form

$$(4.16) \qquad y_{j\pm1} = y_j \pm hy_j' + \frac{h^2}{2}y_j'' \pm \frac{h^3}{6}\widetilde{y^{(3)}},$$

we see that $\tau_j = O(h^2)$.

Now consider the error $\varepsilon_j = y(x_j) - u_j = y_j - u_j$ and subtract the scheme computation for u_j from the definition of the truncation error to get

$$(4.17) \qquad \frac{e_{j+1} - 2e_j + e_{j-1}}{h^2} = \frac{1}{2}\bar{f}_y\left(e_{j+1} + e_{j-1}\right) + \frac{1}{2}\bar{f}_z\left(\frac{e_{j+1} - e_{j-1}}{h}\right) + \tau_j.$$

Here the overbar denotes evaluation at intermediate points, as provided by the Mean–Value Theorem. Now just solve this for e_j; after a bit of algebra you will get

$$(4.18)$$
$$e_j = \frac{1}{2}\left(1 - \frac{h^2}{2}\bar{f}_y - \frac{h}{2}\bar{f}_z\right)e_{j+1} + \frac{1}{2}\left(1 - \frac{h^2}{2}\bar{f}_y + \frac{h}{2}\bar{f}_z\right)e_{j-1} - \frac{h^2\tau_j}{2}.$$

By the bounds on f assumed in (4.11), we have

$$(4.19) \qquad 1 - \frac{h^2}{2}\bar{f}_y \pm \frac{h}{2}\bar{f}_z \geq 1 - \frac{h^2 Q_2}{2} - \frac{hP}{2}.$$

If we now assume that

$$(4.20) \qquad\qquad h^2 Q_2 + hP \leq 2,$$

we can drop the absolute values when estimating $|e_j|$ and can write, for $E = \max_j |e_j|$,

$$|e_j| \leq \frac{1}{2}\left(1 - \frac{h^2}{2}\bar{f}_y - \frac{h}{2}\bar{f}_z\right)E + \frac{1}{2}\left(1 - \frac{h^2}{2}\bar{f}_y + \frac{h}{2}\bar{f}_z\right)E + \frac{h^2|\tau_j|}{2}$$

$$(4.21) \quad \leq \left(1 - \frac{h^2\bar{f}_y}{2}\right)E + \frac{h^2\max_j|\tau_j|}{2}$$

$$\leq \left(1 - \frac{h^2 Q_1}{2}\right)E + \frac{h^2\max_j|\tau_j|}{2}.$$

It follows that

$$(4.22) \qquad E \leq \left(1 - \frac{h^2 Q_1}{2}\right)E + \frac{h^2\max_j|\tau_j|}{2},$$

i.e., that

$$(4.23) \qquad E \le \frac{h^2 \max_j |\tau_j|}{h^2 Q_1} = O(h^2) \quad \text{as} \quad h \to 0.$$

This completes the proof of convergence.

Here is an implementation of this scheme for the special case

$$y'' + y' = 2y + \sin y \quad (0 < x < 1), \quad y(0) = 1, \quad y(1) = 2$$

```
1  /* 2BVPODE.C */
2
3  /*
4  Solution of a nonlinear two-point boundary-value
5  problem for a second-order ODE of the form
6  y" = f(x,y,y'), a < x < b, with boundary conditions
7  y(a)=alpha, y(b)=beta.
8  The hypotheses are -P < Df/Dz < P; 0 < Q1 < Df/Dy < Q2
9  for all x,y,z.
10 It may be necessary to decrease the step size h
11 and/or change the stopping tolerance TOL.
12 */
13
14 # define f(x,y,z) (-1.0*(z)+2.0*(y)+sin(y))
15 /* this example is y'' +y' = y + sin(y) on [0,1] */
16 /* with boundary conditions y[0]=1, y[1]=2 */
17
18 # define MAX(a,b) ((a)>=(b) ?  (a):(b))
19 # define TOL 5.0e-8
20 # include <stdio.h>
21 # include <stdlib.h>
22 # include <math.h>
23 # include <malloc.h>
24 # include "memalloc.c"
25 # include "memalloc.h"
26
27 double maxnum(int m, double *x)
28 {
29 /* returns the maximum norm of vector x */
30 /* indices run over 0 to m-1 */
31 int k;
32 double z;
```

```
33
34              z=MAX(fabs(x[0]),fabs(x[1]));
35              for (k=2;k<=m-1;k++)
36                      z=MAX(fabs(x[k]),z);
37              return z;
38 }
39
40 main ()
41 {
42 int i,N,iter=0;
43 double *x,*e,*u,*v;
44
45 double alpha,beta,a,b,s,h,H2;
46 double maxnum(int m, double *x);
47
48 printf("Enter the number of interior mesh points:  ");
49 scanf("%d",&N);
50 printf("\n");
51
52 printf("\n");
53 printf("Enter the left-hand endpoint:");
54 scanf("%lf",&a);
55 printf("Enter the right-hand endpoint:");
56 scanf("%lf",&b);
57 printf("\n\n");
58
59 printf("Enter the left-hand boundary value:");
60 scanf("%lf",&alpha);
61 printf("Enter the right-hand boundary value:");
62 scanf("%lf",&beta);
63 printf("\n\n");
64
65 x=vecalloc(0,N+1);
66 e=vecalloc(0,N+1);
67 u=vecalloc(0,N+1);
68 v=vecalloc(0,N+1);
69
70 h=(b-a)/(N+1.0);H2=h*h;
71 for (i=0;i<=N+1;i++)
72 x[i]=a+i*h;
73
74 u[0]=v[0]=alpha;
75 u[N+1]=v[N+1]=beta;
```

```
76
77 /* first approximation */
78 for (i=1;i<=N;i++)
79          v[i]=alpha+(beta-alpha)*i*h/(b-a);
80
81 do
82 {
83 for (i=1;i<=N;i++)
84 u[i]=(v[i-1]+v[i+1])/2.0-H2*\
85 f(x[i],(v[i-1]+v[i+1])/2.0,(v[i+1]-v[i-1])/(2.0*h))/2.0;
86
87 for (i=1;i<=N;i++)
88          e[i]=fabs(u[i]-v[i]);
89
90 s=maxnum(N+2,e);
91
92 /* set up next iteration */
93 for (i=1;i<=N;i++)
94          v[i]=u[i];
95
96 if (++iter>1000){
97          printf("Too many iterations.");
98          exit(1);
99          }
100
101 }
102 while (s>TOL*maxnum(N+2,u));
103
104 for (i=0;i<=N+1;i++)
105 printf("x=%12.7lf          u=%12.7lf\n",x[i],u[i]);
106 }
```

AN UNUSUAL ORDINARY DIFFERENTIAL EQUATION

This interesting problem was recently brought to my attention by my colleague, Prof. Peter Sternberg of Indiana University. Let $u(t)$ be a scalar function of the time t which also depends on a parameter x. We write $u = u(t, x)$, where $0 \leq x \leq 1$ and $t \geq 0$. The function u satisfies the ordinary differential equation

$$(4.24) \qquad \frac{du}{dt} = f(u) - \int_0^1 f(u(t, x)) \, dx \qquad \text{with} \quad u(0, x) = u_0(x),$$

where $f(u)$ and $u_0(x)$ are given functions. You might suspect that there is a partial differential equation lurking in the background; there is, but a small parameter there has been set equal to zero, so that the above equation results.

The point of this equation is that the integral average of u is equal to zero: for, we compute

$$(4.25) \qquad \frac{d}{dt} \int_0^1 u(t,x)\,dx = \int_0^1 \left(f(u) - \int_0^1 f(u(t,y))\,dy \right) dx = 0$$

since our x–interval has length one, and the second term here can be brought outside of the integral over x.

The simplest and crudest method for an ordinary differential equation is that of Euler: to approximate a scalar equation $u'(t) = F(t, u(t))$, we can use $u^{n+1} = u^n + \Delta t F(t^n, u^n)$, where $t^n = n\Delta t$ and $u^n \approx u(t^n)$.

But there is a major problem: we have no idea of how u depends on x, since there are no x–derivatives in this equation! Let's begin by writing an approximation for an integral in the form

$$(4.26) \qquad \int_0^1 g(x)\,dx \approx \sum_{k=0}^m a_k g(x_k).$$

Here the points $\{x_k\}$ form some partition of $[0,1]$. We choose below $h = 1/m$ where m is a positive integer, and $x_k = kh$ for $k = 0, 1, \ldots, m$. Recall that the error estimate for such a quadrature formula depends on certain derivatives of g *with respect to* x; we choose the composite trapezoid rule, whose error estimate involves only the second derivative. In fact, for this choice we have $a_0 = a_m = h/2$, $a_k = h$ for $k = 1, 2, \ldots, m-1$.

Replacing the integral by the quadrature formula as above, we have approximately

$$(4.27) \qquad \frac{du}{dt} \approx f(u(t,x)) - \sum_{k=0}^m a_k f(u(t,x_k)).$$

In order to compute the summands here, we evaluate the Euler approximation at each $x_j, j = 0, 1, \ldots, m$. Writing u_j^n for such an expression, we have

$$(4.28) \quad u_j^{n+1} = u_j^n + \Delta t \left(f(u_j^n) - \sum_{k=0}^m a_k f(u_k^n) \right) \quad \text{for} \quad n = 0, 1, \ldots.$$

Of course, we have an initial value $u_0(x)$, with which we can write $u_j^0 = u_0(x_j)$. Thus, for every time step n, we perform such a loop over j and then update u^n.

In the code below, we take $f(u) = u - u^3$ and initially $u_0(x) = \cos(\pi x)$. The results are printed in the format

```
t        x        u
```

to the file mean0.dat. The limiting (as $t \to \infty$) distribution is a step function equal to 1 on $[0, 0.5]$, -1 on $[0.5, 1]$. Can you prove that this behavior must occur for an appropriate class of functions f?

```
1  /* Mean0.c */
2
3  # include <math.h>
4  # include <malloc.h>
5  # include <stdio.h>
6  # include <stdlib.h>
7  # include "memalloc.c"
8  # include "memalloc.h"
9
10 # define PI 3.141592653589793
11 # define f(x) ((x)-(x)*(x)*(x))    /* nonlinear function */
12 # define u0(x) (cos(PI*(x)))              /* initial value */
13 # define DELTAT 0.05
14
15 main()
16 {
17 FILE *fp;
18
19 if (!(fp=fopen("mean0.dat","w"))){
20 printf("MEAN0:    Error opening file mean0.dat\n");
21 }
22
23 else{
24
25 int n,j,k,m=10;
26 double s=0.0,h=1.0/(double)m;
27 double *uold,*unew,*a;
28
29 uold=vecalloc(0,m);
30 unew=vecalloc(0,m);
31 a=vecalloc(0,m);
32
33 a[0]=a[m]=(0.5)*h;
34 for (k=1;k<=m-1;k++){
35          a[k]=h;
```

```
36            uold[k]=u0(k*h); /* initial distribution */
37            }
38
39 uold[0]=u0(0.0);uold[m]=u0(1.0);
40
41 for (n=0;n<=100;n++){                    /* time loop */
42
43            for (j=0;j<=m;j++){
44                    s=0.0;
45                    for (k=0;k<=m;k++){
46                            s += a[k]*f(uold[k]);
47                            }
48            s *= (-1.0);
49            s += f(uold[j]);
50            s *= DELTAT;
51            unew[j]= uold[j]+s;
52            }
53
54 for (j=0;j<=m;j++){
55 fprintf(fp,"%12.7lf %12.7lf %12.7lf\n",\
56            n*DELTAT,j*h,unew[j]);
57 }
58
59 for (j=0;j<=m;j++){
60            uold[j]=unew[j];
61            }
62 }                            /* end time loop */
63
64 }                                /* end if */
65
66 fclose(fp);
67
68 }                                /* end main */
```

THE HEAT EQUATION WITH VARIABLE CONDUCTIVITY

In this section we consider C code for the solution of the partial differential equation

$$(4.29) \qquad \frac{\partial u}{\partial t} = \frac{\partial}{\partial x}\left(s(x)\frac{\partial u}{\partial x}\right) \qquad (0 < x < \pi, \quad t > 0)$$

with a given initial condition $u(x,0) = u_0(x)$ and boundary conditions $u(0,t) = u(\pi,t) = 0$. Before writing the finite–difference algorithm, we digress on the constant–coefficient case (i.e., the heat equation).

The *heat equation* has the form $u_t = u_{xx}$. We assume the same boundary and initial conditions. Subdivide the interval $[0, \pi]$ as usual: $h = \frac{\pi}{N+1}$ and set $x_i = ih$ for $i = 0, 1, \ldots, N+1$. Given $\Delta t > 0$, the standard explicit scheme takes the form (for $n = 0, 1, \ldots$)

$$(4.30) \qquad \frac{u_k^{n+1} - u_k^n}{\Delta t} = \frac{u_{k+1}^n - 2u_k^n + u_{k-1}^n}{h^2} \qquad (k = 1, 2, \ldots, N),$$

where $u_0^n = u_{N+1}^n = 0$ for every n, and $u_k^0 =$ an approximation to $u_0(x_k)$. The numerical integration of partial differential equations is much more difficult than that for ordinary differential equations. This is already seen here in this simple problem: a restriction must be placed on the ratio $\beta \equiv \frac{\Delta t}{h^2} \leq \frac{1}{2}$. The scheme will converge in maximum norm at a rate proportional to Δt when this restriction is met. However, if it is violated, convergence need not take place. Such a restriction, which is severe in this case, is called the *stability condition*; for a large class of linear problems, stability is known to be equivalent to convergence. (This is the Lax–Richtmyer theory, see, e.g., [RM] or [ST].) For a hyperbolic equation such as the wave equation $u_{tt} = u_{xx}$, the restriction is $\Delta t \leq \Delta x$, which is the famous *Courant–Friedrichs–Lewy* (CFL) condition.

A well-known way to eliminate the restriction on β is to use an implicit scheme. Thus, we could try

$$\frac{u_k^{n+1} - u_k^n}{\Delta t} = \frac{u_{k+1}^{n+1} - 2u_k^{n+1} + u_{k-1}^{n+1}}{h^2} \qquad (k = 1, 2, \ldots, N), \quad (n = 0, 1, \ldots),$$

in which the solution of a tridiagonal linear system is involved at each step. Another variation on the theme is the *Crank–Nicolson* scheme, which uses

$$\frac{u_k^{n+1} - u_k^n}{\Delta t} = \frac{1}{2} \frac{u_{k+1}^{n+1} - 2u_k^{n+1} + u_{k-1}^{n+1}}{h^2} + \frac{1}{2} \frac{u_{k+1}^n - 2u_k^n + u_{k-1}^n}{h^2}$$

for the same range of k, n.

The above heat equation can be solved explicitly by means of separation of variables. However, when the conductivity function $s(x)$ is non–constant in the original (variable coefficient) equation (4.29), explicit solutions are out of the question. For the solution of $u_t = (su_x)_x$ we present a standard scheme from [RM]. Only the nondegenerate case is considered: $s(x)$ is to be continuously differentiable and strictly positive on the closed interval $[0, \pi]$. We use a family of schemes depending on a parameter θ with $0 \leq \theta \leq 1$. The case $\theta = 0$ is the fully explicit scheme and requires a restriction on $\beta = \frac{\Delta t}{h^2}$; $\theta = 1$ is fully implicit, and $\theta = 1/2$ is Crank–Nicolson. For the scheme itself define $(\delta u)_i = u_{i+\frac{1}{2}} - u_{i-\frac{1}{2}}$ so that $(\delta^2 u)_i = u_{i+1} - 2u_i + u_{i-1}$. The scheme can be compactly written as

$$(4.31) \qquad \frac{u_k^{n+1} - u_k^n}{\Delta t} = \frac{1}{h^2} \left[\theta \left(\delta(s\delta u) \right)_k^{n+1} + (1 - \theta) \left(\delta(s\delta u) \right)_k^n \right].$$

In explicit detail, we can write

$$-\theta\beta s_{k+\frac{1}{2}}u^{n+1}_{k+1} + \left(1 + \theta\beta s_{k+\frac{1}{2}} + \theta\beta s_{k-\frac{1}{2}}\right)u^{n+1}_k - \theta\beta s_{k-\frac{1}{2}}u^{n+1}_{k-1} =$$

terms known from step n.

As you see, a tridiagonal system is to be solved at each time step (provided $\theta \neq 0$). Recall that the function $s(x)$ is strictly positive. By the well–known theorem on invertibility (cf. Chapter 2 or [IK]), this system always has a unique solution for every n.

Before giving the code listing, we show how the restriction on $\beta = \frac{\Delta t}{h^2}$ naturally arises when making a maximum–norm estimate on the discrete solution in the fully explicit case (i.e., $\theta = 0$). (Such an estimate is the essence of stability.) For this choice the scheme takes the form

$$(4.32) \quad u^{n+1}_k = u^n_k + \beta\left[s_{k+\frac{1}{2}}u^n_{k+1} - \left(s_{k+\frac{1}{2}} + s_{k-\frac{1}{2}}\right)u^n_k + s_{k-\frac{1}{2}}u^n_{k-1}\right],$$

or

$$u^{n+1}_k = \beta s_{k+\frac{1}{2}}u^n_{k+1} + \left(1 - \beta(s_{k+\frac{1}{2}} + s_{k-\frac{1}{2}})\right)u^n_k + \beta s_{k-\frac{1}{2}}u^n_{k-1}.$$

Set $U^n = \max_{0 \leq j \leq N+1}|u^n_j|$. Then replacing $|u^n_{k\pm1}|, |u^n_k|$ crudely on the right side by U^n, we get

$$(4.33) \quad |u^{n+1}_k| \leq \beta s_{k+\frac{1}{2}}U^n + \left|1 - \beta(s_{k+\frac{1}{2}} + s_{k-\frac{1}{2}})\right|U^n + \beta s_{k-\frac{1}{2}}U^n.$$

Notice the absolute value on the middle term here, and recall that $s(x)$ is assumed continuous on the closed interval. Thus, $s(x) \leq s_1$ say, for all x. Therefore,

$$(4.34) \quad 1 - \beta\left(s_{k+\frac{1}{2}} + s_{k-\frac{1}{2}}\right) \geq 1 - 2\beta s_1 \geq 0,$$

provided $\beta \leq \frac{1}{2s_1}$. For this choice of β, we may drop the absolute value in the inequality (4.33) for $|u^{n+1}_k|$. Then all terms but one cancel, and we get

$$|u^{n+1}_k| \leq U^n, \quad \text{hence also} \quad U^{n+1} \leq U^n.$$

On iteration this yields $U^n \leq U^0$ for every n, which is the *discrete maximum principle* in this case. We notice that only an upper bound on $s(x)$ was required when making this estimate; the lower bound would be needed to control lower–order terms, which are absent in this special case. Moreover, if $s(x)$ were the constant function equal to one, the condition just derived reduces to $\beta \leq 1/2$ as mentioned above.

Here is now the complete code:

```
1 /* HEATVARC.C */
2
3 /*
4 Heat Equation with variable conductivity:
5 DtU = Dx(s(x)DxU) on 0 < x < pi, t > 0
6 Results are written to file heatv.dat.
7 Nondegenerate: s(x) strictly positive on [0,pi]
8 Boundary conditions are u = 0 at x = 0,pi
9 Initial condition is u(x,0) = f(x)
10 n is such that (n+1)*(delta x) = pi
11 h = delta x, tau = delta t
12 Scheme from [RM], p.  198.
13 */
14
15 # include <math.h>
16 # include <malloc.h>
17 # include <stdio.h>
18 # include <stdlib.h>
19 # include "memalloc.c"
20 # include "memalloc.h"
21
22 # define PI 3.141592653589793
23
24 void tridiag(int n, double *sub, double *diag,\
25                 double *sup, double *b)
26 { /* this version uses indices from 1 to n */
27
28         int k;
29         double m,det;
30         for (k=2;k<=n;k++){
31                 if (fabs(diag[k-1])<5.0e-20){
32                 printf("Division by zero in tridiag");
33                 exit(1);
34                 }
35                 m=sub[k]/diag[k-1];
36                 diag[k] -= m*sup[k-1];
37                 b[k]  -= m*b[k-1];
38                 }
39
40         det=diag[1];
41         for (k=2;k<=n;k++){
```

```
42                      det *= diag[k];
43                      }
44          if (fabs(det)<5.0e-20){
45                      printf("Singular matrix in tridiag");
46                      exit(1);
47                      }
48
49          b[n] =b[n]/diag[n];
50          for (k=n-1;k>=1;k--)
51                      b[k] =(b[k] - sup[k]*b[k+1])/diag[k];
52 }
53
54 double f(double x)      /* initial condition */
55 {
56          return (x*(PI-x));
57 }
58
59 double s(double x)      /* conductivity function */
60 {
61          return exp(x);
62 }
63
64 main()
65 {
66 void tridiag(int n, double *sub, double *diag,\
67                      double *sup, double *b);
68 double f(double x);
69 double s(double x);
70 FILE *fp;
71 if (!(fp=fopen("heatv.dat","w"))){
72          printf("Error opening file heatv.dat");
73          }
74
75 else{
76
77 int k,j,n;
78 double h,tau,theta,beta,c1,c2,b1,T;
79 double *b,*u,*diag,*sup,*sub;
80
81 printf("Enter the desired number of mesh points:  ");
82 scanf("%d",&n);
83 printf("\n");
84 h=PI/(n+1);
```

```
85
86 printf("Enter the final time:  ");
87 scanf("%lf",&T);
88 printf("\n");
89
90 printf("Enter delta t:  ");
91 scanf("%lf",&tau);
92 printf("\n");
93
94 printf("Enter theta:  ");
95 scanf("%lf",&theta);
96
97 /*
98 theta = 0.5 would be usual Crank Nicolson; theta=1
99 is fully implicit; theta = 0 requires a restriction
100 */
101
102 beta=tau/(h*h);
103
104 diag=vecalloc(1,n);
105 sup=vecalloc(1,n);
106 sub=vecalloc(1,n);
107 b=vecalloc(1,n);
108 u=vecalloc(0,n+1);
109
110 u[0]=u[n+1]=0.0;         /* initial condition */
111 for (j=1;j<=n;j++){
112         u[j]=f(j*h);
113         }
114
115 for (j=0;j<=n+1;j++){
116 fprintf(fp,"%12.6lf %12.6lf %12.6lf\n",0.0,j*h,u[j]);
117 }
118
119 fprintf(fp,"\n");
120
121 c1=(1.0-theta)*beta;
122 c2=theta*beta;
123
124 sub[1]=sup[n]=0.0;
125         for (j=2;j<=n-1;j++){
126                 sub[j]=-c2*s((j-0.5)*h);
127                 sup[j]=-c2*s((j+0.5)*h);
```

```
128                              }
129  sub[n]=-c2*s((n-0.5)*h);
130  sup[1]=-c2*s((1.5)*h);
131
132  for (k=1;k<=(int)floor(T/tau);k++){  /* time loop */
133
134          for (j=1;j<=n;j++){
135              diag[j]=1.0+c2*(s((j+0.5)*h)+s((j-0.5)*h));
136              }
137
138  for (j=1;j<=n;j++){
139  b1  = c1*s((j+0.5)*h)*u[j+1];
140  b1 += (1.0-c1*(s((j+0.5)*h)+s((j-0.5)*h)))*u[j];
141  b1 += c1*s((j -0.5)*h)*u[j-1];
142  b[j] = b1;
143  }
144
145  tridiag(n,sub,diag,sup,b);
146
147  for (j=1;j<=n;j++)
148          u[j]=b[j];
149
150  fprintf(fp,"%12.6lf %12.6lf %12.6lf\n",k*tau,0.0,0.0);
151
152  for (j=1;j<=n;j++){
153  fprintf(fp,"%12.6lf %12.6lf %12.6lf\n",k*tau,j*h,u[j]);
154  }
155
156  fprintf(fp,"%12.6lf %12.6lf %12.6lf\n",k*tau,PI,0.0);
157  fprintf(fp,"\n");
158
159  }   /* end k-loop */
160
161  }
162  fclose(fp);
163
164  }  /* end main */
```

Most of this is fairly straightforward. In lines 24–52 we merely include the code of the tridiagonal solver which has been encountered before. On lines 54–57 we take as initial condition $u_0(x) = x(\pi - x)$. Notice that the boundary conditions should be satisfied by this function for compatibility. The function $s(x)$ is taken to be $\exp(x)$ in lines 59–62.

The results are written to the file `heatv.dat`. The step sizes, final time, etc., are solicited on lines 81–95. You should choose θ equal to 1 or 0.5. The time–loop begins on line 132. Note that the diagonal coefficients of the matrix are reinitialized after each time step. This is because the arguments to `tridiag` are pointers, and the diagonal entries are altered after the function call. The known right–hand side is given on lines 138–143 after which the linear system is solved on line 145. Lines 147–148 simply prepare for the next iteration.

LAGUERRE'S METHOD

This is a classical algorithm for root–finding. We implement it here to find all roots of a *complex–coefficient* polynomial $f(x) = a_0 x^n + a_1 x^{n-1} + \cdots + a_n$. The method requires the computation of f, f' and f'' at each step (this causes no problems for polynomials), and is known to converge *cubically* near a simple zero. Moreover, in the case of real coefficients and real distinct roots, it is *always convergent*. We will begin below with an arbitrary approximation to a root, which is refined by the algorithm. We then deflate (by a version of Horner) to get a polynomial of one lower degree, which is in turn treated in the same way. Of course, complex arithmetic must be used.

We present a derivation of the scheme and most of the details for convergence in the case of real distinct roots. Thus, assume that $f(x)$ is monic and has real zeroes $r_1 < r_2 < \cdots < r_n$. We can write

$$(4.35) \qquad f(x) = \prod_{i=1}^{n} (x - r_i).$$

Differentiating the (complex) logarithm, we get

$$\frac{d}{dx} \ln f(x) = \frac{d}{dx} \sum_{i=1}^{n} \ln(x - r_i) = \sum_{i=1}^{n} \frac{1}{x - r_i},$$

i.e.,

$$(4.36) \qquad \frac{f'(x)}{f(x)} = \sum_{i=1}^{n} \frac{1}{x - r_i} \equiv \Omega_1.$$

Differentiating again, we have

$$(4.37) \qquad \frac{-f(x)f''(x) + f'(x)^2}{f(x)^2} = \sum_{i=1}^{n} \frac{1}{(x - r_i)^2} \equiv \Omega_2.$$

Consider the quadratic equation in y

$$(4.38) \qquad G(y) = (x - y)^2 \sum_{i=1}^{n} \frac{(\lambda - r_i)^2}{(x - r_i)^2} - (\lambda - y)^2 = 0.$$

Here λ, x are real parameters. Think of x as some approximation to one of the roots; thus, we may assume that $x \neq r_i$ for every i. Since the equation for G is quadratic in y, it will have two roots, say z_1, z_2. These roots are distinct provided $\lambda \neq x$, which we now assume. For every k with $1 \leq k \leq n$,

$$G(r_k) = (x - r_k)^2 \sum_{i=1}^{n} \frac{(\lambda - r_i)^2}{(x - r_i)^2} - (\lambda - r_k)^2 = (x - r_k)^2 \sum_{\substack{i \\ i \neq k}} \frac{(\lambda - r_i)^2}{(x - r_i)^2} > 0$$

and

$$G(x) = -(\lambda - x)^2 < 0 \quad \text{because} \quad \lambda \neq x.$$

Now assume that our initial approximation satisfies $r_k < x < r_{k+1}$ for some k with $1 \leq k \leq n - 1$. (The other cases in which $x < r_1$ or $x > r_n$ can be handled similarly.) Then by the intermediate value theorem, G vanishes at two points $z_1 = z_1(\lambda), z_2 = z_2(\lambda)$ where

$$(4.39) \qquad r_k < z_1(\lambda) < x < z_2(\lambda) < r_{k+1}.$$

Thus, we regard $z_1(\lambda), z_2(\lambda)$ as better approximations to the roots r_k, r_{k+1}. The parameter λ will be chosen to maximize $|y - x|$. It would seem that a knowledge of the roots is necessary for this procedure. However, this can be avoided, and in fact λ need not be computed explicitly.

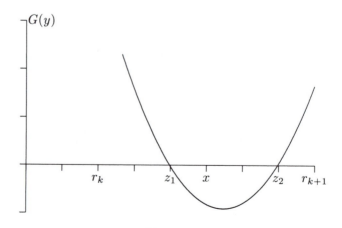

Fig. 4.1

In order to see what the optimal value of λ is, we rewrite the definition of G in terms of the new variables

$$(4.40) \qquad \alpha = \lambda - x, \quad \beta = x - y.$$

Thus,

$$(4.41) \qquad G(y) = \beta^2 \sum_{i=1}^{n} \frac{(\lambda - r_i)^2}{(x - r_i)^2} - (\alpha + \beta)^2,$$

which will be considered as a quadratic in α. To find its roots as a function of α, write

$$\frac{(\lambda - r_j)^2}{(x - r_j)^2} = \frac{(\alpha + x - r_j)^2}{(x - r_j)^2} = \frac{\alpha^2}{(x - r_j)^2} + \frac{2\alpha}{x - r_j} + 1$$

and

$$(\lambda - y)^2 = (\alpha + x - y)^2 = (\alpha + \beta)^2.$$

Therefore,

$$\sum_{i=1}^{n} \frac{(\lambda - r_i)^2}{(x - r_i)^2} = \Omega_2 \alpha^2 + 2\Omega_1 \alpha + n,$$

so that

$$(4.42) \quad \begin{aligned} 0 = G(y) &= \beta^2 \left(\Omega_2 \alpha^2 + 2\Omega_1 \alpha + n \right) - \alpha^2 - 2\beta\alpha - \beta^2 \\ &= \alpha^2 (\beta^2 \Omega_2 - 1) + 2\alpha\beta(\Omega_1 \beta - 1) + (n - 1)\beta^2. \end{aligned}$$

Notice that since λ, x are real, so is α. Thus, the discriminant must be non–negative. Now we can solve explicitly for the roots α using the quadratic formula. After a bit of consideration, you will see that the extreme values desired are just those points where the discriminant vanishes. Setting this discriminant equal to zero, we get

$$(\Omega_1 \beta - 1)^2 - (n - 1)(\beta^2 \Omega_2 - 1), \quad \text{or}$$

$$\left(\Omega_1^2 - (n - 1)\Omega_2 \right) \beta^2 - 2\Omega_1 \beta + n = 0.$$

Now just solve this explicitly by the quadratic formula to get (after some algebra)

$$(4.43) \qquad \beta = \frac{n}{\Omega_1 \pm \sqrt{(n - 1)(n\Omega_2 - \Omega_1^2)}}.$$

As usual, one chooses the sign to maximize the modulus of the denominator. The square root arising here is well–defined, since by the Schwartz inequality

$$(4.44) \qquad \Omega_1^2 = \left| \sum_{i=1}^{n} \frac{1}{x - r_i} \right|^2 \leq \left(\sum_{i=1}^{n} 1 \right) \cdot \left(\sum_{i=1}^{n} \frac{1}{(x - r_i)^2} \right) = n\Omega_2.$$

The scheme may be rewritten in the form of standard fixed–point iteration $x_{j+1} = g(x_j)$ where

$$(4.45) \qquad g(x) = x - \frac{nf(x)}{f'(x) \pm \sqrt{(n-1)^2 f'(x)^2 - n(n-1)f(x)f''(x)}}.$$

Why is the scheme always convergent in the case of real distinct roots? First, let $x = x_1$ be chosen as above: $r_k < x < r_{k+1}$. Please notice that f must retain one sign on (r_k, r_{k+1}); therefore, once we begin with a value $f(x_1)$ of either sign, that sign is preserved. Thus, we can assume that $f(x_1) > 0$. The choice of sign in the scheme (4.45) is dictated by the sign of $f'(x_1)$. Suppose for instance that $f'(x_1) > 0$. Then we choose the plus sign in the denominator of (4.45). From the definition of x_2 as $g(x_1)$ then, $x_2 < x_1$. We claim that a monotonically decreasing sequence is so obtained: $x_1 > x_2 > \cdots$. Since the sequence is bounded below by r_k, it must then converge. Passing to the limit in the scheme $x_{j+1} = g(x_j)$, we see that the limit must in fact be r_k. Of course a similar argument works if $f'(x_1) < 0$.

To establish the claim, we will show that $f'(x_2) > 0$, from which it follows that $x_3 < x_2$ (since $f(x_2) > 0$), and the induction should then be clear. From the definition of Ω_1 we have

$$\frac{f'(x_2)}{f(x_2)} = \sum_{i=1}^{n} \frac{1}{x_2 - r_i}, \qquad \frac{f'(x_1)}{f(x_1)} = \sum_{i=1}^{n} \frac{1}{x_1 - r_i}.$$

The latter sum is assumed to be positive. Since $r_k < x_2 < x_1 < r_{k+1}$, we have $r_i - x_2 > r_i - x_1$ for $i = k+1, \ldots, n$. Therefore,

$$\frac{1}{r_i - x_1} > \frac{1}{r_i - x_2} \qquad \text{for} \quad i = k+1, \ldots, n.$$

Thus,

$$\frac{f'(x_2)}{f(x_2)} = \sum_{i=1}^{k} \frac{1}{x_2 - r_i} + \sum_{i=k+1}^{n} \frac{1}{x_2 - r_i}$$

$$> \sum_{i=1}^{k} \frac{1}{x_2 - r_i} + \sum_{i=k+1}^{n} \frac{1}{x_1 - r_i}$$

$$= \sum_{i=1}^{k} \frac{1}{x_2 - r_i} + \frac{f'(x_1)}{f(x_1)} - \sum_{i=1}^{k} \frac{1}{x_1 - r_i}$$

$$> \sum_{i=1}^{k} \left(\frac{1}{x_2 - r_i} - \frac{1}{x_1 - r_i} \right)$$

$$= (x_1 - x_2) \sum_{i=1}^{k} \frac{1}{(x_2 - r_i)(x_1 - r_i)}$$

$$> 0$$

as desired.

The remaining cases ($x < r_1$ or $x > r_n$) are easily handled as follows. Suppose that $x = x_1 < r_1$. Since there are no roots of f to the left of r_1, either $f(x_1) > 0$ or $f(x_1) < 0$. Assume the former: $f(x_1) > 0$. By equation (4.36),

$$f'(x_1) = f(x_1) \cdot \sum_{i=1}^{n} \frac{1}{x_1 - r_i}.$$

Since each summand is negative, we have $f'(x_1) < 0$. We then choose the minus sign of the denominator in (4.45), and it follows that $x_1 < x_2$. Thus, again the sequence of iterates is monotonically increasing and bounded above by r_1. Passing to the limit in the definition of the scheme $x_{j+1} = g(x_j)$, we see that $x_j \to r_1$, as desired.

In order to obtain the third–order convergence, assume that $r = g(r)$ for g as above. A long computation then shows that $g'(r) = g''(r) = 0$ while $g'''(r) \neq 0$, and a third–order convergence rate follows from this.

The code that follows allows complex coefficients and is fairly lengthy; we present it now with the explanation following the listing.

```
1 /* Laguerre.c */
2
3 /*
4 LAGUERRE'S METHOD FOR A COMPLEX-COEFFICIENT POLYNOMIAL
5 f(x) = a[0]*x^n + a[1]*x^(n-1) + ...   + a[n-1]*x + a[n]
6 */
7
```

```
 8 # include <math.h>
 9 # include <stdio.h>
10 # include <stdlib.h>
11 # include <malloc.h>
12 # include "cpxarith.c"
13 # define TOL 5.0e-9
14
15 struct complex *cpxalloc(int n)
16 {     /* allocation for a complex vector */
17 struct complex *z;
18 z=(struct complex *)calloc(n,sizeof(struct complex));
19 if (!z){
20 fprintf(stderr,"could not allocate memory.");
21 exit(1);
22 }
23 return z;
24 }
25
26 struct complex cpx_horner(int n,struct complex z,\
27                          struct complex *a)
28 {          /* evaluation of a complex polynomial */
29 struct complex *b;
30 int k;
31
32         b=cpxalloc(n+1);
33
34         b[0]=a[0];
35         for (k=1;k<=n;k++)
36                 b[k]=cpxadd(a[k],cpxmult(b[k-1],z));
37         return b[n];
38 }
39
40 void cpxdeflate(int n,struct complex x,struct complex *a)
41 {                  /* deflation via complex Horner */
42         int k;
43         struct complex *b;
44         b=cpxalloc(n);
45
46         b[0]=a[0];
47         for (k=1;k<=n-1;k++){
48                 b[k]=cpxadd(a[k],cpxmult(x,b[k-1]));
49                 }
50         for (k=0;k<=n-1;k++)
```

```
51                  a[k]=b[k];
52 }
53
54 void laguerre(int N, struct complex *X, \
55          struct complex *a, double tol)
56 {
57 /* N=degree, X=initial approximation and */
58 /* returned root, a[ ] = coefficients */
59 int k,iter=0;
60 double e;
61 struct complex *p,*p1,*p2,sqr,den,temp1,temp2;
62 struct complex y,f,fp,fpp,en,en_1,z;
63
64 /* en=complex form of N, en_1 = that of N-1 */
65 en.x=(double)N;en.y=0.0;
66 en_1.x=(double)(N-1);en_1.y=0.0;
67
68 p=cpxalloc(N+1);
69 p1=cpxalloc(N);
70 p2=cpxalloc(N-1);
71
72 do
73 {
74          y=*X;
75
76          for (k=0;k<=N-2;k++){
77                  /* coefficients of f(x) */
78                  p[k]=a[k];
79
80                  /* coefficients of f'(x) */
81                  p1[k].x=(N-k)*a[k].x;
82                  p1[k].y=(N-k)*a[k].y;
83
84                  /* coefficients of f''(x) */
85                  p2[k].x=(N-k)*(N-k-1)*a[k].x;
86                  p2[k].y=(N-k)*(N-k-1)*a[k].y;
87                  }
88
89                  p[N]=a[N];
90                  p[N-1]=a[N-1];
91                  p1[N-1]=a[N-1];
92
93 /* evaluate f(X) via complex Horner, value is f */
```

```
94              f=cpx_horner(N,y,p);
95
96 /* evaluate f'(X) via complex Horner, value is fp */
97          fp=cpx_horner(N-1,y,p1);
98
99 /* evaluate f''(X) similarly, value is fpp */
100          if (N>1){
101                  fpp=cpx_horner(N-2,y,p2);
102                  }
103          else
104                  fpp.x=fpp.y=0.0;
105
106 /* denominator of iteration function */
107 temp1=cpxmult(en_1,fp);
108 temp1=cpxmult(temp1,temp1);
109
110 temp2=cpxmult(en,en_1);
111 temp2=cpxmult(temp2,f);
112 temp2=cpxmult(temp2,fpp);
113
114 temp1=cpxsub(temp1,temp2);
115 sqr=cpxsqrt(temp1);
116
117          /* choice of sign */
118          if (fp.x*sqr.x+fp.y*sqr.y<0.0)
119                  den=cpxsub(fp,sqr);
120          else
121                  den=cpxadd(fp,sqr);
122
123 temp1=cpxmult(en,f);
124 temp1=cpxdiv(temp1,den);
125 *X=cpxsub(*X,temp1);
126
127 e=cabs(cpxsub(*X,z));
128          z=*X;
129          iter++;
130
131 if (iter>100){
132 printf("Failed to converge in %d iterations\n",100);
133 exit(1);
134 }
135
136 }
```

```
137 while (e>cabs(*X)*TOL);          /* end do loop */
138 }
139
140 main()
141 {
142 struct complex *cpxalloc(int n);
143 struct complex cpx_horner(int n, struct complex z,\
144                     struct complex *a);
145 void cpxdeflate(int n,struct complex x,struct complex *a);
146 void laguerre(int n, struct complex *x, \
147                     struct complex *a, double tol);
148 double e;
149 int k,N,order;
150 struct complex *a,*aorig,*root;
151 struct complex X,minus_one;
152
153 minus_one.x=-1.0;
154 minus_one.y=0.0;
155
156 printf("\n\n");
157 printf("Enter the degree of the polynomial:  ");
158 scanf("%d",&N);
159 printf("\n\n");
160 order=N;
161
162 a=cpxalloc(N+1);
163 aorig=cpxalloc(N+1);
164 root=cpxalloc(N);
165
166 printf("\n\n");
167 for (k=0;k<=N;k++){
168 printf("Enter the real part of the coefficient\
169          of x^(%d):",N-k);
170 scanf("%lf",&aorig[k].x);
171 printf("\n");
172 printf("Enter the imag part of the coefficient\
173          of x^(%d):",N-k);
174 scanf("%lf",&aorig[k].y);
175 printf("\n\n");
176 }
177
178 for (k=0;k<=N;k++)
179 a[k]=aorig[k];
```

```
180
181 while (N>1)
182 {
183         X.x=1.000010;X.y=0.00230;
184         laguerre(N,&X,a,TOL);
185         root[N-1]=X;
186
187         cpxdeflate(N,X,a);
188         N--;
189
190 }       /* end while loop */
191
192 /* linear case */
193 root[0]=cpxmult(minus_one,cpxdiv(a[1],a[0]));
194
195 /* good approximations should now be known */
196 /* now clean up - deflation check */
197
198 for (k=0;k<=order-1;k++){
199
200 laguerre(order,&root[k],aorig,TOL);
201
202 printf("Real Part=%12.8lf\t Imag Part=%12.8lf\t \
203         |f(root)|=%2.6e\n", \
204         root[k].x, root[k].y, \
205         cabs(cpx_horner(order,root[k],aorig)));
206 }
207
208 } /* end main */
```

On lines 15–24 we write a function cpxalloc(n) which defines and initializes a block of memory for a *complex vector* of size n. This is similar to
the previous real version. Notice the include file cpxarith.c on line 12.
The function cpx_horner on lines 26–38 enables us to evaluate a complex
polynomial of degree n (with coefficients a[ ]) at a complex point z. It
too is similar to the real version. The next function, cpxdeflate, takes as
input the degree of a polynomial, its coefficients *a and a root x, and returns the coefficients of the polynomial of one less degree which is obtained
via deflation.

The laguerre function begins on line 54. As arguments it takes the
degree N of the polynomial, an approximate (complex) root X, the (complex)
coefficients *a and a stopping tolerance tol. Note that X is defined as a
pointer so that the refined root may be returned in that slot. Notice the

ampersand in the function calls on lines 184 and 200 in **main**. Repeated differentiation gives lines 80–91. Then on lines 93–104 the values of f and its first two derivatives are computed at **X**, the present iterate. On lines 117–121 the choice of sign for the radical is made, as discussed above. The rest of the code in **laguerre** is just implementing fixed–point iteration on the expression given above in (4.45).

In **main**, the degree **N** is solicited on lines 157–158; then the appropriate complex vectors are allocated on lines 162–164. Notice the definition of the integer variable **order** on line 160; this is needed since in the deflation routines, the value of **N** is decremented. The coefficients are then requested in lines 167–176. The deflation loop begins on line 181; we start with an unusual guess, for no particular reason. After the call to **laguerre** in line 184, we enter the refined root into the array **root[ ]**. Then after deflation in line 187 we redo the whole process until a linear polynomial is obtained, whose root is computed on line 193. Finally, on lines 198–200, we use these approximations and call **laguerre** again with the *original* coefficients to verify our results. This is necessary since deflation can be terribly inaccurate. Once a root satisfies the termination condition, it is printed along with the modulus of the original polynomial f at this root.

Lastly, on a UNIX machine the function **cabs** (complex absolute value) may be unavailable (although it should appear in **math.h**). If not, write it yourself: it should return a double value, and take as argument a **struct complex**, say $z = x + iy$: $|z| = \sqrt{x^2 + y^2}$. (See the code for the function **sqr** in Chapter 1).

ROMBERG INTEGRATION

Romberg integration uses extrapolation in connection with the corrected composite trapezoid rule. Given a smooth function $f(x)$, let

$$I(f) = \int_a^b f(x)\, dx$$

and set $h = \frac{b-a}{N}$ for some integer N, $f_i = f(a + ih)$. The composite trapezoid rule asserts that $I(f) \approx T_N(f) \equiv T_N$, where

$$(4.46) \qquad T_N(f) = \frac{h}{2}(f_0 + f_N) + h \sum_{i=1}^{N-1} f_i.$$

We will use the corrected composite trapezoid rule in the form

$$(4.47) \qquad I(f) = T_N + c_1 h^2 + O(h^4),$$

where $c_1 = (f'(a) - f'(b))/12$ and the error term can be expressed as $f^{(4)}(\xi) h^4 (b - a)/720$ for some intermediate point ξ. We first eliminate the dependence on f' as follows: assume that N is even and put $h \to 2h$ in this formula. Then $T_N \to T_{\frac{N}{2}}$ and from (4.47)

$$(4.48) \qquad I(f) = T_{\frac{N}{2}} + 4c_1 h^2 + O(h^4).$$

When we drop the error terms and subtract the last two results, we find that

$$(4.49) \qquad c_1 h^2 = \frac{T_N - T_{\frac{N}{2}}}{3}.$$

Substituting this back into the approximation formula (4.47) above and dropping the error term again, we compute the expression

$$(4.50) \qquad I(f) \approx T_N + c_1 h^2 = T_N + \frac{T_N - T_{\frac{N}{2}}}{3} = \frac{4T_N - T_{\frac{N}{2}}}{3} \equiv T_N^1,$$

which we expect will approximate $I(f)$ with error $O(h^4)$, that is

$$(4.51) \qquad I(f) = T_N^1 + \hat{c}_1 h^4 + o(h^4).$$

Again replace h by $2h$ so that $T_N^1 \to T_{\frac{N}{2}}^1$ to get

$$(4.52) \qquad I(f) = T_{\frac{N}{2}}^1 + 16\hat{c}_1 h^4 + o(h^4).$$

Subtracting this from (4.51) and dropping the error terms again, we get

$$(4.53) \qquad \hat{c}_1 h^4 = \frac{T_N^1 - T_{\frac{N}{2}}^1}{15}.$$

Now this is inserted in (4.51); when we drop the error term we now find

$$(4.54) \qquad I(f) \approx T_N^1 + \hat{c}_1 h^4 = T_N^1 + \frac{T_N^1 - T_{\frac{N}{2}}^1}{15} \equiv T_N^2.$$

We can expect this to be $O(h^6)$–accurate, i.e.,

$$I(f) = T_N^2 + c_2 h^6 + o(h^6), \quad \text{etc.}$$

Given an integer N in the form $N = 2^\nu$ $(\nu = 1, 2, \ldots)$, this process can be repeated to generate a sequence via

$$(4.55) \qquad T_N^\nu \equiv T_N^{\nu-1} + \frac{T_N^{\nu-1} - T_{\frac{N}{2}}^{\nu-1}}{4^\nu - 1},$$

which should be accurate up to order $h^{2\nu+2}$. You will see this formula in lines 27–28 below. An additional simplification results from the following easily derived identity in which N is to be even:

$$T_N = \frac{1}{2}T_{\frac{N}{2}} + h\sum_{i=1}^{\frac{N}{2}} f\left(a + (2i-1)h\right).$$

This formula appears on lines 23–25 in the code below.

The following code implements this procedure.

```
 1 /*  Romberg.c  Romberg Integration */
 2
 3 # include <math.h>
 4 # include <stdio.h>
 5 # define PI (3.141592653589793)
 6
 7 double f(double x)
 8 {
 9 return (sin(x)*sin(x)/x);
10 }
11
12 double romberg(double a,double b,double (*func_ptr)())
13 {
14 int i,k;
15 double h=b-a,s=0.0;
16 double t[9][9];
17
18 t[0][0]=h*((*func_ptr)(a)+(*func_ptr)(b))/2.0;
19
20 for (k=1;k<=8;k++){
21         h /= 2.0;
22         s  = 0.0;
23         for (i=1;i<=(int)pow(2.0,(double)(k-1));i++)
24              s += (h*(*func_ptr)(a+h*(2.0*i-1.0)));
25              t[k][0]=(0.5)*t[k-1][0]+s;
26         for(i=1;i<=k;i++)
27                 t[k][i]=t[k][i-1]+(t[k][i-1]-t[k-1][i-1])\
28                 /(-1.0+pow(4.0,(double)i));
29 }
30 return (t[8][8]);
31 }
32
33 main()
```

```
34 {
35 double a=1.0;                /* left end-point */
36 double b=3.0;                /* right end-point */
37
38 double f(double x);          /* function prototype */
39 double (*func_ptr)()=f; /* function pointer */
40 double romberg(double a,double b,double (*func_ptr) ());
41
42 printf("Value of integral = %12.10lf\n", \
43         romberg(a,b,func_ptr));
44 }
```

The main program is quite short and is set up to estimate

$$\int_1^3 \frac{\sin(x)^2}{x} \, dx.$$

It simply calls the routine **romberg** with arguments equal to the integration limits and a function pointer pointing to the integrand f. Once we have the initial (crude) trapezoidal rule approximation to the integral, we extrapolate eight times as above. You may wish to add an integer argument (replacing the eight above) to this code so that more general intervals and integrands f may be handled. Periodic integrands may cause trouble in Romberg integration; if you need to estimate the integral of such a function over one period, use the trapezoid rule (cf. [IK], p. 340).

FOURIER COEFFICIENTS

We have already been introduced to Gaussian integration, a true gem. Given a smooth function $F(\theta)$, consider the Fourier–coefficient integrals

$$(4.56) \qquad S_n = \int_0^\pi F(\theta) \sin n\theta \, d\theta, \qquad C_n = \int_0^\pi F(\theta) \cos n\theta \, d\theta.$$

One first works out the approximations for $n = 1$. For example,

$$(4.57) \qquad \int_0^\pi F(\theta) \sin \theta \, d\theta = F(\frac{\pi}{4} + \alpha) + F(\frac{3\pi}{4} - \alpha) + \frac{10 - \pi^2}{6} F^{(4)}(\xi)$$

for some point $\xi \in [0, \pi]$. Here

$$(4.58) \qquad \alpha = \frac{\pi}{2} \left(\frac{1}{2} - \sqrt{1 - \frac{8}{\pi^2}} \right) \approx 0.101730773307545.$$

This will be derived by a direct (i.e., algebraic) method; cf. [HI]. Consider S_1 and write

(4.59) $S_1 = w_1 F(x_1) + w_2 F(x_2) + E$

where E is the error. We seek the four unknowns w_1, w_2, x_1, x_2 so that this formula will be exact on all polynomials of degree ≤ 3 (this is the "Gaussian" case). Thus, substituting $F(x) = x^k$ $(k = 0, 1, 2, 3)$ and $E = 0$ for these four cases, we get the system of equations

(4.60)
$$w_1 + w_2 = \int_0^\pi x^0 \sin x \, dx = 2$$
$$w_1 x_1 + w_2 x_2 = \int_0^\pi x^1 \sin x \, dx = \pi$$
$$w_1 x_1^2 + w_2 x_2^2 = \int_0^\pi x^2 \sin x \, dx = \pi^2 - 4$$
$$w_1 x_1^3 + w_2 x_2^3 = \int_0^\pi x^3 \sin x \, dx = \pi^3 - 6\pi.$$

This system is linear in w_1, w_2 but nonlinear in x_1, x_2. Nevertheless it can be solved explicitly via an algebraic trick (cf. [HI]); the results are that $w_1 = w_2 = 1$ and

$$x_1 = \frac{\pi}{4} + \alpha; \quad x_2 = \frac{3\pi}{4} - \alpha,$$

where α is given as above in (4.58).

In order to treat a general integral S_n using the result for S_1, we write

(4.61) $$S_n = \int_0^\pi F(\theta) \sin n\theta \, d\theta$$
$$= \sum_{k=0}^{n-1} \int_{\frac{k\pi}{n}}^{\frac{(k+1)\pi}{n}} F(\theta) \sin n\theta \, d\theta$$
$$= \frac{1}{n} \sum_{k=0}^{n-1} \int_{k\pi}^{(k+1)\pi} F\left(\frac{x}{n}\right) \sin x \, dx$$
$$= \frac{1}{n} \sum_{k=0}^{n-1} \int_0^\pi F\left(\frac{x' + k\pi}{n}\right) \sin(x' + k\pi) \, dx'$$
$$= \frac{1}{n} \sum_{k=0}^{n-1} (-1)^k \int_0^\pi F\left(\frac{x + k\pi}{n}\right) \sin x \, dx$$

to which we can apply the case $n = 1$. The result is

(4.62) $$S_n = \frac{1}{n} \sum_{k=0}^{n-1} (-1)^k \left[F\left(\frac{\frac{\pi}{4} + \alpha + k\pi}{n}\right) + F\left(\frac{\frac{3\pi}{4} - \alpha + k\pi}{n}\right) \right] + E,$$

where for the error E we have

(4.63)
$$E = \frac{10 - \pi^2}{6} \frac{1}{n^5} \sum_{k=0}^{n-1} (-1)^k F^{(4)} \left(\frac{\xi_k}{n} \right)$$

for some points $\xi_k \in (k\pi, (k+1)\pi)$.

For the cosine integral we define

$$\beta = \frac{\sqrt{3\pi^2 - 24}}{2} - \frac{3\pi}{8} \approx 0.006049410017551.$$

This version is not trivial to derive since the cos function changes sign at the midpoint of the interval. Nevertheless the analogous result can be written as

$$C_n = \int_0^\pi F(\theta) \cos n\theta \, d\theta$$

$$= \frac{1}{n(\frac{3\pi}{8} + \beta)} \sum_{k=0}^{n-1} (-1)^k \left[F \left(\frac{\frac{\pi}{8} - \beta + k\pi}{n} \right) - F \left(\frac{\frac{7\pi}{8} + \beta + k\pi}{n} \right) \right] + E,$$

where for a constant $\kappa = (336 - \pi^2(24 + \pi^2))/240 \approx 0.007168347249387$

$$E = -\frac{\kappa}{n^6} \sum_{k=0}^{n-1} (-1)^k F^{(5)} \left(\frac{\xi_k}{n} \right)$$

for some points $\xi_k \in (k\pi, (k+1)\pi)$.

We see that these approximations should be very good for large n, provided the fourth (or fifth) derivative remains under control.

The code below is a straightforward implementation of this as a C function. The last two pointer arguments contain upon return the values of the integrals. A driver routine is not included since it would be the same as that for `romberg.c` given above. One need only write a C function defining the integrand $F(x)$ and then in `main` define and initialize a function pointer which points to F (here PI $\approx \pi$):

```
1 /* trigint.c */
2
3 void trig_integral(int n, double (*func_ptr)(), \
4                         double *c, double *s)
5 {
6 /* returns integrals of (func_ptr)*sin nx (or cos nx) */
7 /* over [0,PI] */
8
```

```
 9 int j;
10 double sums=0.0,sumc=0.0;
11 double alpha=0.5*PI*(0.5-sqrt(1.0-8.0/(PI*PI)));
12 double beta=0.5*sqrt(3.0*PI*PI-24.0)-3.0*PI/8.0;
13
14 for (j=0;j<=n-1;j++){
15 sums += (cos(j*PI)*((*func_ptr)(((j+0.25)*PI+alpha)/n)+\
16              (*func_ptr)(((j+0.75)*PI-alpha)/n)));
17
18 sumc += (cos(j*PI)*((*func_ptr)(((j+1.0/8.0)*PI-beta)/n)-\
19              (*func_ptr)(((j+7.0/8.0)*PI+beta)/n)));
20
21          }
22          sums /= (double)n;
23          sumc /= ((double)n*(3.0*PI/8.0+beta));
24          *s = sums;
25          *c = sumc;
26 }
```

GAUSS–LAGUERRE INTEGRATION

Please recall from Chapter 1 the discussion of Gaussian integration. Briefly, we are given a weight function $w(x)$ on a (possibly infinite) interval (a, b), i.e., $w(x)$ is to be nonnegative and integrable on this interval. In Gaussian quadrature, an approximation of the form

$$(4.64) \qquad I(g) \equiv \int_a^b w(x)g(x)\,dx \approx w_1 g(x_1) + \cdots + w_m g(x_m)$$

is sought which will be as accurate as possible.

The $\{x_k\}$, the *nodes*, are the m zeroes of the orthogonal (with respect to the function $w(x)$) polynomial $\phi_m(x)$ of degree m; the $\{w_k\}$ are called the *weights*. We consider here a special case, that of *Gauss–Laguerre* integration, for which $(a, b) = (0, \infty)$ and $w(x) = \exp(-x)$.

Now we specify the relevant information on Laguerre polynomials, which can be found in any book on special functions (cf. [LB], [AS] or [MOS]). The Laguerre polynomials $L_n(x)$ are defined by

$$(4.65) \qquad L_n(x) = \frac{e^x}{n!} \frac{d^n}{dx^n} \left(x^n e^{-x} \right).$$

Thus, $L_0(x) = 1$, $L_1(x) = 1 - x$, etc. The standard recursions are

$$(4.66) \quad n L_n(x) = (2n - 1 - x)L_{n-1}(x) - (n - 1)L_{n-2}(x) \qquad (n \geq 2),$$

(4.67) $xL_n'(x) = nL_n(x) - nL_{n-1}(x)$ $(n \geq 2)$.

Equivalently,

(4.68) $$L_n(x) = n! \sum_{k=0}^{n} \frac{(-1)^k x^k}{k!^2(n-k)!}.$$

When $\{x_i\}$ are the m zeroes of $L_m(x)$, we have

(4.69) $x_i L_m'(x_i) = -mL_{m-1}(x_i)$,

and a formula for the weights is

(4.70) $$w_i = \frac{x_i}{m^2(L_{m-1}(x_i))^2}.$$

See any numerical analysis book, e.g., [HI], for details. (One must be aware of different normalizing conventions; the Laguerre polynomial of degree n in [HI] differs from those in [AS], [MOS] by a factor of $n!$).

In the following program **gausslag.c** we implement this for ten nodes or less. Recall that from the error formula given in Chapter 1, the use of ten nodes produces in the error term a derivative of g of order 20! It is unlikely that higher derivatives would be known or that their use would be desirable.

On lines 21–36 we write a function **lagpoly** which evaluates L_n at the point x according to a recursion from [AS], p. 789. This recursion sums the power form of the polynomial from (4.68); notice that it runs *backward*, for accuracy considerations. The function **gausslag**, beginning on line 38, returns the nodes in **x[ ]** and the weights in **w[ ]**. We need to begin with rather good approximations to the zeroes of each $L_n(x)$. This asymptotic development, taken from [AS], appears on lines 48–54; these values are called **z**. Then, with these initial approximations in hand, we use Newton's method in a **do loop** to refine these zeroes on lines 56–65. The computation of the weights from (4.70) is performed on lines 68–72. The restriction to ten nodes is essentially due to the finicky nature of Newton's method as applied in this case. The asymptotic form of the zeroes given above is sufficiently accurate for degrees not exceeding six. For $7 \leq n \leq 10$ the initial approximation needs to be taken slightly greater, as we see on line 54.

The function **gausquad** simply computes the above general Gaussian approximation. As you see, it can be used for any Gaussian formula; we need pass it only the appropriate nodes and weights. The code is set up to estimate the integral

$$I(g) = \int_0^\infty \sin(x) \exp(-x)\, dx,$$

whose exact value is 0.5. After prompting for the desired number of nodes, the nodes and weights are printed out, as well as the approximate value of the integral. Here is the full listing:

```
 1 /*  Gausslag.c */
 2
 3 /*
 4 Gauss-Laguerre Integration.
 5 Computes the integral of exp(-x)*g(x) over (0, infinity).
 6 */
 7
 8 # include <stdlib.h>
 9 # include <malloc.h>
10 # include <math.h>
11 # include <stdio.h>
12 # include "memalloc.c"
13 # include "memalloc.h"
14 # define PI 3.141592653589793
15
16 double g(double x)
17 {
18            return (sin(x));
19 }
20
21 double lagpoly(int n, double x)
22 {
23 /* evaluates the Laguerre polynomial of order n */
24 /* at x via the explicit finite sum */
25 /* see [AS], p.  789 */
26
27 int j;
28 double *l;
29 l=vecalloc(0,n);
30
31 l[n]=1.0;
32 for (j=n;j>=1;j--) {
33            l[j-1]=1.0-(n-j+1.0)*x*l[j]/((double)(j*j));
34            }
35 return l[0];
36 }
37
38 void gausslag(int n, double *x, double *w)
39 {
```

```
40 /* returns the nodes and weights in the arrays */
41 /* x,w resp.  for an n-point formula */
42
43 int i;
44 double z1,z,ln,ln_minus1,lprime;
45 double j0,temp,tau=n+.5;
46
47 for (i=1;i<=n;i++){
48 /* z is an asymptotic zero of L_n(x) */
49 /* cf.  [AS], p.  787 */
50
51 /* j0 is approximately the i'th positive zero of J_0(x) */
52 j0=2.4048255577+(i-1)*PI;
53 z=(j0*j0/(4.0*tau))*(1.0+(j0*j0-2.0)/(48.0*tau*tau));
54 if (n>6 && i>n-2) z += 2.0;
55
56 do {
57         ln=lagpoly(n,z);
58         ln_minus1=lagpoly(n-1,z);
59
60 /* lprime=derivative of L_n(z) via std.  recursion */
61         lprime=n*(ln-ln_minus1)/z;
62         z1=z;
63         /* Newton iteration */
64         z=z1-ln/lprime;
65       } while (fabs(z-z1) > fabs(z)*5.0e-12);
66         x[i]=z;
67
68         /* compute weights */
69         temp=1.0/(n*lagpoly(n-1,x[i]));
70         temp *= temp;
71         temp *= x[i];
72         w[i]=temp;
73         }
74 }
75
76 double gausquad(int m, double *x, double *w,\
77         double (*func_ptr)())
78 /*
79 returns the integral of exp(-x)*g(x) over (0, infinity)
80 via Gauss-Laguerre (m-point) quadrature.
81 This function works for any Gaussian method by
82 feeding it appropriate arrays x[ ] and w[ ].
```

```
83 indices run from 1 to m.
84 */
85
86 {
87         double s=0.0;
88         int i;
89         for (i=1;i<=m;i++)
90                 s += ((*func_ptr)(x[i])*w[i]);
91         return s;
92 }
93
94 main()
95 {
96 int i,m;
97
98 double g(double x);
99 double (*func_ptr)()=g;
100
101 double *x,*w;
102 double gausquad(int m, double *x, double *w, \
103                 double (*func_ptr)());
104 void gausslag(int n, double *x, double *w);
105 double lagpoly(int n, double x);
106
107 printf("\n");
108 printf("Enter the number of nodes m (m=2,3,...,10):   ");
109 scanf("%d",&m);
110
111 printf("\n");
112
113 x=vecalloc(1,m);
114 w=vecalloc(1,m);
115
116 gausslag(m,x,w);
117
118 for (i=1;i<=m;i++)
119 printf("x[%d]= %2.12lf\t w[%d]= %1.12e\n",i,x[i],i,w[i]);
120
121 printf("\n");
122
123 printf("Using %d nodes:     Integral= %12.10lf\n", \
124         m,gausquad(m,x,w,func_ptr));
125
```

126 }   /* end main */

As an exercise, write the corresponding program for Gauss–Hermite quadrature in which $(a, b) = (-\infty, \infty)$ and $w(x) = \exp(-x^2)$. The *Hermite polynomials* $H_n(x)$ are defined by

$$H_n(x) = (-1)^n e^{x^2} \frac{d^n}{dx^n} \left(e^{-x^2} \right).$$

Thus, $H_0(x) = 1$, $H_1(x) = 2x$, etc. The standard recursion is

$$H_n(x) = 2x H_{n-1}(x) - 2(n-1) H_{n-2}(x) \quad (n \geq 2).$$

When $\{x_i\}$ are the m zeroes of $H_m(x)$, we have

$$H'_m(x_i) = 2m H_{m-1}(x_i),$$

and a formula for the weights is

$$w_i = \frac{2^{m+1} m! \sqrt{\pi}}{(H'_m(x_i))^2}.$$

Please consult [AS] for the asymptotic approximation of the zeroes of the Hermite polynomials, etc., and be aware of the differing normalization conventions. A related recent publication is [BA3].

EIGENVALUES OF A SYMMETRIC MATRIX

A fascinating problem this is indeed. A major part of the computational background was worked out by J. H. Wilkinson, whose text [WI] is the "bible" for study in this area. Recall that the *eigenvalues* λ of a square matrix A of order n are defined by $\det(A - \lambda I) = 0$. This then is a polynomial of degree n, whose roots we seek. Where does this come from? A (possibly) complex number λ is an *eigenvalue* of A if there exists a non–zero vector x (an *eigenvector*) such that $Ax = \lambda x$. This is the same as $(A - \lambda I)x = 0$. If the matrix here were invertible, we could left multiply by its inverse and obtain $x = 0$, a contradiction. Hence $A - \lambda I$ must be singular, and then you know from linear algebra that the determinant of this matrix must vanish. You *never* use Cramer's Rule to evaluate a determinant; the number of operations required is astronomical.

Fortunately *symmetric* matrices often arise in the applications. These are matrices A whose entries satisfy $a_{ij} = a_{ji}$; it is a simple theorem that all eigenvalues are then *real*. Nonsymmetric A's can have complex eigenvalues. Two matrices A and B are called *similar* if there is a nonsingular matrix

P such that $P^{-1}AP = B$. It is crucial in the modern theory of eigenvalue computation to know that *similar matrices have the same eigenvalues*. If you know the theorem that the determinant of a product equals the product of the determinants, the proof is simple:

$$(4.71) \qquad \det(B - \lambda I) = \det(P^{-1}AP - \lambda I)$$
$$= \det(P^{-1}(A - \lambda I)P)$$
$$= \det P^{-1} \cdot \det(A - \lambda I) \cdot \det P$$
$$= \det(A - \lambda I).$$

No doubt you also know the theorem which tells you when a matrix A can be diagonalized. It says that if the eigenvectors of A span R^n, then $P^{-1}AP = \mathrm{diag}(\lambda_i)$ where the λ_i's are the eigenvalues of A, and the columns of P are the eigenvectors of A. Evidently this will not be very useful in computational studies, although theoretically it is most important.

Recall also that a (real) matrix P is called *orthogonal* if its inverse equals its transpose. Well–known examples are *rotations*, which in two dimensions have the form

$$(4.72) \qquad P = \begin{pmatrix} \sin\theta & \cos\theta \\ \cos\theta & -\sin\theta \end{pmatrix}.$$

Please check directly that $P^T \cdot P = P \cdot P^T = I$. We will also need one crude estimate on the eigenvalues. For any matrix A, recall that the (matrix) norm of A is defined by

$$(4.73) \qquad ||A|| = \sup_{||x||=1} ||Ax|| = \sup_{x \neq 0} \frac{||Ax||}{||x||},$$

where $|| \cdot ||$ is any vector norm. (Thus, for example,

$$||x||_\infty = \max_{1 \leq i \leq n} |x_i|, \quad ||x||_2 = (\sum_{i=1}^{n} x_i^2)^{1/2},$$

etc.) Then any eigenvalue λ satisfies $|\lambda| \leq ||A||$. To see this, recall that the definition of an eigenvector x $(Ax = \lambda x)$ requires that $x \neq 0$. Thus, we have

$$(4.74) \qquad |\lambda| \cdot ||x|| = ||Ax|| \leq ||A|| \cdot ||x||,$$

so that $|\lambda| \leq ||A||$ follows. Most of the powerful modern methods rely on orthogonal transformations. This is true for the classical method of Jacobi, as well as for the "best" of all presently known algorithms, the QR method, which we will study later. We begin with the method of Givens (see [GvL], [WI]) which, while not the fastest of all, is perfect for small to moderate symmetric matrices and allows one to pick out in order the exact number of eigenvalues required (e.g., the two largest, etc.)

One begins with a preliminary reduction to a "canonical" form. The form desired is *tridiagonal*. It is a theorem that any symmetric square matrix A is constructively orthogonally equivalent to a tridiagonal matrix. What does this mean? It means we can find (on the computer and analytically) an orthogonal matrix P such that $P^T A P$ is tridiagonal and hence has the same eigenvalues as our original A. Such a reduction cuts down the work immensely. How do we find P? There are two well–known methods, that of Givens and that of Householder. The latter seems preferable in most situations but is a bit more complicated than that of Givens. We will use the Givens scheme in what follows.

Assume for the time being that we have achieved this reduction to tridiagonal form. How then do we calculate the eigenvalues of A? We will use *Sturm Sequences* and their implementation due to Givens. Basically these compute via a recursion the determinant of a tridiagonal matrix. Consider a tridiagonal matrix (called A again) of the form

$$(4.75) \qquad A = \begin{pmatrix} \alpha_1 & \beta_2 & 0 & 0 & \cdots & 0 \\ \beta_2 & \alpha_2 & \beta_3 & 0 & \cdots & 0 \\ 0 & \beta_3 & \alpha_3 & \beta_4 & \cdots & 0 \\ \vdots & \vdots & \vdots & \vdots & \cdots & \beta_n \\ 0 & 0 & 0 & 0 & \cdots & \alpha_n \end{pmatrix}.$$

Consider the sequence of functions defined by $p_0(\lambda) = 1$, $p_1(\lambda) = \alpha_1 - \lambda$, and

$$(4.76) \qquad p_i(\lambda) = (\alpha_i - \lambda)p_{i-1}(\lambda) - \beta_i^2 p_{i-2}(\lambda) \quad \text{for} \quad i = 2, 3, \ldots, n.$$

Then you can check that $p_j(\lambda)$ is the determinant of the leading principal minor of order j of $A - \lambda I$. Thus, its zeroes are the eigenvalues of the leading principal submatrix A_j of order j. Hence the eigenvalues of A are the zeroes of $p_n(\lambda)$.

Using the Courant Minimax theorem, we can show that the eigenvalues of A_j weakly separate those of A_{j+1}. Then one shows that if all $\beta_i \neq 0$, we have strict separation. The latter statement is easy to establish: if μ were a zero of both $p_j(\lambda)$ and $p_{j-1}(\lambda)$, then putting $i = j$ and $\lambda = \mu$ in the recursion (4.76), we see that $p_{j-2}(\mu) = 0$ since $\beta_j \neq 0$. Running the recursion all the way back to the beginning, we conclude that $p_0(\mu) = 0$, a contradiction. Another related result is that if a symmetric matrix A has an eigenvalue of multiplicity k, then the tridiagonal matrix resulting from orthogonal reduction must have at least $k - 1$ vanishing super–diagonal elements. (Please note that the converse is not true). This statement is used as follows: if all $\beta_i \neq 0$, then A has only simple eigenvalues.

Here is a statement of the Sturm Separation Theorem, due to Givens:

Let A be symmetric tridiagonal, and let $\{p_i(\lambda)\}_{i=0}^n$ be as above in (4.76). Assume all $\beta_i \neq 0$, and let $\mu \in R$. Define $s(\mu)$ by: $s(\mu) =$ the number of agreements in sign of consecutive members of the sequence $\{p_0(\mu), p_1(\mu), \ldots, p_n(\mu)\}$ with the convention that if $p_j(\mu) = 0$, $\operatorname{sgn} p_j(\mu) = -\operatorname{sgn} p_{j-1}(\mu)$. Then $s(\mu)$ is equal to the number of eigenvalues of A which are greater than μ.

In practice the restriction to simple eigenvalues is not too severe, since the tridiagonal reduction will rarely give off-diagonal elements β_i which are *exactly zero*. Furthermore, if some β_i were to vanish, we could decompose the matrix into smaller blocks. As an example of the phrase "agreements in sign," suppose that $n = 4$ and that the signs of the Sturm sequence polynomials appear as $\{+, +, -, +, +\}$. Then there are two agreements in sign.

Here is how we use this theorem. Let A be symmetric with eigenvalues $\lambda_1 \geq \lambda_2 \geq \ldots \geq \lambda_n$. Suppose you wish to locate the kth eigenvalue in decreasing order λ_k. We begin with an interval $[a_0, b_0]$ which contains all of the eigenvalues and which will be continually bisected. From above, we can use $b_0 = -a_0 = \|A\|$. Thus, $s(a_0)$, the number of eigenvalues greater than a_0, is at least as large as k; similarly $s(b_0) < k$. Next we perform a bisection loop over an index j, $1 \leq j \leq N$, which will locate $\lambda_k \in (a_N, b_N)$ with $b_N - a_N = \frac{b_0 - a_0}{2^N}$:

compute $c_j = \frac{1}{2}(a_{j-1} + b_{j-1})$
compute $\{p_0(c_j), p_1(c_j), \ldots, p_n(c_j)\}$ to determine $s(c_j)$
if $s(c_j) \geq k$, set $a_j = c_j$, $b_j = b_{j-1}$; else set $a_j = a_{j-1}$, $b_j = c_j$

As you see, the scheme is computationally simple, once the tridiagonal reduction has been achieved. In the notation of the tridiagonal matrix displayed above, we see that we may choose $\|A\|_\infty = \max_{1 \leq i \leq n}\{|\beta_i| + |\alpha_i| + |\beta_{i+1}|\}$. Actually we take below the initial interval $[a_0, b_0]$ slightly bigger, since there may be an eigenvalue exactly equal to the computed norm of A.

Here are some of the drawbacks. Firstly, it applies only to symmetric matrices and does not return any of the eigenvectors. (While these may also be computed via a recursion, it is not advisable to do so; see [WI]). Secondly, it is rather slow, although the bisection computation may be replaced by a faster algorithm. Lastly, the values of the polynomial elements of the Sturm Sequence may grow terribly quickly with the dimension n of the matrix. Unless you scale these values, you might only be able to use this on matrices of moderate order.

It now remains only to discuss the Givens reduction to tridiagonal form. We illustrate on a 4×4 symmetric matrix A. Consider an orthogonal 4×4 matrix T_1^T which is equal to the identity except in four slots, e.g.,

$$(4.77) \qquad T_1^T = \begin{pmatrix} 1 & 0 & 0 & 0 \\ 0 & c & s & 0 \\ 0 & -s & c & 0 \\ 0 & 0 & 0 & 1 \end{pmatrix}.$$

(The "c" stands for cos, "s" for sin.) T_1^T is called a *rotation in the 2–3 plane*. We form the product $T_1^T A$ with the goal of forcing its 3–1 element to vanish:

$$(4.78) \qquad (T_1^T A)_{31} = (\text{3rd row of } \ T_1^T) \cdot (\text{1st col of } \ A)$$
$$= -s a_{21} + c a_{31}.$$

We choose

$$(4.79) \qquad s = \frac{a_{31}}{\sqrt{a_{21}^2 + a_{31}^2}}, \quad c = \frac{a_{21}}{\sqrt{a_{21}^2 + a_{31}^2}}.$$

Then $(T_1^T A)_{31} = 0$.

In order to keep the eigenvalues invariant, we complete the transformation by right–multiplying by T_1, i.e., our new matrix is $A_1 \equiv T_1^T A T_1$. We need to verify that the 3–1 element remains zero after this right multiplication. As above, we compute

$$(4.80) \qquad (T_1^T A T_1)_{31} = (\text{3rd row of } \ T_1^T A) \cdot (\text{1st col of } \ T_1)$$
$$= (T_1^T A)_{31}$$
$$= 0.$$

Thus, after the first step we have in $A_1 = T_1^T A T_1$ a symmetric matrix with the same eigenvalues as A with the property that its 3–1 element vanishes.

Now we write the elements of A_1 as a_{ij} (with standard abuse of notation) and consider another similarity transformation $A_1 \to A_2 \equiv T_2^T A_1 T_2$ with the goal of forcing its 4–1 element to vanish. Naturally this must be accomplished without disturbing the zero we have already achieved in the 3–1 slot. For T_2^T we take a rotation in the 2–4 plane:

$$(4.81) \qquad T_2^T = \begin{pmatrix} 1 & 0 & 0 & 0 \\ 0 & c & 0 & s \\ 0 & 0 & 1 & 0 \\ 0 & -s & 0 & c \end{pmatrix}.$$

We compute as above that

$$(4.82) \qquad (T_2^T A_1)_{41} = (\text{4th row of } T_2^T) \cdot (\text{1st col of } A_1)$$
$$= -s a_{21} + c a_{41}.$$

This vanishes if we choose

$$(4.83) \qquad s = \frac{a_{41}}{\sqrt{a_{41}^2 + a_{21}^2}}, \quad c = \frac{a_{21}}{\sqrt{a_{41}^2 + a_{21}^2}}.$$

Then we notice as before that right–multiplication by T_2 does not disturb the zero just achieved:

$$(4.84) \qquad (T_2^T A_1 T_2)_{41} = (\text{4th row of } T_2^T A_1) \cdot (\text{1st col of } T_2)$$
$$= (T_2^T A_1)_{41}$$
$$= 0.$$

Now after two steps, we have in $A_2 = T_2^T A_1 T_2$ a symmetric matrix with the same eigenvalues as A with the property that its 3–1 and 4–1 elements are zero. (The 3–1 element remains zero because the third row of T_2^T is the same as that of the identity.) Thus, the first column (and therefore the first row, too) has the desired tridiagonal form.

The last step is now probably clear: we use a rotation T_3^T in the 3–4 plane to perform a similarity transformation on A_2. Thus, consider $A_3 \equiv T_3^T A_2 T_3$ where

$$(4.85) \qquad T_3^T = \begin{pmatrix} 1 & 0 & 0 & 0 \\ 0 & 1 & 0 & 0 \\ 0 & 0 & c & s \\ 0 & 0 & -s & c \end{pmatrix}.$$

The goal is to force the 4–2 element of A_3 to vanish; you can easily check that the choices (writing the elements of A_2 as a_{ij} again)

$$(4.86) \qquad s = \frac{a_{42}}{\sqrt{a_{42}^2 + a_{32}^2}}, \quad c = \frac{a_{32}}{\sqrt{a_{42}^2 + a_{32}^2}}$$

do the job.

Finally, we have in A_3 a symmetric tridiagonal matrix which has the same eigenvalues as A, because

$$(4.87) \qquad A_3 = T_3^T A_2 T_3 = T_3^T T_2^T A_1 T_2 T_3 = T_3^T T_2^T T_1^T A T_1 T_2 T_3.$$

For a general $n \times n$ matrix A the procedure may be outlined as follows:

for $r = 1$ to $n - 2$ {
for $i = r + 2$ to n {
compute sqr $= \sqrt{a_{r+1,r}^2 + a_{r,i}^2}$
compute $c = a_{r+1,r}/\text{sqr}$, $\quad s = a_{r,i}/\text{sqr}$
compute $A \to T^T A T$
} }

Here by the matrix T^T we mean the $n \times n$ matrix equal to the identity except in four slots where

$$T^T_{r+1,r+1} = c, \quad T^T_{r+1,i} = s, \quad T^T_{i,r+1} = -s, \quad T^T_{i,i} = c.$$

Now we present the full code for study, with the explanation following.

```
 1 /* Sturm.c */
 2 /* Eigenvalues of symmetric matrices - Sturm Sequences */
 3 # include <stdlib.h>
 4 # include <math.h>
 5 # include <malloc.h>
 6 # include <stdio.h>
 7 # include "memalloc.c"
 8 # include "memalloc.h"
 9 # define MAX(a,b) ((a)>=(b) ?  (a) :  (b))
10
11 double sgn(double x)
12 {
13         if (x>0.0)
14                 return 1.0;
15         else if (x<0.0)
16                 return -1.0;
17         else
18                 return 0.0;
19 }
20
21 double maxnorm1(int m, double **a)
22
23 /* RETURNS THE MAXIMUM ABSOLUTE ROW SUM OF A[][] */
24 /* INDICES RUN FROM 1 TO m */
25
26 {
27 int k,j;
28 double s,z;
29 double *x;
30 x=vecalloc(1,m);
```

```
31
32          for (k=1;k<=m;k++){
33                  s=0.0;
34                  for (j=1;j<=m;j++)
35                  s += fabs(a[k][j]);
36                  x[k]=s;
37                  }
38
39          z=MAX(fabs(x[1]),fabs(x[2]));
40          for (k=3;k<=m;k++)
41                  z=MAX(fabs(x[k]),z);
42          return z;
43 }
44
45 void givens(int n, double **a)
46
47 /* REDUCES THE MATRIX a[][] TO TRIDIAGONAL FORM */
48 /* INDICES RUN FROM 1 TO n */
49 {
50 int i,j,k;
51 double c,s,x,y,h1,h2;
52
53 for (k=1;k<=n-2;k++){
54 for (i=k+2;i<=n;i++){
55 y=a[k+1][k]*a[k+1][k]+a[i][k]*a[i][k];
56 if (y<5.0e-20){
57          c=1.0;s=0.0;x=sqrt(y);}
58 else{
59 if (fabs(a[k+1][k])<=fabs(a[i][k])){
60 x=fabs(a[i][k])*sqrt(1.0+a[k+1][k]*a[k+1][k]\
61                         /(a[i][k]*a[i][k]));}
62 else{
63 x=fabs(a[k+1][k])*sqrt(1.0+a[i][k]*a[i][k]\
64                         /(a[k+1][k]*a[k+1][k]));}
65
66          c=a[k+1][k]/x;
67          s=a[i][k]/x;
68 }
69
70                      a[k+1][k]=x;
71                      a[i][k]=0.0;
72
73 for (j=k+1;j<=n;j++){
```

```
74              h1=c*a[k+1][j]+s*a[i][j];
75              h2=-s*a[k+1][j]+c*a[i][j];
76              a[k+1][j]=h1;
77              a[i][j]=h2;
78              }
79
80  for (j=1;j<=n;j++){
81              h1=c*a[j][k+1]+s*a[j][i];
82              h2=-s*a[j][k+1]+c*a[j][i];
83              a[j][k+1]=h1;
84              a[j][i]=h2;
85              }
86
87                          }           /* end i-loop */
88                      }           /* end k-loop */
89
90  for (i=3;i<=n;i++){ /* set lower triangle to zero */
91          for (j=1;j<=i-2;j++)
92                  a[i][j]=0.0;
93                  }
94
95  for (i=1;i<=n-2;i++){     /* full tridiagonal form */
96          for (j=i+2;j<=n;j++)
97                  a[i][j]=0.0;
98                  }
99
100 }
101
102 void sturm(int N, int num_ev, double alpha, double beta,\
103             double **a, double *lambda)
104 /* num_ev=number of eigenvalues returned, starting with */
105 /* the largest; N=order of matrix */
106 {
107 int j,k,v;
108 double c,sign;
109 double alphaold=alpha;
110 double betaold=beta;
111 double *y;
112 y=vecalloc(1,N);
113
114 for (k=1;k<=num_ev;k++){
115
116         do{
```

```
117                         c=(alpha+beta)/2.0;
118                         y[1]=a[1][1]-c;
119                         y[2]=(a[2][2]-c)*y[1]-a[2][1]*a[2][1];
120
121                         for (j=3;j<=N;j++){
122                            y[j]=(a[j][j]-c)*y[j-1]-a[j][j-1]*\
123                                   a[j][j-1]*y[j-2];
124                                  }
125
126                         v=0;
127
128                         if (y[1]>0.0)
129                                 v=1;
130
131                         for (j=2;j<=N;j++){
132                                 sign=(y[j-1]>0.0) ?  1.0 :  -1.0;
133
134                                 if (sign*sgn(y[j])<=0.0 )
135                                         continue;
136                                 else
137                                         v++;
138                                 }
139
140                         if (v>=k)
141                                 alpha=c;
142                         else
143                                 beta=c;
144
145                 }while (fabs(beta-alpha)>5.0e-11);
146
147             lambda[k]=(0.5)*(alpha+beta);
148
149                 alpha=alphaold;
150                 beta=betaold;
151
152         }   /* end k loop */
153 }
154
155 main()
156 {
157 int i,j,N,num_ev;
158 double alpha,beta;
159 double *lambda,**a;
```

```
160
161 double sgn(double x);
162 double maxnorm1(int m, double **a);
163 void givens(int n, double **a);
164 void sturm(int n, int num_ev, double alpha, double beta,\
165          double **a, double *lambda);
166
167 printf("\n\n");
168 printf("Enter the order of the matrix:   ");
169 scanf("%d",&N);
170 printf("\n\n");
171
172 printf("Enter the number of eigenvalues desired\
173 (starting with the largest):      ");
174 scanf("%d",&num_ev);
175 printf("\n\n");
176
177 a=matalloc(1,N,1,N);
178 lambda=vecalloc(1,num_ev);
179
180 printf("Enter the upper triangle of the matrix A:\n\n");
181
182         for (i=1;i<=N;i++){
183                 for (j=i;j<=N;j++){
184                 printf("a[%d,%d] = ",i,j);
185                 scanf("%lf",&a[i][j]);
186                 printf("\n");
187                   }
188                 }
189                 for (i=2;i<=N;i++){
190                         for (j=1;j<=i-1;j++)
191                         a[i][j]=a[j][i];
192                         }
193
194 beta=maxnorm1(N,a)+.5;
195 alpha=-beta+0.01;
196
197 givens(N,a);
198
199 sturm(N,num_ev,alpha,beta,a,lambda);
200
201 for (i=1;i<=num_ev;i++){
202 printf("lambda[%d] = %10.10lf\n",i,lambda[i]);
```

203 }
204
205 }

In lines 21–43 we find a routine called `maxnorm1` which computes the maximum norm of a matrix `a`. Notice that the indices run from 1 to m. The `givens` function, on lines 45–100, returns the tridiagonal form of the matrix, as discussed above. The real work is performed by the `sturm` function, beginning on line 102. Here N is the order of the matrix `a`, and [alpha,beta] forms an interval in which all eigenvalues lie. As above, we will take in `main` the number `beta` to be slightly larger than the norm of the matrix, a number returned by `maxnorm1`. The last argument `*lambda` is an array to hold the eigenvalues; the integer argument `num_ev` will allow the user to specify the number of eigenvalues to be computed, starting with the largest.

In the bisection loop beginning on line 116, the integer `v` counts the number of agreements in sign of the members `y[]` of the Sturm Sequence, which are computed via the recursion on lines 118–124. `v` is initialized to zero in 126 and is incremented in the next line should `y[1]>0` (recall that `y[0]=1`). The signs of consecutive members of the sequence are computed on line 132. If these signs do not agree (see line 134), a `continue` statement forces the next iteration. Otherwise, `v` is incremented in 137. The interval is then cut in half appropriately in 140–143. The code in `main` itself is easy and short and should be readily understandable.

THE GENERALIZED EIGENVALUE PROBLEM

In applications the eigenvalue problem $Ax = \lambda Bx$ often arises. We will assume that both A and B are symmetric and that B is positive definite. Your first thought is probably to invert B and reduce to the standard problem via $B^{-1}Ax = \lambda x$. However, the new coefficient matrix need not be symmetric. Instead, we exploit the fact that B is positive definite.

Let's write the usual inner product on R^n as $(x, y) = \sum_{k=1}^{n} x_k y_k$. Recall that an $n \times n$ matrix B is called *positive definite* if $(x, Bx) > 0$ for all nonzero vectors x. Equivalently, all eigenvalues of B are positive. (Recall that the determinant of a matrix is the product of the eigenvalues; hence if B is positive definite, it must be invertible). A special factorization exists for symmetric positive definite matrices, called the *Cholesky Factorization*. It states that if $B = B^T$ is positive definite, there exists a lower–triangular matrix L such that $B = L \cdot L^T$.

We assume this for the moment, and use it as follows: The original equation is $Ax = \lambda Bx = \lambda L \cdot L^T x$. Left–multiply by L^{-1} to get $L^{-1}Ax = \lambda L^T x$. If we now call $y = L^T x$, then the equation can be written as

$$(4.88) \qquad L^{-1}A(L^{-1})^T y = \lambda y,$$

which is in the required standard form, since the coefficient matrix is now symmetric. We can then apply the Sturm sequence algorithm above to find all of the eigenvalues.

It remains to briefly discuss the Cholesky factorization. Let B be positive definite and write $B = L \cdot L^T$ for a lower–triangular matrix L with elements ℓ_{ij}. Thus, by the definition of matrix multiplication,

$$(4.89) \qquad b_{ij} = \sum_{k=1}^{n} \ell_{ik} \ell_{kj}^T = \sum_{k=1}^{n} \ell_{ik} \ell_{jk} = \sum_{k=1}^{\min(i,j)} \ell_{ik} \ell_{jk}.$$

In particular,

$$b_{ii} = \sum_{k=1}^{i} \ell_{ik}^2 = \ell_{ii}^2 + \sum_{k=1}^{i-1} \ell_{ik}^2$$

from which we get

$$(4.90) \qquad \ell_{ii} = \left(b_{ii} - \sum_{k=1}^{i-1} \ell_{ik}^2 \right)^{\frac{1}{2}}.$$

Furthermore, for $j = 1, 2, \ldots, i - 1$,

$$b_{ij} = \sum_{k=1}^{j-1} \ell_{ik} \ell_{jk} + \ell_{ij} \ell_{jj},$$

so that

$$(4.91) \qquad \ell_{ij} = \frac{b_{ij} - \sum_{k=1}^{j-1} \ell_{ik} \ell_{jk}}{\ell_{jj}} \qquad \text{for} \quad j = 1, 2, \ldots, i - 1.$$

These formulae then completely specify the elements of the lower–triangular matrix L, which is easy to invert for the same reason. (We have inverted upper–triangular matrices already.) In the code below we write a function `cholesky(int n, double **a)` which receives an $n \times n$ matrix a and returns (also in a) the lower–triangular matrix L in the Cholesky factorization.

The program is called `stabf.c` and expects three command–line arguments. The first is an integer, the order of the matrices A, B. The second is a data file containing the elements of the upper–triangle of A. The third is also a filename, that containing the elements of the upper–triangle of B. We include with the programs three sets of data files, called `ai.dat,bi.dat` for $i = 5, 16, 33$ (whose significance will be explained below). Thus, after compiling the program, you run it with, for example, the command

```
stabf 5 a5.dat b5.dat
```

The application we have in mind is a classical one in numerical analysis. Consider an "L–shaped" domain Ω in the plane, the union of three unit squares with corners as shown:

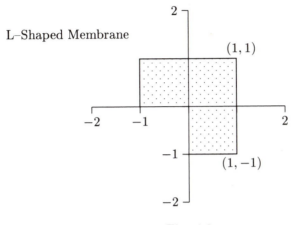

Fig. 4.2

Consider the eigenvalue problem

$$(4.92) \qquad u_{xx} + u_{yy} + \lambda u = 0 \quad ((x,y) \in \Omega), \quad u = 0 \quad \text{on} \quad \partial\Omega.$$

We seek the lowest eigenvalue λ_1, which is easily shown to be positive, as are all eigenvalues. (Multiply the equation by u and integrate by parts using the divergence theorem.) A method of Polya, exposed in [FW], generates a finite–difference approximation to this problem and leads to a matrix problem of the form $Ax = \lambda Bx$. While there are now better methods of approximation known (cf. [FHM]), this spurred much research and is important for that reason. If we sample at n points in each square (excluding the boundary, where the solution is known to vanish), it turns out that the order of the matrices is $(n-1)(3n-1)$. Thus, for $n = 2$ we get 5, for $n = 3$ we get 16 and for $n = 4$ we get 33. This explains the filenames quoted above.

When you run this program, you should get these results:

for order $= 5$, $\quad \lambda_1 = 11.702580043$
for order $= 16$, $\quad \lambda_1 = 10.543067176$
for order $= 33$, $\quad \lambda_1 = 10.161379876$

The actual value is approximately 9.6397.
Here now is the full code; a brief explanation follows it:

```
 1 /* STABF.C */
 2
 3 /*
 4 Eigenvalues of a linear system Ax = (lambda)Bx via Sturm
 5 Sequences.  The upper-triangular parts of A,B
 6 are read from files.    Usage:    stabf order a.dat b.dat.
 7 Data in "a.dat," etc.  are to be separated by spaces.
 8 B is positive definite; both A,B are symmetric.
 9 */
10
11 # include <math.h>
12 # include <malloc.h>
13 # include <stdio.h>
14 # include <stdlib.h>
15 # include "memalloc.c"
16 # include "memalloc.h"
17 # define MAX(a,b) ((a)>=(b) ?  (a) :  (b))
18
19 double sgn(double x)
20 {
21         if (x>0.0)
22                 return 1.0;
23         else if (x<0.0)
24                 return -1.0;
25         else
26                 return 0.0;
27 }
28
29 double maxnorm1(int m, double **a)
30
31 /* RETURNS THE MAXIMUM ABSOLUTE ROW SUM OF a[][] */
32 /* INDICES RUN FROM 1 TO m */
33
34 {
35 int k,j;
36 double s,z;
37 double *x;
38 x=vecalloc(1,m);
39
40         for (k=1;k<=m;k++){
```

```
41                   s=0.0;
42                   for (j=1;j<=m;j++)
43                   s += fabs(a[k][j]);
44                   x[k]=s;
45                   }
46
47          z=MAX(fabs(x[1]),fabs(x[2]));
48          for (k=3;k<=m;k++)
49                   z=MAX(fabs(x[k]),z);
50          return z;
51 }
52
53 void givens(int n, double **a)
54
55 /* REDUCES THE MATRIX a[][] TO TRIDIAGONAL FORM */
56 /* INDICES RUN FROM 1 TO n */
57 {
58 int i,j,k;
59 double c,s,x,y,h1,h2;
60
61 for (k=1;k<=n-2;k++){
62 for (i=k+2;i<=n;i++){
63 y=a[k+1][k]*a[k+1][k]+a[i][k]*a[i][k];
64 if (y<5.0e-20){
65          c=1.0;s=0.0;x=sqrt(y);}
66 else{
67 if (fabs(a[k+1][k])<=fabs(a[i][k])){
68 x=fabs(a[i][k])*sqrt(1.0+a[k+1][k]*a[k+1][k]\
69                      /(a[i][k]*a[i][k]));}
70 else{
71 x=fabs(a[k+1][k])*sqrt(1.0+a[i][k]*a[i][k]\
72                      /(a[k+1][k]*a[k+1][k]));}
73
74          c=a[k+1][k]/x;
75          s=a[i][k]/x;
76 }
77
78                   a[k+1][k]=x;
79                   a[i][k]=0.0;
80
81 for (j=k+1;j<=n;j++){
82          h1=c*a[k+1][j]+s*a[i][j];
83          h2=-s*a[k+1][j]+c*a[i][j];
```

```
84           a[k+1][j]=h1;
85           a[i][j]=h2;
86           }
87
88 for (j=1;j<=n;j++){
89           h1=c*a[j][k+1]+s*a[j][i];
90           h2=-s*a[j][k+1]+c*a[j][i];
91           a[j][k+1]=h1;
92           a[j][i]=h2;
93           }
94
95                              }        /* end i-loop */
96                           }           /* end k-loop */
97
98 for (i=3;i<=n;i++){ /* set lower triangle to zero */
99        for (j=1;j<=i-2;j++)
100                 a[i][j]=0.0;
101              }
102
103 for (i=1;i<=n-2;i++){      /* full tridiagonal form */
104        for (j=i+2;j<=n;j++)
105                 a[i][j]=0.0;
106              }
107
108 }
109
110 void cholesky(int n, double **a)
111 {
112 /*
113 RETURNS LOWER-TRIANGULAR MATRIX L s.t.  L(trL) = a
114 INDICES RUN FROM 1 TO n
115 */
116
117 int i,j,k;
118 double **y,s=0.0;
119 y=matalloc(1,n,1,n);
120
121 y[1][1]=sqrt(a[1][1]);
122
123 if (fabs(y[1][1])<5.0e-20){
124 fprintf(stderr, "Division by zero in Cholesky.c");
125 exit(1);
126 }
```

```
127
128 for (k=2;k<=n;k++)
129         y[k][1]=a[k][1]/y[1][1];
130
131 y[2][2]=sqrt(fabs(a[2][2]-y[2][1]*y[2][1]));
132
133 for (i=3;i<=n;i++){
134 for (j=2;j<=i-1;j++){
135 if (fabs(y[j][j])<5.0e-20){
136         fprintf(stderr, "Division by zero in Cholesky.c");
137         exit(1);
138         }
139
140             s=0.0;
141             for (k=1;k<=j-1;k++)
142                     s += y[i][k]*y[j][k];
143             y[i][j]=(a[i][j]-s)/y[j][j];
144             }
145
146         s=0.0;
147         for (k=1;k<=i-1;k++)
148         s += y[i][k]*y[i][k];
149
150         y[i][i]=sqrt(fabs(a[i][i]-s));
151         }
152
153 for (i=1;i<=n;i++){
154         for (j=1;j<=n;j++)
155                 a[i][j]=y[i][j];
156                 }
157 }
158
159 void sturm(int N, int num_ev, double alpha, double beta,\
160             double **a, double *lambda)
161 /* num_ev=number of eigenvalues returned, starting with */
162 /* the largest; N=order of matrix */
163 {
164 int j,k,v;
165 double c,sign;
166 double alphaold=alpha;
167 double betaold=beta;
168 double *y;
169 y=vecalloc(1,N);
```

```
170
171 for (k=1;k<=num_ev;k++){
172
173          do{
174          c=(alpha+beta)/2.0;
175          y[1]=a[1][1]-c;
176          y[2]=(a[2][2]-c)*y[1]-a[2][1]*a[2][1];
177
178          for (j=3;j<=N;j++){
179 y[j]=(a[j][j]-c)*y[j-1]-a[j][j-1]*a[j][j-1]*y[j-2];
180 }
181
182                  v=0;
183
184                  if (y[1]>0.0)
185                      v=1;
186
187                  for (j=2;j<=N;j++){
188                      sign=(y[j-1]>0.0) ?  1.0 :  -1.0;
189
190                      if (sign*sgn(y[j])<=0.0 )
191                          continue;
192                      else
193                              v++;
194                      }
195
196                  if (v>=k)
197                      alpha=c;
198                  else
199                      beta=c;
200
201          }while (fabs(beta-alpha)>5.0e-11);
202
203          lambda[k]=(0.5)*(alpha+beta);
204
205          alpha=alphaold;
206          beta=betaold;
207
208          }   /* end k loop */
209 }
210
211 void matmult(int n, double **a, double **b, double **c)
212 /* unit offset assumed */
```

```
213 /* matrix product AB returned in matrix C */
214 {
215 int i,j,k;
216 double s;
217
218 for (i=1;i<=n;i++){
219         for (j=1;j<=n;j++){
220                 s=0.0;
221                 for (k=1;k<=n;k++){
222                 s += a[i][k]*b[k][j];
223                 }
224                 c[i][j]=s;
225             }
226         }
227 }
228
229 void transpos(int n, double **a, double **ta)
230 /* unit offset assumed */
231 {
232 int i,j;
233
234 for (i=1;i<=n;i++){
235         for (j=1;j<=n;j++){
236                 ta[i][j]=a[j][i];
237         }
238 }
239 }
240
241 main(int argc, char *argv[])
242 {
243 int N,i,j,k;
244 double alpha,beta,alphaold,betaold,s;
245 FILE *fpa,*fpb;
246
247 double *y,*lambda,**a,**b,**p,**pt;
248
249 double sgn(double x);
250 void sturm(int N, int num_ev, double alpha, double beta,\
251             double **a, double *lambda);
252
253 void cholesky(int n, double **a);
254 double maxnorm1(int m, double **a);
255 void givens(int n, double **a);
```

```
256 void matmult(int n, double **a, double **b, double **c);
257 void transpos(int n, double **a, double **ta);
258
259 printf("\n\n");
260 if (argc!=4){
261         printf("Usage:    stabf order afile bfile");
262         }
263
264 else if (!(fpa=fopen(argv[2],"r"))){
265         printf("STABF: Error opening file %s\n",argv[2]);
266         }
267
268 else if (!(fpb=fopen(argv[3],"r"))){
269         printf("STABF: Error opening file %s\n",argv[3]);
270         }
271
272 else{
273         N=atoi(argv[1]);
274         a=matalloc(1,N,1,N);
275         b=matalloc(1,N,1,N);
276         p=matalloc(1,N,1,N);
277         pt=matalloc(1,N,1,N);
278         lambda=vecalloc(1,N);
279
280         for (i=1;i<=N;i++){
281                 for (j=i;j<=N;j++){
282                         fscanf(fpa,"%lf",&a[i][j]);
283                         }
284                 }
285
286                 for (i=2;i<=N;i++){
287                         for (j=1;j<=i-1;j++)
288                         a[i][j]=a[j][i];
289                 }
290
291         for (i=1;i<=N;i++){
292                 for (j=i;j<=N;j++){
293                         fscanf(fpb,"%lf",&b[i][j]);
294                         }
295                 }
296
297                 for (i=2;i<=N;i++){
298                         for (j=1;j<=i-1;j++)
```

```
299                          b[i][j]=b[j][i];
300                          }
301
302 cholesky(N,b);
303
304 /* COMPUTE p=INVERSE OF b */
305 for (k=1;k<=N;k++)
306          p[k][k]=1.0/b[k][k];
307
308 for (i=2;i<=N;i++){
309          for (j=i-1;j>=1;j--){
310                  s=0.0;
311                  for (k=1;k<=i-1;k++)
312                          s += b[i][k]*p[k][j];
313                  p[i][j]=-s/b[i][i];
314                  }
315          }
316
317 /* COMPUTE pa, call it b */
318 matmult(N,p,a,b);
319
320 /* COMPUTE tr(p), call it pt */
321 transpos(N,p,pt);
322
323 /* COMPUTE final matrix, call it a */
324 matmult(N,b,pt,a);
325
326 beta=maxnorm1(N,a)+.5;
327 betaold=beta;
328 alpha=-beta+0.01;
329 alphaold=alpha;
330
331 givens(N,a);
332
333 sturm(N,N,alpha,beta,a,lambda);
334
335 for (i=1;i<=N;i++)
336          printf("lambda[%d] = %10.10lf\n",i,lambda[i]);
337 }
338 }
```

In lines 29–51 we find the function maxnorm1 which returns the maximum norm of a matrix of order n with indices running over $1 \leq i \leq n$; the givens function (which reduces to tridiagonal form) is on lines 53–108. Both have already been encountered in `sturm.c`. On line 110 the function `cholesky` begins; its code is a straightforward implementation of the algorithm given above, with the exception of several uses of absolute values. These are present to handle matrices which are positive definite but not "numerically positive definite". On return, the matrix `a` is overwritten by the lower-triangular factor L. The `sturm` function is also the same. On lines 211–227 we find a standard routine for matrix multiplication, and a matrix transposition function appears on lines 229–239.

Notice that `main` is declared for command–line input. The matrix `p` (see line 304) is to hold the inverse of L. After the call to `cholesky` on line 302, the matrix `b` holds L. It is then inverted on lines 304–315. We left–multiply `a` by $p = L^{-1}$ in 317–318, and then perform the final right–multiplication of this by p^T on lines 323–324. Now we are reduced to the previous case of the standard symmetric eigenvalue problem.

THE STURM–LIOUVILLE EIGENVALUE PROBLEM

The second–order linear Sturm–Liouville eigenvalue problem in ordinary differential equations appears as

$$(4.93) \qquad (p(x)y')' - q(x)y + \lambda r(x)y = 0 \quad (a < x < b),$$

which is to be solved subject to the *boundary conditions*

$$(4.94) \qquad\qquad y(a) = 0, \quad y(b) = 0.$$

Here one generally assumes that $p(x)$ and $r(x)$ are strictly positive on $[a, b]$ and that $q(x)$ is nonnegative there. From classical theory, there exists a sequence of eigenvalues λ_i with $0 < \lambda_1 \le \lambda_2 \le \cdots \to \infty$ and non-trivial eigenfunctions $y_m(x)$ which satisfy the equation and the boundary conditions, as well as the *orthogonality condition*

$$(4.95) \qquad\qquad \int_a^b r(x)y_n(x)y_m(x)\,dx = \delta_{nm}.$$

We consider in this section numerical approximation of such eigenvalues under the assumption that $q(x) = 0$. We may then arrange it so that $p(x) = 1$ and that $[a, b] = [0, 1]$. This can be achieved by a change of independent variable

$$(4.96) \qquad\qquad \xi = \frac{\int_a^x \frac{dt}{p(t)}}{\int_a^b \frac{dt}{p(t)}}.$$

This defines ξ as a function of x; since $\frac{d\xi}{dx} > 0$, the inverse function makes sense and the equation can be reduced via the chain rule.

Thus, it suffices to consider the problem

$$(4.97) \qquad \frac{d^2 y}{dx^2} + \lambda r(x) y = 0 \quad (0 < x < 1), \quad y(0) = y(1) = 0,$$

where we still assume that $r(x)$ is strictly positive on $[0,1]$. The simplest finite–difference method would be this: partition $[0,1]$ as usual, say $x_i = ih$ for $i = 0, 1, \ldots, n$ where $x_0 = 0$, $x_n = 1$ with $h = \frac{1}{n}$ for some positive integer n. Abbreviating $y(x_i) = y_i$, we know that

$$y''(x_i) = \frac{y_{i+1} - 2y_i + y_{i-1}}{h^2} + O(h^2)$$

for a smooth function y. Thus, a natural approximation would be to define $u_i \approx y(x_i)$ where the u_i satisfy the linear system

$$\frac{u_{i+1} - 2u_i + u_{i-1}}{h^2} + \hat{\lambda}_i r(x_i) u_i = 0, \quad (i = 1, \ldots, n-1)$$

with $u_0 = u_n = 0$. As you see, this is the same as the linear system $Au = \Lambda B u$ where $\Lambda = h^2 \hat{\lambda}$, A is the Dirichlet matrix and B is the diagonal matrix with entries $r(x_i)$. The approximate eigenvalues are therefore given as the roots of $\det(A - \Lambda B) = 0$; we then approximate the actual eigenvalues via $\lambda_i \approx h^{-2} \Lambda_i$.

Another well–known method is the *Ritz–Galerkin* algorithm which has a variational formulation. Consider the functional

$$(4.98) \qquad J[y] = \int_0^1 \left(p(x) y'^2 + q(x) y^2 + 2 f(x) y \right) dx$$

defined on C^1–functions y which satisfy the boundary conditions $y(0) = y(1) = 0$. From the calculus of variations, the Euler Equation of this functional is

$$(4.99) \qquad \left(p(x) y' \right)' - q(x) y = f(x).$$

Hence if $J[y]$ were to attain a minimum at some function y, this Sturm–Liouville equation must necessarily hold. The Ritz–Galerkin solution of this problem proceeds as follows: choose a linearly independent sequence of functions $\phi_i(x)$ $(i = 1, 2, \ldots)$ which satisfy the boundary conditions. For example we may take $\phi_i(x) = \sin(i\pi x)$ or $\phi_i(x) = x^i(1-x)$. Then we attempt an approximate solution $y_n(x)$ of the form

$$(4.100) \qquad y_n(x) = \sum_{k=1}^{n} a_k \phi_k(x).$$

We evaluate $J[y_n]$; it is a quadratic function of the coefficients $\{a_k\}_{k=1}^n$. Then we perform elementary calculus: at a minimum, the partial derivatives of $J[y_n]$ with respect to each a_k must vanish. This leads to a linear system for the determination of the $\{a_k\}_{k=1}^n$.

Now we consider the special eigenvalue problem (4.97) again:

$$\frac{d^2y}{dx^2} + \lambda r(x)y = 0 \quad (0 < x < 1), \quad y(0) = y(1) = 0.$$

When we multiply by y and integrate by parts, we see that any eigenpair (λ, y) must satisfy

$$(4.101) \qquad \lambda = I[y] \equiv \frac{\int_0^1 y'^2 \, dx}{\int_0^1 ry^2 \, dx}.$$

The expression $I[y]$ is called the *Rayleigh Quotient*. If we consider all possible values of $I[u]$ as the function $u(x)$ ranges over all piecewise smooth functions which vanish at the endpoints, then the smallest such value is known to equal the lowest eigenvalue λ_1 of the differential equation. Next we proceed as in Ritz–Galerkin: we try an approximate solution (with ϕ_k as above) of the form

$$(4.102) \qquad U_n(x) = \sum_{k=1}^n z_k \phi_k(x).$$

We calculate

$$\int_0^1 r(x) U_n^2(x) \, dx = \int_0^1 r(x) \sum_{j,k} z_k z_j \phi_k(x) \phi_j(x) \, dx = \sum_{j,k} b_{jk} z_k z_j = (Bz, z),$$

where

$$(4.103) \qquad b_{jk} = \int_0^1 r(x) \phi_k(x) \phi_j(x) \, dx.$$

Similarly,

$$\int_0^1 (U_n'(x))^2 \, dx = \int_0^1 \sum_{j,k} z_k z_j \phi_k'(x) \phi_j'(x) \, dx = \sum_{j,k} a_{jk} z_k z_j = (Az, z),$$

where

$$(4.104) \qquad a_{jk} = \int_0^1 \phi_k'(x) \phi_j'(x) \, dx.$$

Thus, we have

$$I[U_n] = \frac{(Az, z)}{(Bz, z)},$$

where $z = (z_1, \ldots, z_n)^T$ and the matrices A and B have the elements given in (4.103) and (4.104). Clearly A and B are symmetric positive definite.

We now explicitly compute $\frac{\partial I[U_n]}{\partial z_j}$ for $j = 1, 2, \ldots, n$ and set each result equal to zero. A necessary condition is then seen to be the satisfaction of the linear system

(4.105)
$$Az = \frac{(Az, z)}{(Bz, z)} Bz.$$

Then we find the roots of $\det(A - \Lambda B) = 0$, and approximate the lowest eigenvalue (or any of the first n) by $\lambda_1 \approx \Lambda_1$. It is always true that $\lambda_1 \leq \Lambda_1$, but no lower bound on λ_1 is produced by this method. In general, A and B are full matrices. Please notice that the matrix elements are given explicitly, but as integrals. This concludes the brief description of the Ritz–Galerkin method as applied to the Sturm–Liouville eigenvalue problem.

With this introduction, we turn to an example of the *finite–element* method. We present an algorithm of Wendroff [WE]. We will assume an equally spaced mesh $0 = x_0 < x_1 < \ldots < x_{n+1} = 1$ and consider again (4.97):

$$\frac{d^2 y}{dx^2} + \lambda r(x) y = 0 \quad (0 < x < 1), \quad y(0) = y(1) = 0.$$

The function $r(x)$ could be allowed to have discontinuities, but we do not consider this. Everything is the same as above, *except* that the approximating functions are not smooth. In fact, one chooses

(4.106)
$$\phi_k(x) = \begin{cases} 1 & \text{if } x = x_k \\ 0 & \text{if } x = x_j, j \neq k \\ \text{linear} & \text{on each } [x_j, x_{j+1}]. \end{cases}$$

Hat Functions

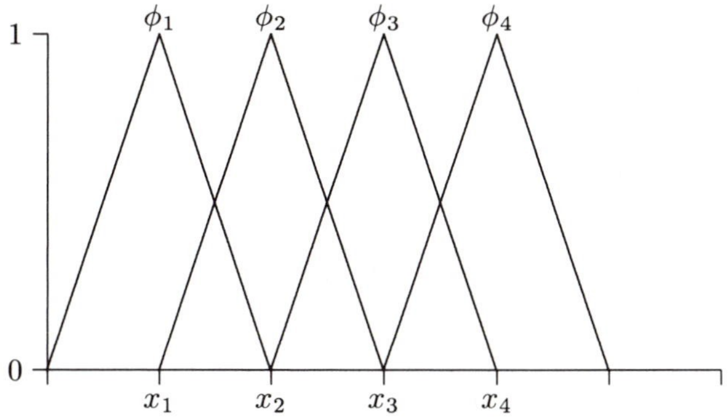

Fig. 4.3

Thus, the functions ϕ_k are "triangular," or "hat" functions. Notice that each satisfies the boundary conditions and that the $\{\phi_k(x)\}$ are linearly independent. One now computes the functional $I[U_n]$ as above, and therefore gets the same matrix coefficients as above. However, note that now A and B are *tridiagonal*. For instance, consider

$$(4.107) \qquad a_{ij} = \int_0^1 \phi_i'(x)\phi_j'(x)\,dx.$$

If $|i - j| > 1$, the supports of ϕ_i and ϕ_j are disjoint, as you can see from the picture. The same is true for the elements of the matrix B. Therefore, $a_{ij} = b_{ij} = 0$ for $|i - j| > 1$.

In this case we may use a special variant of Sturm sequences, as discussed in [WI]. This will be much faster than factoring B via Cholesky and inverting the resulting lower–triangular part, etc. For the elements of the tridiagonal matrices A, B we write $a_{ii} = \alpha_i$, $a_{i+1,i} = a_{i,i+1} = \beta_{i+1}$ and $b_{ii} = \alpha_i'$, $b_{i+1,i} = b_{i,i+1} = \beta_{i+1}'$. Then we get a Sturm Sequence via the recursion $p_0(\lambda) = 1$, $p_1(\lambda) = \alpha_1 - \lambda\alpha_1'$ and
(4.108)
$$p_k(\lambda) = (\alpha_k - \lambda\alpha_k')p_{k-1}(\lambda) - (\beta_k - \lambda\beta_k')^2 p_{k-2}(\lambda) \quad (k = 2, 3, \ldots, n).$$

As before, we then know that the roots of $\det(A - \lambda B) = 0$ are the zeroes of the function $p_n(\lambda)$.

Now we write explicit results for the case of a uniform mesh. Recall that from definition

$$(4.109) \qquad \phi_i(x) = \begin{cases} \frac{x - x_{i-1}}{h} & \text{if } x_{i-1} \le x \le x_i \\ \frac{x_{i+1} - x}{h} & \text{if } x_i \le x \le x_{i+1} \\ 0 & \text{otherwise.} \end{cases}$$

Then clearly

$$(4.110) \qquad a_{ii} = \int_0^1 \phi_i'(x)\phi_i'(x)\,dx = 2\int_{x_{i-1}}^{x_i} h^{-2}\,dx = \frac{2}{h}.$$

Similarly $a_{i,i+1} = -\frac{1}{h}$. Thus, A is the Dirichlet matrix divided by h. Since the function $r(x)$ may be complicated, we perform the integrals for the coefficients b_{ij} via Gaussian Integration. Explicitly, we have

$$(4.111) \quad b_{ii} = \frac{1}{h^2}\int_{x_{i-1}}^{x_i} r(x)(x - x_{i-1})^2\,dx + \frac{1}{h^2}\int_{x_i}^{x_{i+1}} r(x)(x_{i+1} - x)^2\,dx$$

and

$$(4.112) \qquad b_{i,i-1} = \frac{1}{h^2}\int_{x_{i-1}}^{x_i} r(x)(x - x_{i-1})(x_i - x)\,dx.$$

In the program below we solve this eigenvalue problem on any interval $a \leq x \leq b$. In order to use the Gauss–Legendre formula, we perform a linear change of variables in each integral so that the new interval of integration is $[-1, 1]$. When the problem is posed on $[a, b]$ we have

$$y'' + \lambda r(x)y = 0 \quad (a < x < b) \quad y(a) = y(b) = 0.$$

Introduce the change of variables $x = a + (b - a)\xi$ under which the problem becomes

$$\frac{d^2 y(\xi)}{d\xi^2} + \lambda(b - a)^2 r\left(a + (b - a)\xi\right) y(\xi) = 0 \quad (0 < \xi < 1) \quad y(0) = y(1) = 0.$$

Consider the formula for $b_{i,i-1}$:

$$b_{i,i-1} = \frac{(b - a)^2}{h^2} \int_{x_{i-1}}^{x_i} r(a + x(b - a))(x - x_{i-1})(x_i - x)\, dx.$$

Under another change of variables $x = (x_{i-1} + x_i + th)/2$ the set of integration becomes $-1 \leq t \leq 1$ and, after an elementary calculation, we get

$$(4.113) \quad b_{i,i-1} = \frac{h(b - a)^2}{8} \int_{-1}^{1} (1 - t^2)r\left(a + (b - a)(ih - \frac{h}{2} + \frac{ht}{2})\right) dt.$$

In the code below you will see a function called **h1** on lines 54–61 which implements the integrand in (4.113) in a straightforward manner. Similarly, the function **g** (starting on line 43) handles the corresponding transformation for the coefficients b_{ii}.

Wendroff's theorem states the following: let λ_1 be the first eigenvalue of the differential equation, and let Λ_1 be the lowest eigenvalue of our approximate system $Au = \Lambda Bu$. Then $|\lambda_1 - \Lambda_1| \leq \frac{2 \max |r(x)| \Lambda_1 h^2}{3\sqrt{10}}$. The remarkable feature is that a *two–sided* bound is obtained.

We first choose $n = 2$ and compute the approximation. We then double n and extrapolate to find a better value. We continue doubling n and extrapolating until $n = 512$, which gives reasonable approximations. Notice the use of the C–library function **realloc** to achieve this. One other comment: this program uses zero–offset indices.

We employ an eight–point Gaussian formula; the data appear on lines 80–97. In line 117 a lower bound for $r(x)$ is requested. Indeed, we know that $\lambda_1 \leq I[u]$ for all test functions $u(x)$. When we take for simplicity

$u(x) = (x - a)(b - x)$ (which satisfies the boundary conditions), we get

$$I[u] = \frac{\int_a^b (u')^2 \, dx}{\int_a^b r u^2 \, dx}$$

$$= \frac{\int_a^b (a + b - 2x)^2 \, dx}{\int_a^b r(x - a)^2 (b - x)^2 \, dx}$$

$$\leq \frac{\int_a^b (a + b - 2x)^2 \, dx}{r_{\min} \int_a^b (x - a)^2 (b - x)^2 \, dx}$$

$$= \frac{10}{r_{\min}(b - a)^2}.$$

This allows a more reasonable initial guess and therefore speeds things up; it is used in lines 213–214. The Sturm sequence computation starts on line 218 and continues to line 226. It is the altered version as discussed above in (4.108). N is then doubled on line 262, and the entire loop (which began on line 121) is repeated until N=512.

Before giving the full listing, we quickly discuss the special problem considered in the code, namely the problem

$$(4.114) \qquad \left((1 + x)^2 y'\right)' + \lambda y = 0 \quad (0 < x < 1), \quad y(0) = y(1) = 0.$$

Although this has variable coefficients, it is an "equidimensional" ODE and can be solved exactly by seeking a solution in the form $y = (1 + x)^R$. The quadratic $R^2 + R + \lambda = 0$ results, whose roots are $R_\pm = \frac{-1 \pm i\sqrt{4\lambda - 1}}{2}$. (For a nontrivial solution, we must have $4\lambda > 1$.) Since $y(0) = 0$ we get as the solution multiples of the function

$$(4.115) \qquad y = (1 + x)^{-\frac{1}{2}} \sin\left(\frac{\sqrt{4\lambda - 1}\ln(1 + x)}{2}\right).$$

Forcing $y(1) = 0$, we get $\sqrt{4\lambda_1 - 1}\ln 2 = 2\pi$, and thus, $\lambda_1 \approx 20.79228846$.

To reduce to standard form introduce the change of independent variable

$$(4.116) \qquad \xi = \int_0^x \frac{dt}{(1 + t)^2} = \frac{x}{1 + x}.$$

It follows that $0 \leq \xi \leq \frac{1}{2}$ and by inversion $x = \frac{\xi}{1 - \xi}$. The equation is then easily reduced to the form

$$(4.117) \qquad \frac{d^2 y}{d\xi^2} + \frac{\lambda y(\xi)}{(1 - \xi)^2} = 0 \quad \left(y(0) = y(\tfrac{1}{2}) = 0\right),$$

and you will see this formula for $r(\xi)$ in the code to follow on lines 38–41:

```
1 /* Sturmev1.c */
2
3 /*
4 Computes the minimum eigenvalue of y" + (lambda)r(x)y = 0
5 over a<x<b, with boundary conditions y=0 at a,b.
6 r(x) is assumed positive.
7 Method is piecewise linear finite element approximation.
8 cf. [WE], p. 101 ff.
9 Reduces to spectrum of Ax=(lambda)Bx, where
10 A,B are symmetric, tridiagonal and positive definite.
11 Integrals computed via 8 point Gaussian integration.
12 The least eigenvalue then found by Sturm Sequences.
13 Here are some exact results:
14 when a=0,b=pi,r(x)=1, lambda=1
15 when a=0,b=1/2,r(x)=1/(1-x)^2,lambda=20.79228846
16 the latter for ((1+x)^2 y')'+(lambda)y=0, 0<x<1.
17 */
18
19 # include <math.h>
20 # include <malloc.h>
21 # include <stdio.h>
22 # include <stdlib.h>
23 # include "memalloc.c"
24 # include "memalloc.h"
25 # define MAX(a,b) ((a)>=(b) ? (a) : (b))
26
27 double sgn(double x)
28 {
29         if (x>0.0)
30                 return 1.0;
31         else if (x<0.0)
32                 return -1.0;
33         else
34                 return 0.0;
35 }
36
37 /* enter the coefficient function r(x) here */
38 double r(double x)
39 {                        /* 0 < x < 0.5 here */
40         return (1.0/((1.0-x)*(1.0-x)));
41 }
```

```
42
43 double g(double x,int y,double a,double b,double h,\
44          double (*func_ptr)())
45 {    /* for the diagonal elements b[i][i] */
46 double temp  = (h/8.0)*(b-a)*(b-a)*(1.0+x)*(1.0+x);
47 double temp1 = (*func_ptr)(a+(b-a)*(y*h-0.5*h+0.5*h*x));
48 double temp2 = (*func_ptr)(a+(b-a)*(y*h+0.5*h-0.5*h*x));
49 temp2        += temp1
50 temp         *= temp2;
51 return temp;
52 }
53
54 double h1(double x,int y,double a,double b,double h,\
55          double (*func_ptr)())
56 {    /* for the off-diagonal elements b[i][i-1] */
57 double temp = (h/8.0)*(b-a)*(b-a)*(1.0-x*x);
58 double temp1= (*func_ptr)(a+(b-a)*(y*h-0.5*h+0.5*h*x));
59 temp        *= temp1;
60 return temp;
61 }
62
63 main()
64 {
65 int N,i,j,v;
66 double alpha,beta,x[8],w[8];
67 double c,sign,lambda,lambdaold;
68 double a,b,rmin,h,s;
69
70 double *adiag,*asub,*asup,*bdiag,*bsub,*bsup,*y;
71 double (*func_ptr)()=r;
72
73 double sgn(double x);
74 double r(double x);
75 double g(double x,int y,double a,double b,double h,\
76          double (*func_ptr)());
77 double h1(double x,int y,double a,double b,double h,\
78 double (*func_ptr)());
79
80 /* This Gaussian data is from [AS], p.  916 */
81 w[0] = .101228536290376;
82 w[1] = w[0];
83 w[2] = .222381034453374;
84 w[3] = w[2];
```

```
85  w[4] = .313706645877887;
86  w[5] = w[4];
87  w[6] = .362683783378362;
88  w[7] = w[6];
89
90  x[0] = .960289856497536;
91  x[1] = -x[0];
92  x[2] = .7966664774136269;
93  x[3] = -x[2];
94  x[4] = .525532409916329;
95  x[5] = -x[4];
96  x[6] = .18343464249565;
97  x[7] = -x[6];
98
99  N=2;
100
101 /* zero-offset indices here */
102 adiag=vecalloc(0,N-1);
103 asup=vecalloc(0,N-1);
104 asub=vecalloc(0,N-1);
105 bdiag=vecalloc(0,N-1);
106 bsup=vecalloc(0,N-1);
107 bsub=vecalloc(0,N-1);
108 y=vecalloc(0,N-1);
109
110 printf("\n\n");
111 printf("Enter the left-hand endpoint:");
112 scanf("%lf",&a);
113 printf("\n");
114 printf("Enter the right-hand endpoint:");
115 scanf("%lf",&b);
116 printf("\n");
117 printf("Enter a lower bound for r(x) over [a,b]:  ");
118 scanf("%lf",&rmin);
119 printf("\n\n");
120
121 do{
122
123 adiag=(double *)realloc(adiag,N*sizeof(double));
124         if (!adiag) {
125         fprintf(stderr,"could not allocate memory");
126         exit(1);
127         }
```

```
128
129 asub=(double *)realloc(asub,N*sizeof(double));
130         if (!asub) {
131         fprintf(stderr,"could not allocate memory");
132         exit(1);
133         }
134
135 asup=(double *)realloc(asup,N*sizeof(double));
136         if (!asup) {
137         fprintf(stderr,"could not allocate memory");
138         exit(1);
139         }
140
141 bdiag=(double *)realloc(bdiag,N*sizeof(double));
142         if (!bdiag) {
143         fprintf(stderr,"could not allocate memory");
144         exit(1);
145         }
146
147 bsub=(double *)realloc(bsub,N*sizeof(double));
148         if (!bsub) {
149         fprintf(stderr,"could not allocate memory");
150         exit(1);
151         }
152
153 bsup=(double *)realloc(bsup,N*sizeof(double));
154         if (!bsup) {
155         fprintf(stderr,"could not allocate memory");
156         exit(1);
157         }
158
159 y=(double *)realloc(y,N*sizeof(double));
160         if (!y) {
161         fprintf(stderr,"could not allocate memory");
162         exit(1);
163         }
164
165 h=1.0/(N+1.0);
166
167         /* Dirichlet Matrix */
168         for (i=1;i<=N;i++){
169                 adiag[i-1]=2.0;
170                 }
```

```
171
172          asub[0]=0.0;
173          asup[N-1]=0.0;
174
175          for (i=2;i<=N;i++){
176                  asub[i-1]=-1.0;
177                  }
178          for (i=1;i<=N-1;i++){
179                  asup[i-1]=asub[i];
180                  }
181
182 /* elements of B-matrix via Gaussian integration */
183          for (i=1;i<=N;i++){
184          s=0.0;
185          for (j=0;j<=7;j++)
186                  s += (h*w[j]*g(x[j],i,a,b,h,func_ptr));
187                  bdiag[i-1]=s;
188                  }
189
190          for (i=2;i<=N;i++){
191                  s=0.0;
192                  for (j=0;j<=7;j++)
193                  s += (h*w[j]*h1(x[j],i,a,b,h,func_ptr));
194                  bsub[i-1]=s;
195                  }
196
197          bsub[0]=0.0;
198          bsup[N-1]=0.0;
199
200          for (i=1;i<=N-1;i++){
201                  bsup[i-1]=bsub[i];
202                  }
203
204 if (N>2){
205          beta=lambdaold;
206          alpha=0.0;
207          }
208 else{
209          /*
210          crude upper bound from Rayleigh quotient
211          using test function u(x)=(x - a)*(b - x)
212          */
213          beta=10.0/(rmin * (b - a) * (b - a));
```

```
214            alpha=0.0;
215            }
216
217 do{
218 c=(alpha+beta)/2.0;
219 y[0]=adiag[0]-c*bdiag[0];
220 y[1]=(adiag[1]-c*bdiag[1])*y[0]-(asub[1]-c*bsup[0])*\
221                                 (asub[1]-c*bsup[0]);
222
223 for (j=3;j<=N;j++){
224 y[j-1]=(adiag[j-1]-c*bdiag[j-1])*y[j-2]-\
225 (asub[j-1]-c*bsup[j-2])*(asub[j-1]-c*bsup[j-2])*y[j-3];
226            }
227            v=0;
228
229                 if (y[0]>0.0)
230                     v=1;
231
232                 for (j=2;j<=N;j++){
233                     sign=(y[j-2]>0.0) ?  1.0 :  -1.0;
234
235                     if (sign*sgn(y[j-1])<=0.0 )
236                         continue;
237                     else{
238                         v++;
239                     }
240                         }
241
242                 if (v>=N)
243                     alpha=c;
244                 else
245                     beta=c;
246
247            }while (fabs(beta-alpha)>5.0e-11);
248
249            lambda=0.5*(alpha+beta);
250
251 printf("n=%2.2d   minimum lambda = %10.10lf\n",N,lambda);
252
253 if (N==2){
254 printf("\n");
255 }
256 else{
```

```
257 printf("  extrapolated lambda = %10.10lf\n\n",\
258               (4.0*lambda-lambdaold)/3.0);
259 }
260
261 lambdaold=lambda;
262 N *= 2;
263 }
264 while (N<=512);
265
266 }
```

JACOBI'S METHOD

This famous classical method is still quite acceptable for a small to moderate–sized problem involving symmetric matrices whose eigenvalues and eigenvectors are sought. It uses orthogonal transformations $A \rightarrow T^T A T$ as does Givens's method, but in a different manner. When the eigenvalues are distinct, the algorithm is essentially (eventually) quadratically convergent. The idea is to use a sequence of such transformations to reduce the matrix to diagonal form.

Let $A = A^T$ be of order n and write $A_0 = A$. We generate a sequence $A_k = T_k^T A_{k-1} T_k$ by the following procedure. At each step the rotation T_k^T is chosen to make a particular off–diagonal element of A_{k-1} vanish. Each T_k^T is equal to the identity, except for four elements. For example, when $n = 6$ a rotation in the (3,6)–plane has the form

$$(4.118) \qquad T^T = \begin{pmatrix} 1 & 0 & 0 & 0 & 0 & 0 \\ 0 & 1 & 0 & 0 & 0 & 0 \\ 0 & 0 & c & 0 & 0 & s \\ 0 & 0 & 0 & 1 & 0 & 0 \\ 0 & 0 & 0 & 0 & 1 & 0 \\ 0 & 0 & -s & 0 & 0 & c \end{pmatrix}$$

(see the previous discussion of Givens's method). Here $c = \cos\theta$ and $s = \sin\theta$ for some angle θ to be determined.

In general, to eliminate (force to be zero) a given off–diagonal element $a_{pq}^{(k-1)}$, we can use symmetry to assume that $p < q$. The matrix $T^T = T_k^T$ is the identity except for the four elements

$$(4.119) \qquad T_{pp}^T = T_{qq}^T = c, \quad T_{pq}^T = -T_{qp}^T = s.$$

Consider the product $B_k \equiv T^T \cdot A_{k-1}$. It equals A_{k-1} in all rows except rows p and q and, letting R_p be the pth row of R, C_p be the pth column of

R, we have

(4.120)
$$R_p(B_k) = cR_p(A_{k-1}) + sR_q(A_{k-1})$$
$$R_q(B_k) = -sR_p(A_{k-1}) + cR_q(A_{k-1}).$$

Then by the Jacobi transformation

(4.121)
$$A_k = T^T A_{k-1} T = B_k T$$

is the same as B_k in all columns except columns p and q; for these we have

(4.122)
$$C_p(A_k) = cC_p(B_k) + sC_q(B_k)$$
$$C_q(A_k) = -sC_p(B_k) + cC_q(B_k).$$

Now for brevity denote by a'_{ij} the elements of the transformed matrix A_k, and a_{ij} those of A_{k-1}. When these relations are written out in detail, the following equations result:

(4.123)
$$a'_{ip} = ca_{ip} + sa_{iq} \quad (i \neq p, \ i \neq q)$$
$$a'_{iq} = -sa_{ip} + ca_{iq} \quad (i \neq p, \ i \neq q)$$
$$a'_{pp} = c^2 a_{pp} + s^2 a_{qq} + 2cs a_{pq}$$
$$a'_{qq} = s^2 a_{pp} + c^2 a_{qq} - 2cs a_{pq}$$
$$a'_{pq} = cs(a_{qq} - a_{pp}) + (c^2 - s^2)a_{pq}.$$

Now set $a'_{pq} = 0$; after the use of some simple trigonometric identities, we get

(4.124)
$$\tan 2\theta = \frac{2a_{pq}}{a_{pp} - a_{qq}}.$$

We require further that $|\theta| \leq \frac{\pi}{4}$. In the event that $a_{pp} = a_{qq}$, we make the choice $\theta = \frac{\pi}{4}\text{sgn}(a_{pq})$.

The original Jacobi algorithm was, at each step, to search the upper triangle of A_{k-1} to find the element of maximum modulus. This element would then be eliminated as above. In this event we could assume that $a_{pq} \neq 0$. The search time may, however, be nontrivial.

Notice that an element previously reduced to zero may become non-zero on later iterations. For the eigenvectors, suppose that to working accuracy we have after ν iterations

(4.125)
$$\left(T_\nu^T T_{\nu-1}^T \cdots T_1^T\right) A \left(T_1 T_2 \cdots T_\nu\right) = \text{diag}(\lambda_i).$$

Then the columns of

(4.126)
$$P_\nu \equiv T_1 T_2 \cdots T_\nu$$

are the approximate eigenvectors of A.

In practice, one uses the *special serial Jacobi method*. We eliminate the elements in a definite order by rotating in the planes

$$(1,2),(1,3),\ldots,(1,n)$$

$$(2,3),(2,4),\ldots,(2,n)$$

$$\vdots$$

$$(n-1,n).$$

A *sweep* is one complete loop of this process. Thus, the total number of rotations involved in a single sweep is $(n-1)+(n-2)+\cdots+1 = \frac{n(n-1)}{2}$. We then return to the $(1,2)$ element again, and repeat the entire process. This special method can be shown to converge under appropriate conditions; see [WI], pp. 270–271 for more details. For some time the Jacobi method was considered to be a relic, but recent work in parallel computation has revived interest in it.

Before looking at the code, we make a comment on the accurate computation of the rotation angle θ. From above we have

$$(4.127) \qquad \tan 2\theta = \frac{2a_{pq}}{a_{pp} - a_{qq}} \equiv \alpha^{-1}.$$

This came from requiring that $a'_{pq} = 0$, where

$$(4.128) \qquad a'_{pq} = cs(a_{qq} - a_{pp}) + (c^2 - s^2)a_{pq}.$$

When we set $\tan = \frac{s}{c}$, the equation $a'_{pq} = 0$ can be rewritten as a quadratic

$$(\tan)^2 + 2\alpha(\tan) - 1 = 0.$$

The smaller root of this is

$$\tan = \frac{\operatorname{sgn}\alpha}{|\alpha| + \sqrt{1+\alpha^2}}.$$

It then follows that

$$(4.129) \qquad c = \frac{1}{\sqrt{1+\tan^2}}, \qquad s = c \cdot \tan.$$

Below we present code to implement this algorithm. The elements of the upper–triangle of A are read from a file in lines 50–54, after which A is symmetrized. The matrix **eig** will hold the eigenvectors; it is initialized

to the identity. The current iterate is called a[i][j]; the next iterate is
b[i][j]. If a given element a[p][q] is small, the rotation is skipped.
This is seen in lines 76–80. The rotation angle for a given elimination is
computed on lines 82–95. The rest of the code is, hopefully, sufficiently well
commented.

Each eigenvalue is displayed, followed by the corresponding eigenvector. The program uses command–line arguments as follows: assume that
the upper triangle of A has been entered in a file called jacin.dat; we plan
to write the results out to another file, say jacout.dat. Let the order of
A be n. Then after compilation we execute the program by entering the
command

```
jacobi n jacin.dat jacout.dat
```

```
1  /* Jacobi.c */
2  /*
3  Jacobi method for the eigenvalues and eigenvectors
4  of a symmetric N by N matrix A.  A sequence of
5  similarity transformations converts the matrix into
6  diagonal form, whose entries are the eigenvalues.
7  The eigenvectors are the columns of the accumulated
8  product of the rotation matrices P.
9  A SWEEP is a complete set of N(N-1)/2 rotations.
10 The elements of the upper triangle of A are read from
11 a file.  USAGE:  jacobi order infile.dat outfile.dat
12 */
13
14 # include <math.h>
15 # include <malloc.h>
16 # include <stdio.h>
17 # include <stdlib.h>
18 # include "memalloc.h"
19 # include "memalloc.c"
20 # define PI 3.141592653589793
21 # define MAX(a,b) ((a)>=(b) ?  (a):(b))
22
23 main(int argc, char *argv[])
24 {
25 int i,j,p,q,N,isweep=0;
26 double det=1.0,theta,tan,sgn,alpha,e,c,s,x1,x2;
27 double **a,**b,**eig;
28
29 FILE *fpin,*fpout;
30
```

```
31 if (argc!=4){
32 printf("Usage:     jacobi order infile.dat outfile.dat");
33 }
34
35 else if (!(fpin=fopen(argv[2],"r"))){
36 printf("JACOBI:  Error opening file %s\n",argv[2]);
37 }
38
39 else if (!(fpout=fopen(argv[3],"w"))){
40 printf("JACOBI:  Error opening file %s\n",argv[3]);
41 }
42
43 else{
44
45 N=atoi(argv[1]);
46 a  =matalloc(1,N,1,N);
47 eig=matalloc(1,N,1,N);
48 b  =matalloc(1,N,1,N);
49
50 for (i=1;i<=N;i++){
51         for (j=i;j<=N;j++){
52                 fscanf(fpin,"%lf",&a[i][j]);
53                         }
54                 }
55
56 for (i=2;i<=N;i++){
57         for (j=1;j<=i-1;j++)
58                 a[i][j]=a[j][i];
59                 }
60
61 for (i=1;i<=N;i++){
62         for (j=1;j<=N;j++)
63                 eig[i][j]=0.0;
64                 }
65
66 for (i=1;i<=N;i++)
67         eig[i][i]=1.0;
68
69 for (i=1;i<=N;i++){
70         for (j=1;j<=N;j++)
71                 b[i][j]=a[i][j];
72                 }
73
```

```
74 do
75 {
76 for (p=1;p<=N-1;p++){
77         for (q=p+1;q<=N;q++){
78                 /* skip rotation if a[p][q] is nearly 0 */
79                 if (fabs(a[p][q])<5.0e-20)
80                         continue;
81
82         if (fabs(a[p][p]-a[q][q])<5.0e-20){
83                 sgn=(a[p][q]>0.0) ?  1.0 :  -1.0;
84                 theta=sgn*PI/4.0;
85                 c=cos(theta);
86                 s=sin(theta);
87                 }
88
89         else{
90         alpha = (a[p][p]-a[q][q])/(2.0*a[p][q]);
91         sgn=(alpha>0.0) ?  1.0 :  -1.0;
92         tan=sgn/(fabs(alpha)+sqrt(1.0+alpha*alpha));
93         c=1.0/sqrt(1.0+tan*tan);
94         s=c*tan;
95         }
96
97 /* row p in the upper triangle of the next iterate */
98         for (j=p+1;j<=q-1;j++)
99         b[p][j]=c*a[p][j]+s*a[j][q];
100        b[p][q] = 0.0;
101                for (j=q+1;j<=N;j++)
102                        b[p][j]=c*a[p][j]+s*a[q][j];
103
104 /* this gives row q as in the above remark */
105        for (j=q+1;j<=N;j++)
106        b[q][j]=-s*a[p][j]+c*a[q][j];
107
108 /* the only two diagonal elements that change */
109        b[p][p]=c*c*a[p][p]+2.0*c*s*a[p][q]+s*s*a[q][q];
110        b[q][q]=s*s*a[p][p]-2.0*c*s*a[p][q]+c*c*a[q][q];
111
112 /* column p in the upper triangle:  */
113        for (j=1;j<=p-1;j++)
114        b[j][p]=c*a[j][p]+s*a[j][q];
115
116 /* column q in the upper triangle:  */
```

```
117            for (j=1;j<=p-1;j++)
118            b[j][q]=-s*a[j][p]+c*a[j][q];
119            for (j=p+1;j<=q-1;j++)
120            b[j][q]=-s*a[p][j]+c*a[j][q];
121
122 /* build up the products of the rotations */
123 /* to compute the eigenvectors:   */
124
125 for (i=1;i<=N;i++){
126            x1=eig[i][p];
127            x2=eig[i][q];
128            eig[i][p]=c*x1+s*x2;
129            eig[i][q]=-s*x1+c*x2;
130            }
131
132
133 for (i=1;i<=N;i++){
134            for (j=i;j<=N;j++)
135                    a[i][j]=b[i][j];
136                    }
137
138 }                      /* end q-loop */
139 }                      /* end p-loop */
140
141 e = 0.0;
142 for (i=1;i<=N-1;i++){
143            for (j=i+1;j<=N;j++)
144            e = MAX(e,fabs(b[i][j]));
145            }
146
147 isweep++;
148 }
149
150 while (e>5.0e-11 && isweep<20);
151
152 for (i=1;i<=N;i++)
153            det *= b[i][i];
154
155 for (i=1;i<=N;i++){
156 fprintf(fpout,"eigenvalue[%d] = %14.10lf\n",i,b[i][i]);
157 fprintf(fpout,"The corresponding eigenvector is:  \n");
158 fprintf(fpout,"\n");
159
```

```
160 for (j=1;j<=N;j++)
161          fprintf(fpout,"x[%d] = %14.10lf\n",j,eig[j][i]);
162          fprintf(fpout,"\n");
163
164 }
165 fprintf(fpout,"\n");
166 fprintf(fpout,"determinant = %16.10e\n", det);
167 fprintf(fpout,"\n");
168 fprintf(fpout,"sweeps required = %d\n",isweep);
169 fprintf(fpout,"\n\n");
170
171 }
172 fclose(fpin);fclose(fpout);
173 }
```

We include here a proof that the classical Jacobi method converges. The statement is: as $k \to \infty$, $A_k \to \text{diag}(\lambda_i)$, where $\{\lambda_i\}$ are the eigenvalues of A. It is convenient to use the Hilbert–Schmidt (or Frobenius) norm of a matrix $B = (b_{ij})$, defined by

$$(4.130) \qquad \|B\| \equiv \left(\sum_{k,j} b_{kj}^2 \right)^{\frac{1}{2}}.$$

We write

$$(4.131) \qquad A_k = \text{diag}(a_{ii}^{(k)}) + \mathcal{B}_k,$$

where $\mathcal{B}_k = \mathcal{B}_k^T$ denotes the off–diagonal elements of A_k. We claim that $\|\mathcal{B}_k\| \to 0$ as $k \to \infty$.

In order to show this, consider the expression

$$\sum_{\substack{i \\ i \neq p,q}} \left[(a_{ip}^{(k)})^2 + (a_{iq}^{(k)})^2 \right] = \sum_{\substack{i \\ i \neq p,q}} \left[(ca_{ip}^{(k-1)} + sa_{iq}^{(k-1)})^2 + (-sa_{ip}^{(k-1)} + ca_{iq}^{(k-1)})^2 \right]$$

$$= \sum_{\substack{i \\ i \neq p,q}} \left[(a_{ip}^{(k-1)})^2 + (a_{iq}^{(k-1)})^2 \right].$$

This follows from (4.123). Under the transformation $A_{k-1} \to A_k$, the element $a_{pq}^{(k)}$ becomes 0. Therefore, the left–hand side here equals $\|\mathcal{B}_k\|^2$. The right–hand side is $\|\mathcal{B}_{k-1}\|^2$, except for the omission of the term $2(a_{pq}^{k-1})^2$ (by symmetry). Hence,

$$(4.132) \qquad \|\mathcal{B}_k\|^2 = \|\mathcal{B}_{k-1}\|^2 - 2 \left(a_{pq}^{(k-1)} \right)^2.$$

By choice, $a_{pq}^{(k-1)}$ is the element of maximum modulus. Therefore,

(4.133)
$$\|\mathcal{B}_{k-1}\|^2 = 2 \sum_{\substack{l,j \\ j>l}} [(\mathcal{B}_{k-1})_{lj}]^2$$

$$\leq 2 \left[a_{pq}^{(k-1)}\right]^2 [(n-1) + (n-2) + \cdots + 1]$$

$$= \left[a_{pq}^{(k-1)}\right]^2 \cdot (n-1)n.$$

It now follows that

(4.134)
$$\|\mathcal{B}_k\|^2 \leq \|\mathcal{B}_{k-1}\|^2 \left[1 - \frac{2}{(n-1)n}\right].$$

When this is iterated, we get

$$\|\mathcal{B}_k\|^2 \leq \left[1 - \frac{2}{(n-1)n}\right]^k \|\mathcal{B}_0\|^2$$

(4.135)
$$\to 0, \quad \text{as} \quad k \to \infty.$$

THE SYMMETRIC QR ALGORITHM

This famous method dates from 1961 and the work of Francis; see [WI] for more details. For general matrices it is the most widely used method for eigenvalue computation. It computes both the eigenvalues and eigenvectors and implicitly contains a very stable deflation technique. After a brief introduction, we describe and code the application of the algorithm to eigenvalue calculation in the symmetric case.

The basis of the method is the *QR factorization theorem*: any real square matrix A can be factored in the form $A = QR$ where Q is orthogonal and R is upper–triangular. Given our previous discussion of rotation matrices and the Givens reduction, the proof is easy. We illustrate on a 3×3 matrix A:

$$A = \begin{pmatrix} a_{11} & a_{12} & a_{13} \\ a_{21} & a_{22} & a_{23} \\ a_{31} & a_{32} & a_{33} \end{pmatrix}.$$

Consider the effect of left–multiplying by a rotation T_1^T of the form

$$T_1^T = \begin{pmatrix} c & s & 0 \\ -s & c & 0 \\ 0 & 0 & 1 \end{pmatrix}.$$

We choose the elements c, s so that we will have

$$
T_1^T A = \begin{pmatrix} c & s & 0 \\ -s & c & 0 \\ 0 & 0 & 1 \end{pmatrix} \cdot \begin{pmatrix} a_{11} & a_{12} & a_{13} \\ a_{21} & a_{22} & a_{23} \\ a_{31} & a_{32} & a_{33} \end{pmatrix} = \begin{pmatrix} \hat{a}_{11} & \hat{a}_{12} & \hat{a}_{13} \\ 0 & \hat{a}_{22} & \hat{a}_{23} \\ a_{31} & a_{32} & a_{33} \end{pmatrix}.
$$

The zero is achieved provided $-sa_{11} + ca_{21} = 0$ and we choose

$$
s = \frac{a_{21}}{\sqrt{a_{11}^2 + a_{21}^2}}, \qquad c = \frac{a_{11}}{\sqrt{a_{11}^2 + a_{21}^2}}.
$$

Now we left–multiply this result by another rotation T_2^T to achieve a zero in the 3–1 slot:

$$
T_2^T T_1^T A = \begin{pmatrix} c & 0 & s \\ 0 & 1 & 0 \\ -s & 0 & c \end{pmatrix} \cdot \begin{pmatrix} \hat{a}_{11} & \hat{a}_{12} & \hat{a}_{13} \\ 0 & \hat{a}_{22} & \hat{a}_{23} \\ a_{31} & a_{32} & a_{33} \end{pmatrix} = \begin{pmatrix} \tilde{a}_{11} & \tilde{a}_{12} & \tilde{a}_{13} \\ 0 & \hat{a}_{22} & \hat{a}_{23} \\ 0 & \tilde{a}_{32} & \tilde{a}_{33} \end{pmatrix}
$$

provided $-s\hat{a}_{11} + ca_{31} = 0$. We choose

$$
s = \frac{a_{31}}{\sqrt{(\hat{a}_{11})^2 + a_{31}^2}}, \qquad c = \frac{\hat{a}_{11}}{\sqrt{(\hat{a}_{11})^2 + a_{31}^2}}.
$$

Finally, left–multiplying this by

$$
T_3^T = \begin{pmatrix} 1 & 0 & 0 \\ 0 & c & s \\ 0 & -s & c \end{pmatrix}
$$

for appropriate c, s we obtain

$$
T_3^T T_2^T T_1^T A = \text{upper triangle} \equiv R.
$$

It follows that

$$
A = T_1 T_2 T_3 R \equiv QR,
$$

which is the desired factorization in this simple illustrative case.

The QR algorithm itself is deceptively simple. Define $A_1 \equiv A$ and factor A_1 as above: $A_1 = Q_1 R_1$. Then the next iterate A_2 is defined to be $A_2 = R_1 Q_1$. This new matrix A_2 is factored via $A_2 = Q_2 R_2$ and we set $A_3 = R_2 Q_2$, etc. Notice that at each step we have a similarity transformation: e.g., for A_2 we have $A_2 = R_1 Q_1 = Q_1^{-1} A_1 Q_1 = Q_1^{-1} A Q_1$. Moreover, each A_k is symmetric if A itself is. The QR factorization is not unique, but uniqueness may be shown if it is required that the diagonal elements of R are positive.

In general the workload for a full matrix is prohibitive, so A is first reduced to a special canonical form. For nonsymmetric A we reduce via similarity transformations to (upper) *Hessenberg* form, which means that $a_{ij} = 0$ for $i \geq j + 2$. If A were symmetric, we can reduce to a tridiagonal form, as was seen previously. Moreover one must show that a product $T_1 T_2 \cdots T_N$ of rotations as above is Hessenberg and that whenever R is upper–triangular and Q is Hessenberg, the product RQ remains Hessenberg.

Consider now the symmetric case. By our previous work, we can assume that A has been orthogonally reduced to tridiagonal form from the outset by use of, say, the Givens algorithm. Therefore, to achieve the QR factorization, we need only reduce the elements $a_{i+1,i}$ to zero for $1 \leq i \leq n - 1$. Thus, T_1^T can be chosen to be, in our previous notation, a rotation in the 1–2 plane:

$$T_1^T = \begin{pmatrix} c & s & 0 & \cdots & 0 \\ -s & c & 0 & \cdots & 0 \\ 0 & 0 & 1 & \cdots & 0 \\ \vdots & \vdots & \vdots & \ddots & \vdots \\ 0 & 0 & 0 & \cdots & 1 \end{pmatrix}.$$

Similarly, T_2^T is a rotation in the 2–3 plane:

$$T_2^T = \begin{pmatrix} 1 & 0 & 0 & \cdots & 0 \\ 0 & c & s & \cdots & 0 \\ 0 & -s & c & \cdots & 0 \\ \vdots & \vdots & \vdots & \ddots & \vdots \\ 0 & 0 & 0 & \cdots & 1 \end{pmatrix},$$

etc. Here is a statement of a basic convergence theorem:

Let the eigenvalues of the $n \times n$ matrix A satisfy

$$|\lambda_1| > |\lambda_2| > \cdots > |\lambda_n| > 0.$$

If A is symmetric, then the QR–iterates A_k converge to a diagonal matrix whose entries are the $\{\lambda_i\}$.

The proof is too long to be given here; cf. [WI] or [CI]. Much more than this is generally true. Indeed, if it is assumed that A is already in Hessenberg form, many properties of the QR algorithm have been rigorously established.

The last issue to be addressed is speed of convergence. As given above, the method converges much too slowly to be practical. It is well–known that convergence of eigenvalue algorithms can be enhanced by shifting the origin, i.e., by considering, instead of A itself, the matrix $A - wI$ for an appropriate choice of a parameter w. A typical choice for w is $w = a_{nn}^{(k)}$ where the notation means the nn–element of the matrix A_k. While this usually works, a better choice is to shift as follows: compute the eigenvalues of the 2×2 matrix in the lower right–hand corner of the iterate A_k; call them $\alpha_k \pm i\beta_k$. If $\beta_k \neq 0$, Wilkinson ([WI], p. 512) chooses $w = w_k = \alpha_k$. If these eigenvalues are real and distinct, say $\alpha_k \neq \beta_k \in R^1$, the choice is

$$
w_k = \begin{cases} \alpha_k & \text{if } |\alpha_k - a_{nn}^{(k)}| < |\beta_k - a_{nn}^{(k)}| \\ \beta_k & \text{else.} \end{cases}
$$

It is this latter shift which we employ below.

Here then is the full program with an explanation to follow:

```
1  /* QRSYM.c */
2
3  /*
4  QR method for real symmetric matrices.
5  The upper triangle of the matrix is read from a file
6  at the command line.    Usage:    qrsym order datafile.
7  */
8
9  # include <math.h>
10 # include <malloc.h>
11 # include <stdio.h>
12 # include <stdlib.h>
13 # include "memalloc.c"
14 # include "memalloc.h"
15
16 void givens(int n, double **a)
17
18 /* REDUCES THE MATRIX a[][] TO TRIDIAGONAL FORM */
19 /* INDICES RUN FROM 1 TO n */
20 {
21 int i,j,k;
22 double c,s,x,y,h1,h2;
23
24 for (k=1;k<=n-2;k++){
25 for (i=k+2;i<=n;i++){
26 y=a[k+1][k]*a[k+1][k]+a[i][k]*a[i][k];
27 if (y<5.0e-20){
28         c=1.0;s=0.0;x=sqrt(y);}
29 else{
30 if (fabs(a[k+1][k])<=fabs(a[i][k])){
```

```
31 x=fabs(a[i][k])*sqrt(1.0+a[k+1][k]*a[k+1][k]\
32                         /(a[i][k]*a[i][k]));}
33 else{
34 x=fabs(a[k+1][k])*sqrt(1.0+a[i][k]*a[i][k]\
35                         /(a[k+1][k]*a[k+1][k]));}
36
37             c=a[k+1][k]/x;
38             s=a[i][k]/x;
39 }
40
41                     a[k+1][k]=x;
42                     a[i][k]=0.0;
43
44 for (j=k+1;j<=n;j++){
45         h1=c*a[k+1][j]+s*a[i][j];
46         h2=-s*a[k+1][j]+c*a[i][j];
47         a[k+1][j]=h1;
48         a[i][j]=h2;
49         }
50
51 for (j=1;j<=n;j++){
52         h1=c*a[j][k+1]+s*a[j][i];
53         h2=-s*a[j][k+1]+c*a[j][i];
54         a[j][k+1]=h1;
55         a[j][i]=h2;
56         }
57
58                     }            /* end i-loop */
59                 }                /* end k-loop */
60
61 for (i=3;i<=n;i++){ /* set lower triangle to zero */
62         for (j=1;j<=i-2;j++)
63                 a[i][j]=0.0;
64                 }
65
66 for (i=1;i<=n-2;i++){    /* full tridiagonal form */
67         for (j=i+2;j<=n;j++)
68                 a[i][j]=0.0;
69                 }
70
71 }
72
73 void matmult(int n, double **a, double **b, double **c)
```

```
74 /* unit offset assumed */
75 /* matrix product AB returned in matrix C */
76 {
77 int i,j,k;
78 double s;
79
80 for (i=1;i<=n;i++){
81         for (j=1;j<=n;j++){
82                 s=0.0;
83                 for (k=1;k<=n;k++){
84                 s += a[i][k]*b[k][j];
85                 }
86                 c[i][j]=s;
87             }
88         }
89 }
90
91 void transpos(int n, double **a, double **ta)
92 /* unit offset assumed */
93 {
94 int i,j;
95
96 for (i=1;i<=n;i++){
97         for (j=1;j<=n;j++){
98                 ta[i][j]=a[j][i];
99         }
100 }
101 }
102
103 void qrsym(int n, double **a, double *lambda)
104 {
105 int i,j,k,order,iter=0;
106 double c,s,w,k1,k2,d,oldlambda,p1,p2,discr;
107 double **q,**t,**r;
108
109 t=matalloc(1,n,1,n);
110 q=matalloc(1,n,1,n);
111 r=matalloc(1,n,1,n);
112
113 while (n>1){
114
115 /* compute the shift-cf.  [WI], p.  512 */
116 /* these are the eigenvalues of the 2x2 matrix in the */
```

```
117 /* lower right-hand corner of the matrix.  */
118
119 k1=a[n][n]+a[n-1][n-1];
120 k2=-4.0*a[n][n]*a[n-1][n-1]+4.0*a[n-1][n]*a[n-1][n];
121 discr=k1*k1+k2;
122
123 if (discr <= 0.0)                   /* compute shift */
124         w=k1/2.0;
125 else{
126 p1=(k1+sqrt(fabs(discr)))/2.0;
127 p2=(k1-sqrt(fabs(discr)))/2.0;
128 w=(fabs(p1-a[n][n]) < fabs(p2-a[n][n])) ?  p1 :  p2;
129 }
130
131 for (i=1;i<=n;i++)                   /* perform shift */
132         a[i][i] -= w;
133
134 for (i=1;i<=n-1;i++){ /* loop over subdiagonals */
135 /* subdiagonal element nearly 0 */
136 if (fabs(a[i+1][i])<5.0e-20){
137         c=1.0;
138         s=0.0;
139         }
140 else {
141 if (fabs(a[i][i])<=fabs(a[i+1][i]))
142 d=fabs(a[i+1][i])*sqrt(1.0+a[i][i]*a[i][i]\
143             /(a[i+1][i]*a[i+1][i]));
144 else{
145         if (fabs(a[i][i])<5.0e-20)
146         d=fabs(a[i+1][i]);
147         else
148         d=fabs(a[i][i])*sqrt(1.0+a[i+1][i]*a[i+1][i]\
149             /(a[i][i]*a[i][i]));
150         }
151
152 c=a[i][i]/d;     /* cos and sin of rotation angle */
153 s=a[i+1][i]/d;
154 }
155
156 for (k=1;k<=n;k++) /* diagonal elements of tr(T) */
157         t[k][k]=1.0;
158
159 t[i][i]=t[i+1][i+1]=c;
```

```
160 t[i][i+1]=s;t[i+1][i]=-s;
161
162 for (j=1;j<=n;j++){                 /* tr(T) times A */
163         k1=c*a[i][j]+s*a[i+1][j];
164         k2=-s*a[i][j]+c*a[i+1][j];
165         a[i][j]=k1;
166         a[i+1][j]=k2;
167         }
168
169 if (i>1){
170         for (k=1;k<=n;k++){ /* build up Q: product */
171                             /* of rotations */
172                 k1=c*q[k][i]+s*q[k][i+1];
173                 k2=-s*q[k][i]+c*q[k][i+1];
174                 q[k][i]=k1;
175                 q[k][i+1]=k2;
176                 }
177             }
178 else
179         transpos(n,t,q);      /* at first iteration */
180                               /* define Q */
181
182 t[i][i+1]=t[i+1][i]=0.0;  /* clear T for next iterate */
183
184 }                                    /* end i-loop */
185
186 matmult(n,a,q,r);                    /* product R times Q */
187
188 if (fabs(r[n][n]+w-oldlambda)<5.0e-10){
189 lambda[n]=oldlambda=r[n][n]+w;
190 n--;
191 }
192
193 else
194         oldlambda=r[n][n]+w;
195
196 for (j=1;j<=n;j++){ /* prepare for next iterate */
197         for (k=1;k<=n;k++){
198                 a[j][k]=r[j][k];
199                 }
200         }
201
202 for (j=1;j<=n;j++)             /* restore shift */
```

```
203            a[j][j] += w;
204
205 if (++iter > 50 ){
206            fprintf(stderr,"Too many iterations");
207            exit(1);
208            }
209 }                                  /* end while loop */
210 lambda[1]=a[1][1];
211 }                                      /* end function */
212
213 main(int argc, char *argv[])
214 {
215 int N,i,j,order;
216 double *lambda;
217 double **a;
218
219 void givens(int n, double **a);
220 void matmult(int n, double **a, double **b, double **c);
221 void transpos(int n, double **a, double **ta);
222 void qrsym(int n, double **a, double *lambda);
223
224 FILE *fp;
225 printf("\n\n");
226 if (argc != 3){
227 printf("Usage:    qrsym order afile");
228 }
229
230 else if (!(fp=fopen(argv[2],"r"))){
231 printf("qrsym:    Error opening file %s\n",argv[2]);
232 }
233
234 else{
235            N=order=atoi(argv[1]);
236            a=matalloc(1,N,1,N);
237            lambda=vecalloc(1,N);
238
239        for (i=1;i<=N;i++){
240            for (j=i;j<=N;j++){
241                fscanf(fp,"%lf",&a[i][j]);
242                }
243            }
244
245            for (i=2;i<=N;i++){
```

```
246                          for (j=1;j<=i-1;j++)
247                          a[i][j]=a[j][i];
248                          }
249
250 givens (N,a);
251 qrsym(N,a,lambda);
252
253 for (i=1;i<=order;i++){
254         printf("Eigenvalue[%d]=%10.10lf\n",i,lambda[i]);
255         }
256 }                                    /* end else */
257
258 }                                    /* end main */
```

At the top of the program are listed three routines givens, matmult and transpos which we have encountered before. The function qrsym, starting on line 103, receives a matrix a and its order n as arguments, and returns in the array lambda the eigenvalues. The shift is computed on lines 115–129. On lines 131–132 we subtract the value of the shift from the diagonal elements and begin the QR factorization on line 134.

To eliminate the element $a_{i+1,i}$ ($1 \leq i \leq n - 1$) of the tridiagonal form we compute the rotation cosine and sine in lines 135–154. After defining the elements of the rotation T^T in lines 156–160, we compute the product $T^T A$ on lines 162–167. Then the matrix Q is built up by successive rotations in lines 169–180. Of course, at the first iterate, Q is not yet defined, which explains lines 178–180. Then the matrix r in line 186 contains the next iterate. Once convergence is attained in line 188, n is decremented and the entire process is repeated, but now on a matrix of size $(n - 1) \times (n - 1)$. This "deflation" is very well–behaved. At the conclusion of the while loop, the matrix is simply a scalar, and hence the last remaining eigenvalue is assigned on line 210.

As usual, main is short and simple. It should be self–explanatory. We only point out that it uses command–line arguments. After compilation, we run the program with the command

qrsym order adatafile

where the file adatafile is to contain the upper triangle of the matrix A.

CUBIC SPLINES

Consider a finite interval $[a, b]$ and a grid $a = x_0 < x_1 < \cdots < x_n = b$, not necessarily evenly spaced. We say that a function $\Phi(x)$ is a *cubic spline* on R^1 if

i) On each subinterval $(-\infty, x_0], [x_0, x_1], \ldots, [x_n, \infty)$, $\Phi(x)$ is a cubic polynomial;

ii) Φ, Φ' and Φ'' are continuous on R^1.

Cubic splines are a popular choice for smoothing large sets of data. They avoid the often wildly oscillatory behavior of high–degree polynomial interpolation. If no other information were available, you could (hopefully) approximate the derivative of the data by the derivative of the cubic spline.

Suppose we are given $n+1$ values $y_0, \ldots, y_n$; we seek such a function $\Phi(x)$ so that $\Phi(x_j) = y_j$ for $j = 0, 1, \ldots, n$. On each subinterval $[x_{j-1}, x_j]$ we must have

$$(4.136) \qquad \Phi(x) = \alpha_j + \beta_j x + \gamma_j x^2 + \delta_j x^3 \quad (x_{j-1} \leq x \leq x_j).$$

Thus, there are $4n$ coefficients to be determined. The constraints are

$$(4.137) \qquad \Phi(x_i) = y_i \quad (i = 0, 1, \ldots, n);$$

$$(4.138) \qquad \frac{d^k \Phi(x_i^+)}{dx^k} = \frac{d^k \Phi(x_i^-)}{dx^k} \quad (k = 0, 1, 2), \quad (i = 1, 2, \ldots, n-1).$$

Thus, there are $4n - 2$ constraints in all; we therefore expect to be able to impose two additional conditions freely, since there are two degrees of freedom.

We call $C_i = \Phi''(x_i)$ for $i = 0, 1, \ldots, n$. Then, since Φ is cubic on each subinterval, Φ'' is linear there. It follows that on $[x_i, x_{i+1}]$

$$(4.139) \qquad \Phi''(x) = \frac{(x_{i+1} - x)C_i + (x - x_i)C_{i+1}}{\Delta_i} \quad (i = 0, 1, \ldots, n-1),$$

where

$$(4.140) \qquad \Delta_i = x_{i+1} - x_i.$$

Notice that Φ'' is continuous on $[x_0, x_n]$. Integrating this twice to get Φ, we then have for $i = 0, 1, \ldots, n-1$

$$(4.141) \quad \Phi(x) = \frac{(x_{i+1} - x)^3 C_i + (x - x_i)^3 C_{i+1}}{6\Delta_i} + \gamma'(x_{i+1} - x) + \delta'(x - x_i).$$

Now just impose the conditions $\Phi(x_i) = y_i$, $(i = 0, 1, \ldots, n)$ to find γ', δ' and to get a first formula for $\Phi(x)$ on $x_i \leq x \leq x_{i+1}$, $i = 0, 1, \ldots, n-1$:

$$
\begin{aligned}
\Phi(x) = {} & \frac{(x_{i+1} - x)^3 C_i + (x - x_i)^3 C_{i+1}}{6\Delta_i} + \frac{(x_{i+1} - x)y_i + (x - x_i)y_{i+1}}{\Delta_i} \\
(4.142) \qquad & - \frac{\Delta_i}{6} \left((x_{i+1} - x)C_i + (x - x_i)C_{i+1} \right).
\end{aligned}
$$

Stare at this for a moment and convince yourself that this $\Phi(x)$ is continuous on $[x_0, x_n]$. Hence Φ is completely determined once the C_i's are known.

It remains to enforce the continuity of $\Phi'(x)$ at each grid point, i.e., to require that

$$(4.143) \qquad \lim_{x \to x_i^+} \Phi'(x) = \lim_{x \to x_i^-} \Phi'(x) \quad (i = 1, 2, \dots n - 1).$$

Now use the formula (4.142) above to explicitly compute $\Phi'(x)$ first on $[x_i, x_{i+1}]$ and then on $[x_{i-1}, x_i]$. In each of these two expressions we let $x \to x_i$ and then set the resulting limits equal. When we do, the following linear system results: for $i = 1, 2, \dots, n - 1$,

$$(4.144) \quad \frac{\Delta_{i-1} C_{i-1}}{6} + \frac{(\Delta_i + \Delta_{i-1}) C_i}{3} + \frac{\Delta_i C_{i+1}}{6} = \frac{y_{i+1} - y_i}{\Delta_i} - \frac{y_i - y_{i-1}}{\Delta_{i-1}}.$$

These are $n - 1$ linear equations for $n + 1$ unknowns $C_0, \dots, C_n$. Thus, there are two degrees of freedom, as expected. A typical choice is the *natural boundary conditions* which set $C_0 = C_n = 0$. Then the above system is linear tridiagonal and invertible, as you should confirm using the Gerschgorin theorem (see below).

Here is a straightforward implementation of this procedure:

```
1 /* SPLINE.C */
2
3 /*
4 Read pairs of data values from a file, compute
5 the cubic spline interpolant and write the
6 results out to another data file at steps of 0.005.
7 The data are not assumed equally spaced.
8 Natural boundary conditions are used.
9 Usage:    spline infile.dat outfile.dat
10 */
11
12 # include <stdlib.h>
13 # include <stdio.h>
14 # include <math.h>
15 # include <malloc.h>
16 # include "memalloc.c"
17 # include "memalloc.h"
18 # define MAX(a,b) ((a)>=(b) ?  (a):(b))
19 # define MIN(a,b) ((a)>=(b) ?  (b):(a))
20
21 double maxnum(int m,double *x)
```

```
22 {         /* zero offset indices */
23 int k;
24 double z;
25
26         z=MAX(x[0],x[1]);
27         for (k=2;k<=m-1;k++)
28                 z=MAX(x[k],z);
29         return z;
30 }
31
32 double minnum(int m,double *x)
33 {         /* zero offset indices */
34 int k;
35 double z;
36
37         z=MIN(x[0],x[1]);
38         for (k=2;k<=m-1;k++)
39                 z=MIN(x[k],z);
40         return z;
41 }
42
43 void tridiag(int n, double *sub, double *diag, \
44                 double *sup, double *b)
45 {                         /* zero offset indices */
46 int k;
47 double m;
48 for (k=1;k<=n-1;k++){
49         m =*(sub+k)/(*(diag+k-1));
50         *(diag+k) -= m*(*(sup+k-1));
51         *(b+k) -= m*(*(b+k-1));
52         }
53         *(b+n-1)=*(b+n-1)/(*(diag+n-1));
54         for (k=n-2;k>=0;k--)
55         *(b+k)=(*(b+k)-*(sup+k)*(*(b+k+1)))/(*(diag+k));
56
57 }
58
59 double spline(double x,double xi,double xi_plus1,\
60 double h,double fi,double fi_plus1,double si,\
61 double si_plus1)
62 {
63         double temp1=xi_plus1-x;
64         double temp2=x-xi;
```

```
65          double temp=si*temp1*temp1*temp1/(6.0*h);
66          temp += (si_plus1*temp2*temp2*temp2/(6.0*h));
67          temp += ((fi_plus1/h-h*si_plus1/6.0)*temp2);
68          temp += ((fi/h-h*si/6.0)*temp1);
69          return (temp);
70 }
71
72 main(int argc, char *argv[ ])
73 {
74 int i,n;
75 void tridiag(int n,double *sub,double *diag,\
76                 double *sup,double *b);
77 double spline(double x,double xi,double xi_plus1,\
78 double h,double fi,double fi_plus1, double si,\
79 double si_plus1);
80 double maxnum(int m,double *x);
81 double minnum(int m,double *x);
82 double *h,*x,*y,*s,*f;
83 double *sub,*sup,*diag,*b;
84 double dum,xmax,xmin,ymax,ymin;
85
86 FILE *fpin,*fpout;
87
88 x=vecalloc(0,511);
89 s=vecalloc(0,511);
90 f=vecalloc(0,511);
91 h=vecalloc(0,511);
92
93 sub=vecalloc(0,511);
94 sup=vecalloc(0,511);
95 diag=vecalloc(0,511);
96 b=vecalloc(0,511);
97
98 if (argc != 3){
99 printf("Usage:    spline indatafile outdatafile");
100 }
101
102 else if (!(fpin=fopen(argv[1],"r"))){
103 printf("SPLINE: Error opening file %s\n",argv[1]);
104 }
105
106 else if (!(fpout=fopen(argv[2],"w"))){
107 printf("SPLINE: Error opening file %s\n",argv[2]);
```

```
108 }
109
110 else{
111
112 n=0;
113         while (!feof(fpin)){
114                 fscanf(fpin,"%lf %lf\n",&x[n],&f[n]);
115                 n++;
116                 if (n>512){
117                         printf("Too many data points.");
118                         exit(1);
119                         }
120                 }
121
122 xmax=maxnum(n,x);
123 xmin=minnum(n,x);
124 ymax=maxnum(n,f);
125 ymin=minnum(n,f);
126 }
127
128 fclose(fpin);
129
130 x=(double *)realloc(x,n*sizeof(double));
131 s=(double *)realloc(s,n*sizeof(double));
132 f=(double *)realloc(f,n*sizeof(double));
133 h=(double *)realloc(h,(n-1)*sizeof(double));
134
135 sub=(double *)realloc(sub,(n-2)*sizeof(double));
136 sup=(double *)realloc(sup,(n-2)*sizeof(double));
137 diag=(double *)realloc(diag,(n-2)*sizeof(double));
138 b=(double *)realloc(b,(n-2)*sizeof(double));
139
140 for (i=0;i<=n-2;i++){
141         h[i]=x[i+1]-x[i];
142         }
143
144 for (i=1;i<=n-4;i++){
145 *(sub+i)=*(sup+i)=h[i]/6.0;
146 *(diag+i)=(h[i]+h[i+1])/3.0;
147 }
148
149 *diag=(h[0]+h[1])/3.0;
150 *(diag+n-3)=(h[n-3]+h[n-2])/3.0;
```

```
151 *sup=h[0]/6.0;
152 *(sup+n-3)=0.0;
153 *sub=0.0;
154 *(sub+n-3)=h[n-3]/6.0;
155
156 for (i=1;i<=n-2;i++)
157 *(b+i-1)=(*(f+i+1)-(*(f+i)))\
158 /h[i]-(*(f+i)-(*(f+i-1)))/h[i-1];
159 /* natural BC's:  second derivative = 0 at endpoints */
160 *s=0.0;
161 *(s+n-1)=0.0;
162
163 tridiag(n-2,sub,diag,sup,b);
164
165 for (i=1;i<=n-2;i++)
166         s[i]=b[i-1];
167
168 fprintf(fpout,"minx=%8.6lf maxx=%8.6lf miny=%8.6lf \
169         maxy=%8.6lf\n\n",xmin,xmax,ymin,ymax);
170
171 for (i=0;i<=n-2;i++){
172 for (dum=x[i];dum<=x[i+1];dum += 0.005){
173 fprintf(fpout,"%lf %lf\n",dum,spline(dum,x[i],x[i+1],\
174         h[i],f[i],f[i+1],s[i],s[i+1]));
175                                 }
176                         }
177
178 fclose(fpout);
179
180 } /* end of main */
```

Firstly, please be aware that the indices in this program are zero–offset. The functions **maxnum** and **minnum** return the maximum (minimum) elements of the arrays passed to them; these appear on lines 21–41. The tridiagonal system solver we have used before, but here we use a form with pointer arithmetic, for no other purpose than to illustrate this. The function in lines 59–70, **spline**, computes the function $\Phi(x)$ as shown above in (4.142). Here xi means x_i, si means C_i, h means Δ_i and fi means y_i.

Initially, all vectors are allocated for 512 units of double storage. (Of course you may edit this to accommodate your input file.) This occurs on lines 88–96. The program uses command–line arguments. Two files are opened, first on line 102 (for reading the data in) and then on line 106 (for writing the data out). The input file itself is read on line 112–120 in the **while** loop. Each line of this file should have the format `xvalue yvalue`

with space–delimited entries.

After the maximum and minimum of the input file have been determined, all vectors are reallocated (using `realloc`) on lines 130–138. On lines 144–154 we specify the coefficient matrix and, below that, the right-hand side of the linear system. Notice that n in the program is "n+1" in the discussion. The natural boundary conditions appear on lines 160–161. After the call to `tridiag` in line 163, the results are written out to the output file, and the program concludes.

To conclude this section we prove the *Gerschgorin Theorem*: Every eigenvalue λ of an $n \times n$ matrix A lies in one of the circles

$$(4.145) \qquad |\lambda - a_{ii}| \le \sum_{\substack{j \\ j \ne i}} |a_{ij}|.$$

For the proof, let $Ax = \lambda x$ with $x \ne 0$. Let k be that index with $|x_k| = \|x\|_\infty$. In component form, this matrix equation is

$$(4.146) \qquad \sum_j a_{kj} x_j = \lambda x_k,$$

or

$$(4.147) \qquad a_{kk} x_k + \sum_{\substack{j \\ j \ne k}} a_{kj} x_j = \lambda x_k.$$

Rewriting this as

$$(4.148) \qquad (\lambda - a_{kk}) x_k = \sum_{\substack{j \\ j \ne k}} a_{kj} x_j,$$

we get, by taking absolute values and using the triangle inequality,

$$(4.149) \qquad |\lambda - a_{kk}||x_k| \le \sum_{\substack{j \\ j \ne k}} |a_{kj}| \|x\|.$$

Dividing by $\|x\|_\infty$ we obtain the desired result.

LINEAR SYSTEMS

Here we implement the famous procedure of *Gaussian Elimination* to solve a linear system of equations $Ax = b$. Here x and b are n–vectors, and A is a square matrix of order n. As you know, the goal is to reduce the system to upper–triangular form, after which the solution is simple. Since this procedure is probably well–known, we only sketch the method.

We proceed column by column, reducing to zero all elements below the diagonal. Write $Ax = b$ as $A^{(1)}x = b^{(1)}$ with $A^{(1)} = A$, $b^{(1)} = b$. Assuming that $a_{11}^{(1)} \neq 0$, we define the multipliers

$$(4.150) \qquad \qquad \mu_{i1} = \frac{a_{i1}^{(1)}}{a_{11}^{(1)}} \qquad (i = 2, 3, \ldots, n).$$

We can use these to eliminate the variable x_1 from equations 2 through n by computing

$$(4.151) \qquad \qquad a_{ij}^{(2)} = a_{ij}^{(1)} - \mu_{i1}a_{ij}^{(1)} \quad (i, j = 2, \ldots, n)$$
$$b_i^{(2)} = b_i^{(1)} - \mu_{i1}b_1^{(1)}.$$

Notice that the system $A^{(2)}x = b^{(2)}$ has its first row unchanged, while all elements in the first column below the diagonal are now reduced to zero. Next we eliminate all elements in the second column below the diagonal by a similar procedure. This process can clearly be repeated. In general, we eliminate the variable x_k from equations $k + 1$ through n as follows: assuming that $a_{kk}^{(k)} \neq 0$, we define the multipliers

$$(4.152) \qquad \qquad \mu_{ik} = \frac{a_{ik}^{(k)}}{a_{kk}^{(k)}} \qquad (i = k + 1, \ldots, n).$$

Then, as above, we compute

$$(4.153) \qquad \qquad a_{ij}^{(k+1)} = a_{ij}^{(k)} - \mu_{ik}a_{kj}^{(k)} \quad (i, j = k + 1, \ldots, n)$$
$$b_i^{(k+1)} = b_i^{(k)} - \mu_{ik}b_k^{(k)}.$$

At the conclusion of this process, an upper–triangular form of the coefficient matrix has been achieved; we call it U. When the entries μ_{ik} are appropriately inserted into a unit lower–triangular matrix, the canonical factorization $A = L \cdot U$ results. There is a practical problem, however: in the computation of the multipliers above, we may have divided by some rather small numbers, spoiling accuracy. For this reason, *pivoting* is used. At step k, after the variables $x_1, \ldots, x_{k-1}$ have been eliminated, we scan the column of values to be reduced to zero, starting with the diagonal element. These values are $a_{kk}^{(k)}, \ldots, a_{nk}^{(k)}$. The maximum element in absolute value is found. Let's say that this maximum element occurs in row j; partial pivoting then requires that we swap the elements of rows k and j. This renders all of the multipliers no greater than unity in absolute value and improves accuracy greatly.

The code below is a direct implementation of this procedure. No scaling is performed, so it is of the "plain vanilla" variety. It uses command–line arguments and reads the data from files. You would run it with, for example, the command

linsyst n a.dat b.dat

where n is the order of the coefficient matrix A, a.dat is an ASCII file containing the elements of A, and b.dat is a file with the entries of the given right–hand side b.

The actual elimination is performed by the function gausselm, beginning on line 31. You see that it takes as arguments the order N of the matrix A (written **a), the right–hand side *b (in which the solution is returned), and a double pointer *det. The loop on i, beginning on line 43, executes the elimination on column i. The test for pivoting starts on line 45; the checking appears on lines 51–59 in a do loop. Lines 76–83 contain the computation of the multipliers and of the new matrix elements, etc.

main itself is characteristically short. It opens the data files for reading, after checking that the number of command–line arguments is correct. Then it simply calls gausselm followed by uppertri, an upper–triangular system solver which we have encountered before. Please notice that all indices in this program are unit offset. Here is the full listing:

```
1  /*   LINSYST.C   */
2  /*   SOLUTION OF Ax = b VIA GAUSS ELIMINATION   */
3
4  # include <math.h>
5  # include <stdio.h>
6  # include <stdlib.h>
7  # include <malloc.h>
8  # include "memalloc.c"
9  # include "memalloc.h"
10 # define MAX(a,b) ((a)>=(b) ?  (a) :  (b) )
11
12 void swap(double *x, double *y)
13 {
14 double temp;
15 temp=*x;
16 *x=*y;
17 *y=temp;
18 }
19
20 double maxnum(int m,double *x)
```

```
21 {
22 int k;
23 double z;
24
25         z=MAX(fabs(x[1]),fabs(x[2]));
26         for (k=3;k<=m;k++)
27                 z=MAX(fabs(x[k]),z);
28         return z;
29 }
30
31 void gausselm(int N, double **a, double *b, double *det)
32 /* unit-offset indices used.  */
33 {
34 int i,j,k;
35 double *u,*m;
36 double maxentry;
37 void swap(double *x, double *y);
38 double maxnum(int m, double *x);
39
40 u=vecalloc(1,N);
41 m=vecalloc(1,N-1);
42
43 for (i=1;i<=N-1;i++){
44
45 /* determine if pivoting is needed:  */
46 for (k=0;k<=N-i;k++)
47         u[k+1]=a[k+i][i];
48
49 maxentry=maxnum(N-i+1,u);
50
51 if (fabs(fabs(a[i][i])-maxentry)> 5.0e-15){
52 /* perform partial pivoting */
53
54 j = 0;
55 do{
56 j++;
57 if (j==N-i) break;
58 }
59 while (fabs(fabs(a[i+j][i])-maxentry)> 5.0e-15);
60
61 for (k=i;k<=N;k++)
62         swap(&a[i+j][k],&a[i][k]);
63
```

```
64 swap(&b[i+j],&b[i]);
65
66 *det *= -(1.0);
67 }
68
69 if (fabs(a[i][i])<5.0e-15) {
70 fprintf(stderr,"\aMatrix singular to working accuracy.");
71 exit(1);
72 }
73
74 else{
75
76 for (k=1;k<=N-i;k++)
77         m[k]=-a[k+i][i]/a[i][i];
78
79         for (k=i+1;k<=N;k++){
80         b[k] += (m[k-i]*b[i]);
81         for (j=i+1;j<=N;j++)
82         a[k][j] += (m[k-i]*a[i][j]);
83         }                               /* end k-loop */
84 }                               /* end if      */
85 }                               /* end i-loop */
86
87 for (i=1;i<=N;i++)
88         *det *= a[i][i];
89 }
90
91 void uppertri (int n, double **u, double *b)
92 /* unit-offset indices used.  */
93 {
94 int j,k;
95 double s=0.0;
96
97 if (fabs(u[n][n])<5.0e-15){
98 fprintf(stderr,"\aMatrix singular to working accuracy.");
99 exit(1);
100 }
101
102 b[n]  /= u[n][n];
103 for (k=n-1;k>=1;k--){
104
105 if (fabs(u[k][k])<5.0e-15){
106 fprintf(stderr,"\aMatrix singular to working accuracy.");
```

```
107 exit(1);
108 }
109
110         s=0.0;
111         for (j=k+1;j<=n;j++)
112         s += u[k][j]*b[j];
113
114         b[k] = (b[k]-s)/u[k][k];
115         }
116 }
117
118 main(int argc, char *argv[ ])
119 {
120 void gausselm(int N, double **a, double *b, double *det);
121 void uppertri(int n, double **a, double *b);
122 FILE *fpa,*fpb;
123
124 int N,i,j;
125 double *b,**a;
126
127 double s=0.0,det=1.0,maxentry;
128
129 printf("\n\n");
130 if (argc != 4){
131 printf("Usage:    LINSYST order afile bfile");
132 }
133
134 else if (!(fpa=fopen(argv[2],"r"))){
135 printf("LINSYST: Error opening file %s\n",argv[2]);
136 }
137
138 else if (!(fpb=fopen(argv[3],"r"))){
139 printf("LINSYST: Error opening file %s\n",argv[3]);
140 }
141
142 else{
143 N=atoi(argv[1]);
144 b=vecalloc(1,N);
145 a=matalloc(1,N,1,N);
146
147 for (i=1;i<=N;i++){
148         for (j=1;j<=N;j++){
149         fscanf(fpa,"%lf",&a[i][j]);
```

```
150              }
151 }
152
153 for (i=1;i<=N;i++){
154         fscanf(fpb,"%lf",&b[i]);
155 }
156
157 gausselm(N,a,b,&det);
158 uppertri(N,a,b);
159
160 printf("The solution components are:\n\n");
161 for (i=1;i<=N;i++)
162 printf("x[%d] = %10.10lf\n",i,b[i]);
163 printf("\n\n");
164 printf("determinant = %10.10e\n\n",det);
165
166 }   /* end else */
167
168 }   /* end main() */
```

We end this section with a comment on matrix inversion. You may remember that you never invert a matrix unless you really have to. In case you do, the code above can be easily used as follows. Let A be $n \times n$, and let e^i be the ith coordinate basis vector. That is, component k of e^i equals δ_{ik}. Finding the inverse of A is the same as solving the matrix equation $AX = I$ where X is $n \times n$. One solves n linear systems $Ax^i = e^i$ $(i = 1, 2, \ldots, n)$ by the above method and then forms the matrix X whose columns are the vectors x^i. This matrix X is the inverse of A. For efficiency, the function gausselm should be rewritten so that it returns the factorization $A = LU$ and does not alter b. In this manner only one call to gausselm would be required.

NEWTON'S METHOD FOR SYSTEMS

The first thing you want to be aware of is that nonlinear systems are very difficult. The present state is this: if you have a good initial approximation, then it can be refined beautifully and quickly. However, finding a "good" initial guess for a nonlinear system is a nasty problem in general and is a topic of current research.

Here we present simple code for Newton's method. Let $f(x)$ be an n–component vector function of a vector variable $x \in R^n$. We wish to solve $f(x) = 0$ for x. What should the scheme be? With the one–dimensional case in mind, you probably see that the algorithm should follow the same pattern, once we have a suitable replacement for the ordinary one–dimensional derivative used in the scalar case. A bit of thought (and your study of multidimensional calculus) will lead you to the guess that the appropriate quantity is the *Jacobian matrix* J_f of f. The ijth element of J_f is $\frac{\partial f_i}{\partial x_j}$, and, by analogy to the one–dimensional case, the scheme is

$$(4.154) \qquad x^{(k+1)} = x^{(k)} - J_f^{-1}(x^{(k)}) f(x^{(k)}) \quad (k = 0, 1, \ldots),$$

with $x^{(0)}$ the initial (vector) approximation.

As was pointed out earlier, you should never invert a matrix unless you must. Thus, we rewrite the scheme as

$$(4.155) \qquad J_f(x^{(k)}) \left(x^{(k)} - x^{(k+1)} \right) = f(x^{(k)}) \quad (k = 0, 1, \ldots).$$

Once this linear system is solved, the new approximation $x^{(k+1)}$ is easily recovered.

What about convergence? You may remember the phrase "it should converge if the initial approximation is good enough." Just what does this mean? Here is a statement of the famous theorem of Kantorovich, which addresses the issue directly:

Let $f \in C^2$. Assume that, at the initial approximation $x^{(0)}$, the matrix J_f is invertible and satisfies

$$(4.156) \qquad \|J_f^{-1}(x^{(0)})\|_\infty \le a.$$

Furthermore, assume that

$$(4.157) \qquad \|x^{(1)} - x^{(0)}\|_\infty = \|J_f^{-1}(x^{(0)}) f(x^{(0)})\|_\infty \le b$$

and

$$(4.158) \qquad \sum_{j,k=1}^n \left| \frac{\partial^2 f_i}{\partial x_j \partial x_k}(x) \right| \le c \quad (i = 1, \ldots, n)$$

for all x satisfying $\|x - x^{(0)}\|_\infty \le 2b$.

Then if $abc \le \frac{1}{2}$, the Newton iterates $x^{(k)}$ converge quadratically to a vector α which satisfies $f(\alpha) = 0$. I refer you to [IK] or [HE] for a proof.

The code below should be easy to understand. The function `vectorfn` (on line 13) computes the vector function f and the Jacobian matrix J_f at the input vector x. We use here standard unit–offset mathematical notation for vectors and the matrix J_f. We have already encountered the functions gausselm and uppertri in the previous program, so there is nothing new until the iteration loop, beginning on line 191, and this code fragment is a straightforward implementation of the algorithm above. Several examples are given in the vectorfn body; all but one are commented out. There are a multitude of reasons for this program to refuse to cooperate. Refinement of the initial guess should always be your first attempt.

```
1  /* SYSTEMS.C */
2  /* Nonlinear Systems via NEWTON's Method */
3
4  # include <stdio.h>
5  # include <stdlib.h>
6  # include <math.h>
7  # include <malloc.h>
8  # include "memalloc.c"
9  # include "memalloc.h"
10 # define PI 3.141592653589793
11 # define MAX(a,b) ((a)>=(b) ?  (a) :  (b) )
12
13 void vectorfn(double *x, double **Jf, double *f)
14 {
15 /* f is the vector function */
16 /* Jf is the Jacobian matrix */
17
18 /* solution near (-0.5,0.25) */
19 /*
20 Jf[1][1] = 6.0*x[1];
21 Jf[1][2] = 8.0*x[2];
22 Jf[2][1]=  -24.0*x[1]*x[1];
23 Jf[2][2]=  3.0*x[2]*x[2];
24 f[1]=3.0*x[1]*x[1]+4.0*x[2]*x[2]-1.0;
25 f[2] =x[2]*x[2]*x[2]-8.0*x[1]*x[1]*x[1]-1.0;
26 */
27
28 /* solution near (-.5,.25) */
29 /*
30 Jf[1][1] = 8.0*x[1];
31 Jf[1][2] = 2.0*x[2];
32 Jf[2][1]=  1.0-cos(x[1]-x[2]);
33 Jf[2][2]=  1.0+cos(x[1]-x[2]);
34 f[1]=4.0*x[1]*x[1]+x[2]*x[2]-4.0;
35 f[2] =x[1]+x[2]-sin(x[1]-x[2]);
36 */
```

```
37
38 /* start near (.1,.1,-.1) , [BF], p.539 */
39 Jf[1][1] = 3.0;
40 Jf[1][2] = x[3]*sin(x[2]*x[3]);
41 Jf[1][3] = x[2]*sin(x[2]*x[3]);
42
43 Jf[2][1] = 2.0*x[1];
44 Jf[2][2] = -162.0*(x[2]+0.1);
45 Jf[2][3] = cos(x[3]);
46
47 Jf[3][1] = -x[2]*exp(-x[1]*x[2]);
48 Jf[3][2] = -x[1]*exp(-x[1]*x[2]);
49 Jf[3][3] = 20.0;
50
51 f[1]=3.0*x[1]-cos(x[2]*x[3])-0.5;
52 f[2] =x[1]*x[1]-81.0*(x[2]+0.1)*(x[2]+0.1)+sin(x[3])+1.06;
53 f[3]=exp(-x[1]*x[2])+20.0*x[3]+(10.0*PI-3.0)/3.0;
54
55 }
56
57 void swap(double *x, double *y)
58 {
59 double temp;
60 temp=*x;
61 *x=*y;
62 *y=temp;
63 }
64
65 double maxnum(int m,double *x)
66 {
67 int k;
68 double z;
69
70         z=MAX(fabs(x[1]),fabs(x[2]));
71         for (k=3;k<=m;k++)
72                 z=MAX(fabs(x[k]),z);
73         return z;
74 }
75
76 void gausselm(int N, double **a, double *b, double *det)
77 /* unit-offset indices used.  */
78 {
79 int i,j,k;
```

```
80  double *u,*m;
81  double maxentry;
82  void swap(double *x, double *y);
83  double maxnum(int m, double *x);
84
85  u=vecalloc(1,N);
86  m=vecalloc(1,N-1);
87
88  for (i=1;i<=N-1;i++){
89
90  /* determine if pivoting is needed:  */
91  for (k=0;k<=N-i;k++)
92          u[k+1]=a[k+i][i];
93
94  maxentry=maxnum(N-i+1,u);
95
96  if (fabs(fabs(a[i][i])-maxentry)> 5.0e-15){
97  /* perform partial pivoting */
98
99  j = 0;
100 do{
101 j++;
102 if (j==N-i) break;
103 }
104 while (fabs(fabs(a[i+j][i])-maxentry)> 5.0e-15);
105
106 for (k=i;k<=N;k++)
107         swap(&a[i+j][k],&a[i][k]);
108
109 swap(&b[i+j],&b[i]);
110
111 *det *= -(1.0);
112 }
113
114 if (fabs(a[i][i])<5.0e-15) {
115 fprintf(stderr,"\aMatrix singular to working accuracy.");
116 exit(1);
117 }
118
119 else{
120
121 for (k=1;k<=N-i;k++)
122         m[k]=-a[k+i][i]/a[i][i];
```

```
123
124            for (k=i+1;k<=N;k++){
125            b[k] += (m[k-i]*b[i]);
126            for (j=i+1;j<=N;j++)
127            a[k][j] += (m[k-i]*a[i][j]);
128            }                                    /* end k-loop */
129 }                                        /* end if     */
130 }                                        /* end i-loop */
131
132 for (i=1;i<=N;i++)
133            *det *= a[i][i];
134 }
135
136 void uppertri (int n, double **u, double *b)
137 /* unit-offset indices used.   */
138 {
139 int j,k;
140 double s=0.0;
141
142 if (fabs(u[n][n])<5.0e-15){
143 fprintf(stderr,"\aMatrix singular to working accuracy.");
144 exit(1);
145 }
146
147 b[n] /= u[n][n];
148 for (k=n-1;k>=1;k--){
149
150 if (fabs(u[k][k])<5.0e-15){
151 fprintf(stderr,"\aMatrix singular to working accuracy.");
152 exit(1);
153 }
154
155            s=0.0;
156            for (j=k+1;j<=n;j++)
157            s += u[k][j]*b[j];
158
159            b[k] = (b[k]-s)/u[k][k];
160            }
161 }
162
163 main()
164 {
165 int iter=0,i,N;
```

```
166 double det=1.0;
167 double *xold,*xnew,*y,*f,*e,**Jf;
168 void vectorfn(double *x, double **Jf, double *f);
169 double maxnum(int m,double *x);
170 void swap(double *x, double *y);
171 void gausselm(int N, double **a, double *b, double *det);
172 void uppertri (int n, double **u, double *b);
173
174         printf("\n\n");
175         printf("Enter the number of equations:  ");
176             scanf("%d",&N);
177         printf("\n\n");
178
179     Jf  =matalloc(1,N,1,N);     /* Jacobian */
180     f   =vecalloc(1,N); /* vector function */
181     xold =vecalloc(1,N);  /* present iterate */
182     xnew =vecalloc(1,N);     /* next iterate */
183     y    =vecalloc(1,N);      /* xold - xnew */
184     e    =vecalloc(1,N);
185
186 for (i=1;i<=N;i++){
187 printf("Enter the initial approximation for x[%d]:  ",i);
188             scanf("%lf",&xold[i]);
189                 }
190
191             do{
192             vectorfn(xold,Jf,f);
193             for (i=1;i<=N;i++){
194               y[i]=f[i];
195               }
196
197 gausselm(N,Jf,y,&det); /* LU - factorization */
198 uppertri(N,Jf,y);                 /* backsolve */
199 for (i=1;i<=N;i++){
200         xnew[i]=xold[i]-y[i];
201         e[i]=fabs(xnew[i]-xold[i]); /* error vector */
202         }
203
204             for (i=1;i<=N;i++){
205               xold[i]=xnew[i];    /* next iterate */
206               }
207
208
```

```
209        if (++iter>100){
210        fprintf(stderr,"Too many iterations.");
211             exit(1);
212             }
213        }
214        while (maxnum(N,e)>maxnum(N,xnew)*5.0e-11);
215
216        printf("\n");
217        printf("Solution:\n");
218        for (i=1;i<=N;i++){
219        printf("x[%d]=%14.10lf\n",i,xnew[i]);
220        printf("Function[%d] value=%1.8e\n",i,f[i]);
221             }
222        printf("\n");
223        printf("%d iterates were required.",iter);
224        printf("\n");
225
226 }
```

POISSON'S EQUATION AND SOR

Poisson's Equation is the elliptic partial differential equation

$$(4.159) \qquad u_{xx} + u_{yy} = f(x, y) \quad ((x, y) \in \Omega)$$

with a given function f and given boundary conditions on $\partial\Omega$. Below we take Ω to be a square with edge length a and zero boundary conditions on all edges. We employ the standard second–order centered finite–difference scheme: given an integer N, set $h = \frac{a}{N+1}$ and write $u(jh, kh) \approx u_{j,k}$. Then the scheme is

$$(4.160) \qquad \frac{u_{j+1,k} - 2u_{j,k} + u_{j-1,k}}{h^2} + \frac{u_{j,k+1} - 2u_{j,k} + u_{j,k-1}}{h^2} = f_{j,k}.$$

Here $1 \leq j, k \leq N$ and we set $u_{j,k} = 0$ for $j = 0, N + 1$ for all k, and $u_{j,k} = 0$ for $k = 0, N + 1$ for all j.

We can rewrite this scheme as

$$(4.161) \qquad u_{j,k} - \frac{u_{j+1,k} + u_{j-1,k}}{4} - \frac{u_{j,k+1} + u_{j,k-1}}{4} = -\frac{h^2}{4} f_{j,k}.$$

Since the coefficient matrix is symmetric, the Gauss–Seidel iteration is a natural choice. It turns out that this is much too slow, however, so faster methods have been developed. A favorite choice is *successive over–relaxation*, or *SOR*. For a linear system $Ax = b$, the Gauss–Seidel iteration is replaced by a two–step process involving a parameter w: for $i = 1, 2, \ldots, n$ we use

$$(4.162) \qquad \hat{x}_i^{(m+1)} = \frac{1}{a_{ii}} \left(b_i - \sum_{j=1}^{i-1} a_{ij} x_j^{(m+1)} - \sum_{j=i+1}^{n} a_{ij} x_j^{(m)} \right)$$

$$(4.163) \qquad x_i^{(m+1)} = w \hat{x}_i^{(m+1)} + (1 - w) x_i^{(m)}.$$

How should we choose the parameter? Certainly it should be chosen to maximize the rate of convergence. In practice, however, the optimal choice of w is extremely difficult. For a square the result is known explicitly:

$$(4.164) \qquad w = \frac{2}{1 + \sqrt{1 - \rho_J^2}},$$

where ρ_J is the spectral radius of the Jacobi iteration for the same geometry. In the code below ρ_J is called η (on line 57). Please see [IK] or [GvL] for details, which are too lengthy to be given here. In our case here, the SOR iteration can be written in the explicit form $(m = 0, 1, \ldots)$

$$u_{j,k}^{(m+1)} = \frac{w}{4} \left(u_{j+1,k}^{(m)} + u_{j,k+1}^{(m)} + u_{j-1,k}^{(m+1)} + u_{j,k-1}^{(m+1)} - h^2 f_{j,k} \right) + (1 - w) u_{j,k}^{(m)}.$$

The computation is done in the following manner. We can begin with the initial approximation $u_{j,k}^{(0)} = 0$. We proceed row by row, starting at the bottom. In any given row, we compute from left to right. Then we iterate on m until some desired convergence criterion is met.

Below we take a simple and contrived example in which $a = 1$, $N = 19$ and

$$f(x, y) = -\sin(\pi x) \left(\pi^2 y (1 - y) + 2 \right).$$

Uniqueness follows from the maximum principle; the exact solution is found to be

$$u(x, y) = \sin(\pi x) y (1 - y).$$

Here is a straightforward implementation of this SOR algorithm.

```
1 /* POISSON.C */
2
3 /*
4 Fast Poisson solver using SOR on a
5 square  R: 0 < x,y < a
6 PDE is Laplacian(u) = f in R, u = 0 on the boundary of R
7 */
```

```
 8
 9 # include <math.h>
10 # include <malloc.h>
11 # include <stdio.h>
12 # include "memalloc.c"
13 # include "memalloc.h"
14 # define MAX(a,b) ((a)>=(b) ?  (a) :  (b))
15 # define PI 3.141592653589793
16
17 double maxnum(int m, double *x)
18 {
19 int k;
20 double z;
21
22          z=MAX(fabs(x[1]),fabs(x[2]));
23          for (k=3;k<=m;k++)
24                  z=MAX(fabs(x[k]),z);
25          return z;
26 }
27
28 double f(double x, double y)
29 {
30 return (-sin(PI*x)*(2.0+PI*PI*y*(1.0-y)));
31 }
32
33 main (int argc, char *argv[ ])
34 {
35 int k,j,N;
36 double a,eta,w,h,rsum;
37 double f(double x, double y);
38 double maxnum(int m, double *x);
39 double *e,**uold,**unew;
40 FILE *fp;
41
42 if (argc != 2){
43 puts("Usage:    poisson outfile ");
44 }
45
46 else if (!(fp=fopen(argv[1],"w"))){
47 printf("POISSON: Error opening file %s\n",argv[1]);
48 }
49
50 else{    /* enter data here */
```

```
51
52 a=1.0;     /* length in either direction */
53 N=19;      /* number of interior points  */
54
55 h=a/(N+1.0);
56
57 eta=1.0-2.0*sin(PI/(2.0*(N+1.0)))*sin(PI/(2.0*(N+1.0)));
58
59 w=2.0/(1.0+sqrt(1.0-eta*eta));
60
61 e=vecalloc(1,N);
62 uold=matalloc(0,N+1,0,N+1);
63 unew=matalloc(0,N+1,0,N+1);
64
65 do{
66
67 for (k=1;k<=N;k++){
68 for (j=1;j<=N;j++){
69
70 unew[j][k]  = (0.25)*w*(uold[j+1][k]+uold[j][k+1]+\
71                 unew[j-1][k]+unew[j][k-1]-\
72                 h*h*f(j*h,k*h))+(1.0-w)*uold[j][k];
73
74 }         /* end j loop */
75 }         /* end k loop */
76
77 for (j=1;j<=N;j++){
78         rsum=0.0;
79         for (k=1;k<=N;k++){
80            rsum += fabs(unew[j][k]-uold[j][k]);
81            e[j]  = rsum;
82            }
83         }
84
85 for (j=1;j<=N;j++){
86         for (k=1;k<=N;k++){
87            uold[j][k]=unew[j][k];
88            }
89         }
90
91 }while (maxnum(N,e)>5.0e-9);
92
93 for (j=0;j<=N+1;j++){
```

```
 94          for (k=0;k<=N+1;k++){
 95
 96 fprintf(fp,"%12.6lf %12.6lf %12.6lf\n",j*h,k*h,unew[j][k]);
 97 }
 98 }
 99
100 fprintf(fp,"\n\n");
101
102 }   /* end else */
103
104 }   /* end main */
```

APPENDIX I

COMPLEX
ARITHMETIC FUNCTIONS

Here we list the complex arithmetic functions in the file cpxarith.c.

```
1  /* CPXARITH.C */
2  /* COMPLEX ARITHMETIC FUNCTIONS */
3
4  # include <math.h>
5  # include <stdlib.h>
6  # include <stdio.h>
7
8  /* remove the following comment */
9  /* if struct complex is undefined */
10 /*
11 struct complex{
12         double x;
13         double y;
14 };
15 */
16
17 /* remove the following comment if cabs is undefined */
18 /*
19 double cabs(struct complex z)
20 {
21 if (z.x==0.0 && z.y==0.0)
22         return 0.0;
23
```

```
24 else if (fabs(z.x) <= fabs(z.y))
25 return fabs(z.y)*sqrt(1.0+z.x*z.x/(z.y*z.y));
26 else
27 return fabs(z.x)*sqrt(1.0+z.y*z.y/(z.x*z.x));
28 }
29 */
```

```
1 struct complex cpxadd( struct complex z, struct complex w)
2 {
3         struct complex Z;
4         Z.x=z.x+w.x;
5         Z.y=z.y+w.y;
6         return Z;
7 }
```

```
1 struct complex cpxsub( struct complex z, struct complex w)
2 {
3         struct complex Z;
4         Z.x=z.x-w.x;
5         Z.y=z.y-w.y;
6         return Z;
7 }
```

```
1 struct complex cpxmult(struct complex z, struct complex w)
2 {
3         struct complex Z;
4         Z.x=(z.x)*(w.x)-(z.y)*(w.y);
5         Z.y=(z.y)*(w.x)+(z.x)*(w.y);
6         return Z;
7 }
```

```
1 struct complex cpxdiv(struct complex n,struct complex d)
2 {
3 struct complex Z;
4 double temp1,temp2;
5
6 if (cabs(d)<(5.0e-20)*cabs(n)){
7         fprintf(stderr,"division by zero in cpxdiv");
8         exit(1);
9         }
10
11 if (fabs(d.x)<=fabs(d.y)){
12         temp1=d.x/d.y;
13         temp2=d.y+temp1*d.x;
```

```
14          Z.x=(temp1*n.x+n.y)/temp2;
15          Z.y=(temp1*n.y-n.x)/temp2;
16          }
17
18 else{
19          temp1=d.y/d.x;
20          temp2=d.x+temp1*d.y;
21          Z.x=(n.x+temp1*n.y)/temp2;
22          Z.y=(n.y-temp1*n.x)/temp2;
23          }
24
25 return Z;
26 }
```

```
1 struct complex cpxsqrt(struct complex z)
2 {
3          struct complex Z;
4          double phi,r=sqrt(cabs(z));
5
6          double theta=atan2(z.y,z.x);
7          phi=theta/2.0;
8          Z.x=r*cos(phi);
9          Z.y=r*sin(phi);
10          return Z;
11 }
```

```
1 struct complex cpxexp(struct complex z)
2 {
3          struct complex Z;
4          Z.x=exp(z.x)*cos(z.y);
5          Z.y=exp(z.x)*sin(z.y);
6          return Z;
7 }
```

```
1 struct complex cpxsin(struct complex z)
2 {
3          struct complex Z;
4          Z.x=sin(z.x)*cosh(z.y);
5          Z.y=cos(z.x)*sinh(z.y);
6          return Z;
7 }
```

```
1 struct complex cpxcos(struct complex z)
2 {
```

```
3          struct complex Z;
4          Z.x=cos(z.x)*cosh(z.y);
5          Z.y=-sin(z.x)*sinh(z.y);
6          return Z;
7 }
```

```
 1 struct complex cpxipow(struct complex z, int n)
 2 {
 3          /* returns z^n for integral n */
 4          struct complex Z;
 5          double r=cabs(z);
 6          double theta=atan2(z.y,z.x);
 7          Z.x=pow(r,(double)n)*cos((double)n*theta);
 8          Z.y=pow(r,(double)n)*sin((double)n*theta);
 9          return (Z);
10 }
```

```
1 struct complex cpxlog(struct complex z)
2 {
3          struct complex Z;
4          double r=cabs(z);
5
6          Z.y=atan2(z.y,z.x);
7          Z.x=log(r);
8          return (Z);
9 }
```

A header file cpxarith.h for such functions follows:

```
 1 /* CPXARITH.H */
 2
 3 struct complex cpxadd(struct complex z, struct complex w);
 4 struct complex cpxsub(struct complex z, struct complex w);
 5 struct complex cpxmult(struct complex z,struct complex w);
 6 struct complex cpxdiv(struct complex a, struct complex b)
 7 struct complex cpxsqrt(struct complex z);
 8 struct complex cpxexp(struct complex z);
 9 struct complex cpxsin(struct complex z);
10 struct complex cpxcos(struct complex z);
11 struct complex cpxipow(struct complex z, int n);
12 struct complex cpxlog(struct complex z);
```

APPENDIX II

MEMORY
ALLOCATION FUNCTIONS

Throughout the book we have defined and allocated vectors and matrices using the functions vecalloc and matalloc, both of which are written for double values. If an error occurs when including the file malloc.h, simply comment that line out. Here are the contents of memalloc.c:

```
 1 # include <malloc.h>
 2 # include <stdlib.h>
 3 # include <stdio.h>
 4
 5 double *vecalloc(int low,int high)
 6 {
 7 double *x;
 8
 9 x=(double *)calloc((unsigned)(high-low+1),sizeof(double));
10 if (x==NULL){
11 fprintf(stderr,"unable to allocate memory");
12 exit(1);
13 }
14 return (x-low);
15 }
16
17 double **matalloc(int rowlow, int rowhigh,\
18 int collow,int colhigh)
19 {
20 int k;
```

```
21 double **x;
22 x=(double **) calloc((unsigned) (rowhigh-rowlow+1),\
23 sizeof(double *));
24 if (x==NULL){
25 fprintf(stderr,"unable to allocate memory");
26 exit(1);
27 }
28 x -= rowlow;
29
30 for(k=rowlow;k<=rowhigh;k++) {
31 x[k]=(double *) calloc((unsigned) (colhigh-collow+1),\
32                        sizeof(double));
33 if (x[k]==NULL){
34 fprintf(stderr,"unable to allocate memory");
35 exit(1);
36 }
37 x[k] -= collow;
38 }
39         return x;
40 }
```

Here are the contents of the simple header file `memalloc.h`:

```
1 double *vecalloc(int low, int high);
2 double **matalloc(int rowlow, int rowhigh,\
3                   int collow, int colhigh);
```

APPENDIX III

PLOTTING FILES

PLOTTING FILES IN MATHEMATICA

The program Mathematica is well–known for its beautiful graphics. Let's say you have completed a computation and wish to plot the results. We include here two simple "functions" which produce graphics output in Mathematica.

For the case of two–dimensional graphs, suppose you have written pairs of data values to a file, called out2.dat, which is assumed to lie in an accessible directory. The format of this file should be

$$x_1 \quad y_1$$
$$x_2 \quad y_2$$
$$\vdots$$

where y_1 is the value of the function at x_1, etc. Notice that on each line the data is space–delimited. Now enter the Mathematica program and type the following:

```
FilePlot2D[file_String]:=ListPlot[ReadList[file,
{Number,Number}]]
```

Then at the Mathematica prompt, enter

```
FilePlot2D["out2.dat"]
```

Your data file will be displayed with automatically chosen axes, ticks, etc. If you don't care for the point size, try this command after displaying the graph:

```
Show[%,Prolog->AbsolutePointSize[1]]
```

Of course, any other options can be implemented by later use of the Show command. See [MA].

The case of three–dimensional plots is somewhat different. We are restricted to plotting a surface over a square domain in two dimensions. Moreover, only "z" values are to be entered into the file. For the purpose of graphing such a file, enter this "function":

```
FilePlot3D[file_String,n_]:=
ListPlot3D[ReadList[file,Table[Number,{n}]],Ticks->None]
```

There are to be exactly n entries on each grid line parallel to the axes. The Ticks statement turns off the axes ticks, which may be incorrect if not excised. Assume your data file is called out3.dat. If, for example, there are n=21 points on each grid line, enter at the Mathematica prompt

```
FilePlot3D["out3.dat",21]
```

PLOTTING FILES WITH GNUPLOT

For two–dimensional graphs, suppose you have written pairs of data values to a file, called out2.dat. The format of this file should be

$x_1 \quad y_1$
$x_2 \quad y_2$
$\vdots$

The top line in the file must not be blank. Notice that on each line the data is space–delimited. Use the command

```
set samples N
```

where N is at least equal to the number of pairs of data points. One generates the plot with the command

```
plot "out2.dat"
```

For a three–dimensional plot, the format of your data file (called out3.dat) should be

$x_1 \quad y_1 \quad z_1$
$x_2 \quad y_2 \quad z_2$
$\vdots$

Enter the command

```
set parametric
```

Then your file will be plotted with the command

```
splot "out3.dat"
```

APPENDIX IV

C KEYWORDS

C is a small language with very few keywords. Here they are:

C KEYWORDS			
auto	break	case	char
const	continue	default	do
double	else	enum	extern
float	for	goto	if
int	long	register	return
short	signed	sizeof	static
struct	switch	typedef	union
unsigned	void	volatile	while

Some compilers also reserve `asm`, `entry` and `fortran`.

REFERENCES

[AA] Anderson, G. and Anderson, P. **The UNIX C Shell Field Guide.** Prentice Hall, Englewood Cliffs, New Jersey, 1986.

[AK] Akhiezer, N.I. **The Calculus of Variations.** Blaisdell, New York, 1962.

[AS] Abramowitz, M. and Stegun, I. **Handbook of Mathematical Functions.** Dover, New York, 1965.

[AT] Atkinson, K. **An Introduction to Numerical Analysis.** J. Wiley & Sons, New York, 1978.

[BA1] Baker, L. **C Tools for Scientists and Engineers.** McGraw Hill, New York, 1989.

[BA2] Baker, L. **More C Tools for Scientists and Engineers.** McGraw Hill, New York, 1991.

[BA3] Baker, L. **C Mathematical Function Handbook.** McGraw Hill, New York, 1992.

[BF] Burden, R. and Faires, J. **Numerical Analysis**, Fourth Edition, PWS Kent, Boston, 1989.

[CB] Conte, S. and de Boor, C. **Elementary Numerical Analysis.** Third Edition, McGraw Hill, New York, 1980.

[CI] Ciarlet, P. **Introduction to Numerical Linear Algebra and Optimisation.** Cambridge University Press, Cambridge, 1989.

[CL] Coddington, E. and Levinson, N. **Theory of Ordinary Differential Equations.** McGraw Hill, New York, 1955.

[CY] **C For Yourself**, Microsoft QuickC 2.5 Documentation, Microsoft Corporation, Redmond, WA. 1988.

[FE] Feibel, W. **Using Quick C: Second Edition.** Osborne McGraw Hill, Berkeley, CA. 1989.

[FHM] Fox, L., Henrici, P. and Moler, C. **S.I.A.M. J. Num. Anal.**, 4 (1967), 89–102.

[FL] Fletcher, R. **Practical Methods of Optimization** (Second Edition.) J. Wiley and Sons, New York, 1987.

[FW] Forsythe, G. and Wasow, W. **Finite Difference Methods for Partial Differential Equations.** J. Wiley and Sons, New York, 1960.

[FX] Fox, L. **An Introduction to Numerical Linear Algebra.** Oxford University Press, New York, 1965.

[GE] Gear, C. **Numerical Initial Value Problems in Ordinary Differential Equations.** Prentice–Hall, Englewood Cliffs, N.J. 1971.

[GF] Gelfand, I.M. and Fomin, S.V. **Calculus of Variations.** Prentice–Hall, Englewood Cliffs, N.J. 1963.

[GvL] Golub, G. and van Loan, C.F. **Matrix Computations.** (Second Edition) Johns Hopkins University Press, Baltimore, 1989.

[HE] Henrici, P. **Discrete Variable Methods in Ordinary Differential Equations.** J. Wiley and Sons, New York, 1962.

[HI] Hildebrand, F.B. **Introduction to Numerical Analysis.** McGraw Hill, New York, 1974.

[HO] Householder, A. **The Numerical Treatment of a Single Nonlinear Equation.** McGraw Hill, New York, 1970.

[HO2] Householder, A. **The Theory of Matrices in Numerical Analysis.** Dover, New York, 1975.

[HP] Hall, C.A. and Porsching, T.A. **Numerical Analysis of Partial Differential Equations.** Prentice Hall, Englewood Cliffs, N.J. 1990.

[HS] Harbison, S. and Steel, G. **C: A Reference Manual** (Third Edition.) Prentice Hall, Englewood Cliffs, N.J. 1991.

[IK] Isaacson, E. and Keller, H. **Analysis of Numerical Methods.** John Wiley and Sons, New York, 1966.

[JA1] Jamsa, K. **Microsoft C: Secrets, Shortcuts and Solutions.** Microsoft Press, Redmond, WA. 1989.

[JA2] Jamsa, K. **Graphics Programming with Microsoft C and Microsoft QuickC.** Microsoft Press, Redmond, WA. 1990.

[JC] Johnson, C. **Numerical Solution of Partial Differential Equations by the Finite Element Method.** Cambridge University Press, Cambridge, 1990.

[JO1] John, F. **Partial Differential Equations.** Springer, New York, 1982.

[JO2] John, F. **Lectures on Advanced Numerical Analysis.** Gordon and Breach, New York, 1967.

[KC] Kincaid, D. and Cheney, W. **Numerical Analysis.** Brooks/Cole, Pacific Grove, CA. 1991.

[KH] Kocak, H. **Differential and Difference Equations through Computer Experiments** (Second Edition.) Springer Verlag, New York, 1989.

[KK] Kantorovich, L. and Krylov, V. **Approximate Methods of Higher Analysis.** Interscience, Groningen, 1964.

[KL] Keller, H.B. **Numerical Solution of Two Point Boundary Value Problems.** CBMS–NSF Conference Series # 24, S.I.A.M., Philadelphia, 1984.

[KR] Kernighan, B. and Ritchie, D. **The C Programming Language** (Second Edition.) Prentice Hall, Englewood Cliffs, New Jersey, 1988.

[LB] Lebedev, N. **Special Functions and their Applications.** Dover, New York, 1972.

[LE] Lesser, M. **Advanced QuickBasic 4.0.** Bantam Books, Toronto, 1988.

[MA] Wolfram, S. **Mathematica: A System for doing Mathematics by Computer** (Second Edition.) Addison Wesley, Redwood City, CA. 1991.

[MOS] Magnus, W., Oberhettinger, F. and Soni, R. **Formulas and Theorems for the Special Functions of Mathematical Physics** (Third Edition.) Springer Verlag, New York, 1966.

[NA] Nash, J.C. **Compact Numerical Methods for Computers** (Second Edition.) Adam Hilger, Bristol, 1990.

[NR] Press, W., Flannery, B., Teukolsky, S., and Vetterling, W. **Numerical Recipes in C.** Cambridge University Press, Cambridge, 1989.

[RH] Rheinboldt, W. **Methods for Solving Systems of Nonlinear Equations.** CBMS–NSF Conference Series # 14, S.I.A.M., Philadelphia, 1987.

[RL] Ralston, A. **A First Course in Numerical Analysis**. McGraw Hill, New York, 1965.

[RM] Richtmyer, R. and Morton, K. **Difference Methods for Initial Value Problems** (Second Edition.) Interscience, New York, 1967.

[SF] Strang, G. and Fix, G. **An Analysis of the Finite Element Method**. Prentice–Hall, Englewood Cliffs, N.J. 1973.

[SR] Strauss, W. **Nonlinear Wave Equations.** CBMS–NSF Regional Conference Series in Mathematics, # 73, Amer. Math. Soc., Providence, 1989.

[ST] Strikwerda, J. **Finite Difference Schemes and Partial Differential Equations.** Wadsworth & Brooks/Cole, Pacific Grove, CA., 1989.

[SZ] Szegö, G. **Orthogonal Polynomials**. American Mathematical Society, Providence, 1939.

[WE] Wendroff, B. **Theoretical Numerical Analysis.** Academic Press, New York, 1966.

[WI] Wilkinson, J. **The Algebraic Eigenvalue Problem.** Oxford University Press, Oxford, 1965.

[WR] Wilkinson, J., and Reinsch, C. *Linear Algebra*, Vol. II of **Handbook for Automatic Computation**. Springer Verlag, New York, 1971.

INDEX

A

a.out, 5, 125
absolute value fn.,
  see fabs
address of operator
  &, 12, 17, 72–73, 123
Adams methods, 139–140
\a (alert), 33
AND, 33, 123
ANSI, 2, 5, 14, 34, 43, 45, 82
argc, 107, 109
argv[ ], 107, 109–110
arrays, 1, 44–45, 51, 54–55, 66,
  81–82, 85, 88–89, 95,
  106–107, 110, 123, 126, 131,
  144, 175, 197, 238, 244
ASCII, 107, 110, 129, 247
assignment operator, 34, 123
associativity, 122–123
asymptotic expansion, 49–51,
  117, 182, 186
atan function, 61, 128
atan2 function, 60
atof, 129
atoi, 110, 129
atol, 129
automatic variables, 130
awk, 130

B

back substitution, 47, 95
backslash \, 33
backspace \b, 33
Bairstow's method, 119
Bashforth methods, 140
Bernoulli's method, 110
Bessel functions, 140
birthday problem, 15

bisect method, 24, 28, 43,
  189, 197
boundary–value problems,
  114–115, 126, 145–146, 150,
  158, 208
break, 18–19, 66–69

C

C functions, 9, 32, 34–35, 40,
  43–45, 53, 80–81, 88, 97,
  110–111, 113, 117, 122,
  131, 180
cabs (fn.), 61–62, 175
Calculus of Variations, 209
call
  by value, 34, 36, 62, 132
  by reference, 34, 62, 71–72,
    165, 175
calloc, 72, 82–84, 89, 91, 120
case, 66
case sensitive, 13
cast, 13, 39, 75, 83, 91, 123
Cauchy sequence, 16
ceil (fn.), 14
centered differences, 115, 125,
  151, 258
CFL, 159
char, 13, 129
char array, 44, 107, 128–129
Chebyshev polynom., 39
Cholesky, 197–198, 212
comma operator, 123–124
command–line arguments, 63,
  71, 107, 109, 129, 135, 198,
  224, 238, 244, 247
comments, 7, 131
complex arithmetic, 2, 56, 62,
  165
complex deflation, 174–175